Past and Present Publications

SMYTHE LIBRARY

**Stamp this label with the date for return.
Contact the Librarian if you wish to renew this book.**

Past and Present Publications

General Editor: PAUL SLACK, *Exeter College, Oxford*

Past and Present Publications comprise books similar in character to the articles in the journal *Past and Present*. Whether the volumes in the series are collections of essays – some previously published, others new studies – or monographs, they encompass a wide variety of scholarly and original works primarily concerned with social, economic and cultural changes, and their causes and consequences. They will appeal to both specialists and non-specialists and will endeavour to communicate the results of historical and allied research in readable and lively form.

For a list of titles in Past and Present Publications, see end of book.

Geography, technology, and war

Studies in the maritime history of the Mediterranean, 649–1571

JOHN H. PRYOR

Associate Professor of History, University of Sydney

CAMBRIDGE
UNIVERSITY PRESS

Published by the Press Syndicate of the University of Cambridge
The Pitt Building, Trumpington Street, Cambridge CB2 1RP
40 West 20th Street, New York, NY 10011–4211, USA
10 Stamford Road, Oakleigh, Victoria 3166, Australia

First published 1988
First paperback edition 1992

British Library cataloguing in publication data
Pryor, John H.
Geography, technology, and war: studies
in the maritime history of the Mediterranean
649–1571. – (Past and Present
Publications).
1. shipping – Mediterranean Region –
History
I. Title   II. Series
387.5′09182′2 HE722

Library of Congress cataloguing in publication data
Pryor, John H., 1947–
Geography, technology, and war.
(Past and Present Publications)
Bibliography.
Includes index.
1. Navigation – Mediterranean Region – History.
2. Mediterranean Region – History, Naval.   I. Title.
II. Series.
VK55.P79   387.5′091638   87–13338

ISBN 0 521 34424 7 hardback
ISBN 0 521 42892 0 paperback

Transferred to digital printing 2000

Patri matrique

Contents

Tables

Figures

Figure sources

All drawings have been made by the author. Figures 2, 3, 23, 26, 27, 28, and 29 are original. The others are based on the following source material:

1 Caffaro, *Annali genovesi di Caffaro e de' suoi continuatori dal MXCIX al MCCXCIII*, ed. L. T. Belgrano, vol. 2 (Genoa, 1901), p. 23

4 TOP HALF
   G. F. Bass, ed., *A history of seafaring based on underwater archaeology* (London, 1972), plate 4, p. 149

22 Caffaro, *Annali genovesi*, vol. 2, p. 8
24 V. Minorsky, *The Chester Beatty Library: a catalogue of the Turkish manuscripts and miniatures* (Dublin, 1958), MS. 413, fol. 28
25 Bryer, 'Shipping in the empire of Trebizond', fig. 7, p. 10

Preface

This book has been many years in gestation. On the one hand, it grew out of research on medieval maritime commerce and commercial law in the Mediterranean. On the other, it emerged from an interest in the Crusades. These two interests were drawn together in earlier research on shipping, transportation, and naval warfare during the era of the Crusades. A great deal of work still remains to be done in these areas, particularly in that of naval warfare in the Mediterranean during the period from the rise of the Italian maritime republics in the eleventh century to the end of the Crusades in the fourteenth. These concerns will be the subject of another work, yet to be completed, on the naval history of the Crusades.

In the meantime these studies are offered as a contribution to wider concerns with relations between Islam and Christendom across the Mediterranean over a more extended period of time. 'Across the Mediterranean' rather than 'in the Mediterranean, or Mediterranean world' because here the sea itself is the focus and centre of attention. It is considered at one and the same time as both the unique centripetal force bonding together the various peoples on all of its shores and also as the principal centrifugal element separating them and lying at the heart of their distinct historical developments. As Saint Basil appreciated, the sea was God's gift to mankind: a highway for communications, travel, commerce, and the passage of armies:

The sea is beautiful in the eyes of God, especially, because it surrounds the islands of which it is at one and the same time the adornment and protection; because it brings together the most far-removed lands and gives to sailors unhindered intercourse: through them it furnishes to us the history of what was previously unknown: it provides the fortune of the merchant abroad; it improves easily the needs of life, allowing the well endowed to export their excess, and to the poor it furnishes amendment of what they lack.[1]

[1] Basil of Caesarea, St, *Homélies sur l'hexaéméron*, ed. & trans. S. Giet (Paris, 1949), IV.7 (pp. 274–5).

xiii

Yet at the same time the sea did not offer an easy passage to those who wished to pass along its roads in antiquity and the Middle Ages. Given the technology available to man in these periods, the architecture of his ships, the crossing of the sea was not always achieved without difficulty. The Mediterranean, although a reasonably quiescent body of water by comparison to other seas around the world, still held its terrors and posed its own difficulties to navigators. The capabilities of ancient and medieval ships were barely adequate to give man that mastery of his physical world which he desired and for which he designed them. To a large degree man had to make his crossings of the sea in harmony with the forces of nature rather than in spite of them or against them. As a consequence, the most practical routes for crossing the sea in the Middle Ages and antiquity were not always those which today might appear most obvious.

In the course of research on many different aspects of maritime traffic and the conduct of naval warfare in the Mediterranean during the Middle Ages, I have been drawn back ever more consistently to the foundations of man's endeavours: to the nature and peculiarities of the physical world in which he operated. I have become ever more convinced that certain aspects of the physical geography of the Mediterranean Sea, when considered in relation to the capabilities of the maritime technology of the time, exercised a profound effect on the course of conflict and competition between Islam and Christendom over a very long period of time. That is not to say that there were not many changes and developments as the centuries succeeded each other. Of course there were. The influence of the physical world on human history was not uni-directional. The winds of change blew from different quarters at different times. Nevertheless, there was a certain consistency in the influence of the nexus between maritime technology and the physical world on man's endeavours during the various periods which are the object of this book. I am persuaded that traditional historical periodizations are meaningless as far as the focus of these studies is concerned: the relations between the physical conditions of the sea, maritime technology, and economic and military competition between Islam and Christendom. The period from the seventh to the sixteenth centuries was one at sea, even if it was not in other aspects of man's history.

Over the course of preparation of these studies I have incurred a debt of gratitude to many people. My knowledge of Greek and Arabic extends to no more than a few words and I am grateful to those who have helped me with sources in those languages: at my own university Professor Michael Jeffreys and Dr Elizabeth Jeffreys of the Department of Modern Greek, Dr Ahmed Shboul of the Department of Semitic studies, and in the Department of History Associate Professor R. K. Sinclair, Dr J. O'Neil, and Miss S. Rovik; and at the Hebrew University of Jerusalem the late Professor Eliyahu Ashtor. Dr Colin Imber of the University of Manchester provided me with copies of his works on the Ottoman navy. Professor Michel Balard of the Université de Rheims gave me invaluable references to water supplies carried on Genoese and Venetian galleys. Sr Federico Foerster of Barcelona shared with me his knowledge of Catalan shipping and naval warfare in the thirteenth century. Professor Vassilios Christides of the University of Athens provided me with a copy of his work on Byzantine and Muslim manuals of naval warfare which was unavailable in Australia. Professor John Guilmartin of the United States Air Force Academy, whose work on Mediterranean galley warfare in the sixteenth century has become seminal to the subject, commented helpfully on my analysis of the naval battles of Roger of Lauria. Professor John Dotson of the University of Southern Illinois at Carbondale shared with me his work on the voyage of Simone Leccavello and commented generously on my work on thirteenth-century naval architecture. Mr S. Jaffe of the Israel Meteorological Services kindly provided data on wind direction frequencies in Haifa Bay. Professor Victor Goldsmith of the Israel National Institute of Oceanography shared with me his knowledge of sea conditions in Levantine waters and provided me with copies of his publications. Professoressa Laura Balletto of the Università di Genova helpfully furnished me with a copy of Belgrano's edition of Genoese documents which was unavailable in Australia. Professors David Ayalon, Joshua Prawer, and David Jacoby of the Hebrew University of Jerusalem shared their own work with me and gave helpful criticism of a version of chapter 5 given as a seminar in Jerusalem in 1984. At the University of Haifa, Professor Aryeh Grabois sent me a copy of his work on Mediterranean navigation in the eighth century and Professor Avner Raban responded helpfully to my queries about water supplies carried on Muslim ships in the Middle Ages. Professor Geo Pistarino, director of the Istituto di paleographia e storia medioevale of the Università di Genova, generously provided me with copies of many of the invaluable publications of his Institute. Professor Hector Williams of the University of British Columbia kindly sent me a copy of

Purpura's report on the twelfth-century ship recently discovered at Marsala.

Earlier versions of this book were read by Professor Roy Macleod of my own department, Professors B. Z. Kedar and Eliyahu Ashtor of the Hebrew University of Jerusalem, Dr David Abulafia of Gonville and Caius College, Cambridge, and Dr Judith Herrin of the University of Birmingham. To all these I am grateful for their useful comments, criticisms, and further references. The uses to which I have put their assistance are entirely my own responsibility.

A special and invaluable debt is owed to Professor A. Dvoretzky and the staff of the Institute for Advanced Studies of the Hebrew University of Jerusalem. Much of the essential research for these studies was conducted during a stay at the Institute as a Visiting Fellow in 1984. The generosity and kindness of the Institute and its staff permitted me to accomplish more during those six months than I would normally have done in years.

Finally, to my wife and children, who have patiently endured my long absences from their company, my appreciation ought to be recorded.

Preface to the paperback edition

The reissue of this book in paperback form provides a welcome opportunity to address some of the issues concerning the studies that comprise it which have been raised by friends, colleagues, and students, both in print and informally. Because this is a book which is focused on issues and developed through theses, it has, in fact, attracted a good deal of comment. Naturally, I have been gratified by the favourable nature of much of that comment. However, not everyone has agreed either with the theses concerning the nature of Mediterranean geography and medieval technology or with the application of these to particular historical studies. Some of the more critical comment that has been made stems from a misunderstanding of the purpose of the book and from a tendency to attribute to it a wider compass than its limitations permit. Readers should be aware from the outset that this book is not, and never was intended to be, a general maritime history of the Mediterranean world in the Middle Ages. The subtitle is very deliberate. The studies contained in chapters 4 to 8 are both selective and selectively treated. They are intended to provide historical testing grounds for the theses developed in the first three geographical and technological chapters, and no more than that. They encompass neither the entire maritime history of the Mediterranean in the period nor even all aspects of the conflict and competition between the civilisations with which they deal.

The central thesis of the book is that in the Middle Ages the meteorological and oceanographic conditions of the Mediterranean had a profound influence on the course of human history because medieval maritime technology gave only very partial mastery of the elements. The capabilities of both wind-powered sailing ships and man-powered galleys were very limited. Because of this, the natural elements themselves were important conditioners of the outcome of historical events. Meteorological and oceanographic patterns therefore become important objects of historical study in themselves. In the studies contained here, ancient and medieval observations of winds, currents, and tides have been used to explore the parameters of meteorological and oceanographic conditions. However, because these observations are very fragmentary, extensive use has also been made of data compiled in the modern era on prevailing wind directions and currents, the two factors most relevant to wind- and man-powered shipping in the medieval Mediterranean. This raises immediately the question of how we may be confident that conclusions drawn from modern data are relevant to medieval conditions, given that there has been significant climatic change both over the period covered by this book and also between that and the modern era.

I am, in fact, convinced that the conclusions drawn from modern data are applicable to the medieval period. The history of climate is a complex field,[1] and to have demonstrated in detail the validity of this assertion would have required an additional chapter on historical climatic change and its implications which I did not want to undertake here. However, in brief, the argument is as follows. In general terms there is no doubt that the climate of Europe warmed and grew drier from late Roman times to *c.* 1200 A.D., after which it cooled and became wetter till *c.* 1450. This was followed by a short period of warming to *c.* 1525, after which Europe moved into its 'Little Ice Age'. In periods of cooling the influence of the North Atlantic low pressure system and the Mongolian high in winter extended further to the south and prolonged the duration of winter conditions (see figure 3, p. 17). The reverse was the case in periods of warming. In those periods the influence of the tropical Azores high and Indo-Persian low in summer extended further north, and summer conditions were prolonged. However, the point is that because both the polar and also the tropical pressure systems generate prevailing winds in the Mediterranean varying from north-west to north-east, alternations in their influence over time should have created no great difference in prevailing wind directions. They would have created variation in the incidence of storms, cloud, and precipitation, but not in that of prevailing wind directions. Ancient and medieval meteorological observations support this conclusion.[2] I have found no evidence of any

---

[1] See, in the first instance, H. H. Lamb, *Climate: past, present, and future*, vol. 2: *Climatic history and the future* (London, 1977), esp. ch. 17; Lamb, *Climate, history, and the modern world* (London and New York, 1982), esp. chs. 10–12; Lamb, *Weather, climate, and human affairs: a book of essays and other papers* (London and New York, 1988), esp. chs. 3–9; E. le Roy Ladurie, *Times of feast, times of famine: a history of climate since the year 1000* (London, 1971), esp. ch. 6.

[2] See William H. Murray, 'Do modern winds equal ancient winds', *Mediterranean Historical Review*, 2 (1987), 139–67.

type which suggests that climatic change affected meteorological conditions in the Middle Ages in any way which would affect the conclusions about prevailing wind directions drawn from modern data in this book. The same is true of oceanographic conditions. Medieval and ancient observations of current circulation agree with modern oceanographic analysis of currents, and tides in certain narrows, in the Mediterranean.

The historical studies of chapters 4 to 8 do not pretend to be comprehensive surveys of the maritime history of the periods and regions in question. They address selected themes only. By way of particular example, I am perfectly well aware that the situation in Levantine waters during the Crusader period was complicated beyond the picture presented in chapter 5 by rivalry and conflict between the Italian maritime republics, by the operations of corsairs, by the increasing magnitude of Western maritime traffic, and by the influence of internal developments within the Muslim world such as the political unification or division of Syria/Palestine and Egypt at various times. However, this chapter is specifically structured to present an analysis of the limitations on the operations of the Egyptian fleets in the light of the geographical and technological theses. It does not attempt to do more than that. It does not pretend to offer the explanation for the survival of the Crusader states for two centuries. Nor is it a maritime history of the Crusades. In more general terms, the disavowal in the Introduction (p. 10) of any belief that conflict and competition between the three great civilisations of Islam, Byzantium, and the West were monolithic in nature should be borne in mind throughout. If it appears that in discussions of particular situations I have written as though it were otherwise, this is because certain aspects only of that conflict and competition and those situations are being addressed, not their entirety.

This is not a book about people. To some readers it may appear that I have de-humanised history. There is little acknowledgement in this book of the importance in history of either individual human genius and incompetence or of human motivation and skill. In reality, I am perfectly well aware of the importance of the human element in history and have addressed the issue of individual genius in maritime history elsewhere.[3] In particular circumstances, human skills, motivation, genius, or foolishness can be decisive if other factors are equal. For example, there

---

[3] J. H. Pryor, 'The naval battles of Roger of Lauria', *Journal of Medieval History*, 9 (1983), 179–216.

is no doubt that the motivation of the early Muslims played an important role in their struggle with the Byzantines, who were more skilled at naval warfare, in the seventh and eighth centuries. Similarly, Venetian skill and training was instrumental in permitting the Serenissima to sustain for so long her resistance to the vast numbers of the Ottomans in the fifteenth to seventeenth centuries. But this is a book which is concerned specifically with the other factors. It attempts to isolate and analyse the non-human elements. It attempts to provide a physical and technological board on which the interplay of human chess pieces in history may be seen to have moved. It attempts to provide explanations over the long term, when human elements ought to have cancelled themselves out. If these attempts have been successful, readers will have a sound under-standing of the conditions in which humans in history operated.

Since the manuscript of this work was originally completed in 1987 some important new works have appeared which have added consider-ably to our knowledge of Muslim and Byzantine shipping and should now be added to the bibliography. In a seminal article in 1989, David Nicolle provided important new iconographic evidence for early Muslim ship types.[4] We had previously believed that there were no surviving Muslim depictions of ships before the thirteenth century (see p. 28). Nicolle's work was complemented by a study of Muslim ships on pottery bowls from eleventh-century Majorca by Pryor and Bellabarba.[5] On late Byzantine shipping, a subject about which little was known, we now have the important study of Georgios Makris,[6] although it is rather disappointing on ship types and makes no use of iconographic evidence. One general work has appeared which should be added to the bibli-ography on relations between Islam, Byzantium and the medieval West: Archibald Lewis's *Nomads and crusaders*. The book that he and Timothy Runyan published in 1985, which was not known to me in 1987, *European naval and maritime history, 300–1500*, is also useful.[7]

John H. Pryor
Sydney, 15 September 1991

---

[4] D. Nicolle, 'Shipping in Islamic art: seventh through sixteenth century AD', *American Neptune*, 49 (1989), 168–97.

[5] J. H. Pryor and S. Bellabarba, 'The medieval Muslim ships of the Pisan *bacini* ', *The Mariner's Mirror*, 76 (1990), 99–113.

[6] G. Makris, *Studien zur spätbyzantinischen Schiffahrt* (Genoa, 1988).

[7] A. R. Lewis, *Nomads and crusaders A.D. 1000–1368* (Bloomington and Indianapolis, 1988); A. R. Lewis and R. J. Runyan, *European naval and maritime history, 300-1500* (Bloomington, 1985).

Abbreviations

A.E.M.	*Anuario de estudios medievales*
Annales: E.S.C.	*Annales: Economies, sociétés, civilizations*
D.O.P.	*Dumbarton Oaks papers*
I.J.N.A.	*International journal of nautical archaeology and underwater exploration*
M.M.	*The mariner's mirror*
P.P.T.S.L.	*Palestine Pilgrims' Text Society library*
R.H.C. Occ.	*Recueil des historiens des Croisades. Historiens Occidentaux*
R.H.C. Or.	*Recueil des historiens des Croisades. Historiens Orientaux*

Note on orthography and typography

Medieval Latin, Greek, and Arabic orthography varied wildly, and modern transcription of it, particularly of Arabic, similarly varies greatly. Throughout these studies I have preserved the particular orthography which I have found in the various editions of works which I have used, both in the case of edited texts and in references to technical terms found in secondary works. I have, however, standardized the orthography of some terms in the interests of consistency where various texts and modern authors have used differing orthographies. Thus, for example, the Arabic *tarida, ṭarīda, tarīda, tarrīda*, and *ṭarrāda* have been standardized as *ṭarīda*. In all cases, 'classical' Latin, Greek, and Arabic forms have been used except where reference is made to specific medieval texts or references; which is, in fact, in most cases.

In quotations of texts, parentheses ( ) refer to parenthetical explanations, either my own or those of editors of the texts. Square brackets [ ] refer to my own interpolations.

Introduction

Ibn Jubayr, a twelfth-century Muslim pilgrim and traveller from Andalusia, left Acre on 18 October 1184 on a Genoese ship bound for Messina. Of his departure he wrote that:

Our stay there [at Acre] was prolonged twelve days, through the failure of the wind to rise. The blowing of the winds in these parts has a singular secret. It is that the east wind does not blow except in spring and autumn, and, save at those seasons, no voyages can be made and merchants will not bring their goods to Acre. The spring voyages begin in the middle of April, when the east wind blows until the end of May . . . The autumn voyages are from the middle of October, when the east wind (again) sets in motion . . . it blows for (only) fifteen days, more or less. There is no other suitable time, for the winds then vary, that from the west prevailing . . . at daybreak of . . . the 18th of October the ship set sail . . . Steadily, we sailed on, under a propitious wind of varying force, for five days. Then the west wind came out of ambuscade and blew into the ship's bows. The captain and ruler of the ship, a Genoese Rumi, who was perspicacious in his art and skilled in the duties of a sea captain, made shift to elude this wind by tacking right and left, and sought to return not on his tracks. *The sea was calm and gentle.* At midnight, or near to it, on the night of . . . the 27th of October, the west wind fell on us and broke a spar of the mast known as the 'ardimun', throwing half of it, with the attaching sails, into the sea.[1]

Ibn Jubayr made three voyages on Genoese ships during his pilgrimage to Mecca in 1183–5: from Ceuta to Alexandria, from Acre to Messina, and from Trapani to Cartagena. His narratives of these voyages show a high degree of perspicacity for, and sensitivity to, problems of sea travel. He understood ships and the men who sailed

---

[1] Ibn Jubayr, *The travels of Ibn Jubayr*, trans. R. J. C. Broadhurst (London, 1952), pp. 326–7. The italics are mine.

1

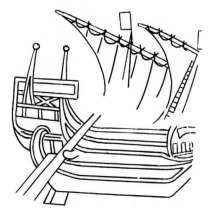

Figure 1 Genoese round ship to illustrate the ship which brought Conrad of Montferrat from Constantinople to Tyre in 1187, from the continuation of Caffaro's *Annales januenses*

them. In fact, it seems to me, he may well have had previous experience of the sea, for his narratives are devoid of that unreasonable fear of the deep which characterizes so many contemporary Christian records of sea voyages made by landlubbers. For the twelfth century at least, his accounts are unrivalled for the light they cast on sea travel in the Mediterranean.

The Genoese merchant ship on which Ibn Jubayr sailed from Acre was probably one of the largest and most advanced types of Mediterranean sailing ships of its day. Information which he gives about the ship suggests that its construction was very similar to that of the ship depicted in the famous marginal illumination to the continuation of the *Annales januenses* of Caffaro, illustrating the arrival of Conrad of Montferrat at Tyre in 1187.[2] Yet the voyage of Ibn Jubayr's Genoese ship in 1184 was a disaster from beginning to end.

The captain sailed from Acre at the end of the autumn sailing season, just in time, it was hoped, to reach Sicily before the onset of true winter weather conditions made navigation excessively dangerous. According to Ibn Jubayr, the ship set out before dawn with an easterly wind which blew at that time of the year and which had given rise to an Arabic name, *al-salibiyah* (cross-like), for the sailing season

[2] Bib. Nat. Paris, MS. Suppl. lat., 773, fol. 108r. See figure 1 and pp. 29–32 below.

Table 1. *Haifa Bay: frequency of easterly winds as percentage*[4]

January	31%	May	15%	September	4%
February	27%	June	3%	October	11%
March	24%	July	1%	November	31%
April	22%	August	1%	December	30%

from the fact that with the wind astern ships could set their two lateen sails *musallabah* (goose winged) across the ship.[3] Modern meteorological data support Ibn Jubayr's assertion that at Acre favourable conditions for leaving the West occurred only in two short periods of the year.

Because of the interference of terrestrial geographical phenomena, wind direction frequencies recorded at coastal stations often do not reflect accurately prevailing wind conditions out to sea. However, in this case the data from Haifa Bay are confirmed for the eastern Mediterranean from 30° east longitude to the coast of Israel and from Cyprus south to Egypt by data compiled from observations taken at sea by ships over the years 1949–78.[5] Taken together, the data from both Haifa Bay and from observations taken at sea show that easterly winds favourable to sailing ships leaving Acre for the West are most common from mid October through to mid May; throughout the winter, in effect.

In the twelfth century commercial shipping rarely ventured to sea from November through to mid March.[6] Thirteenth-century data confirm that the majority of ships bound for the Holy Land left the West in the last weeks of March and in early April.[7] With an average passage eastwards taking about four to six weeks,[8] ships would not arrive in Acre before mid to late April. William of Tyre confirmed that

---

[3] Ibn Jubayr, *Travels*, pp. 313, 332, 383 n. 132.

[4] Data supplied through the kind offices of Mr S. Jaffe, Acting Director of the Israel Meteorological Services. In general, these figures are supported by those of the British Air Ministry Meteorological Office for wind direction frequencies at Haifa and Beirut. See Great Britain, Air Ministry, Meteorological Office, *Weather in the Mediterranean*, 2nd edn (London, 1962), vol. 2, pp. 74–5.

[5] V. Goldsmith & S. Sofer, 'Wave climatology of the Southeastern Mediterranean', *Israel journal of earth sciences*, 32 (1983), 1–51; here pp. 24–6 and fig. 20.

[6] See below, pp. 87–9.

[7] J. H. Pryor, *Business contracts of medieval Provence: selected notulae from the cartulary of Giraud Amalric of Marseilles, 1248* (Toronto, 1981), pp. 43, 69–72.

[8] See below, pp. 36, 51–3.

this was so. According to him, Easter was 'circa transitum vernalem'.[9]
With a minimum turn-around time of two or three weeks, ships would
not have been ready to return to the West before late April or early
May. Bearing in mind that few shipmasters would have wished to
spend the winter in the Holy Land because of the economic costs of
being tied up unproductively, prospective voyagers to the West in the
spring would normally have had to wait until arriving ships were
ready to begin their return voyages. In the autumn, because the
voyage westwards regularly took two months or more,[10] ships on
normal commercial business would not have attempted to leave the
Holy Land after the beginning of November for fear of being caught
at sea en route by winter storms. Late October was, then, the last
suitable period in which to set out. Again assuming a turn-around
time of two or three weeks, ships would have needed to have arrived
during the last weeks of September. Once again William of Tyre
confirms that this was so. The arrival of pilgrim ships as summer gave
way to autumn was 'iuxta consuetudinem', he said.[11] These considerations make sense of Ibn Jubayr's seasons of *al-salibiyah*. It was not
that easterlies blew out on to Haifa Bay only for the few weeks that he
specified. In fact they were more frequent during the winter proper.
But, in the twelfth century commercial shipping rarely sailed during
the winter proper. And, in the summer easterlies were extremely
uncommon. The seasons of *al-salibiyah* were, then, two short periods
during which the beginning and end of favourable meteorological
conditions coincided with the availability of shipping; an availability
very largely determined by correlations between geography and
technology: the inadequacy of the technology of twelfth-century ships
to allow them to sail the winter seas with confidence.

In the case of Acre, the general problems of setting out from the
Holy Land against the prevailing winds were very probably exacerbated by the peculiar topography of the port and by the influence of
terrestrial geographical and meteorological conditions. The harbour
entrance was narrow, only about eighty metres across, and ships had
to set a course south-south-west to exit from it and then perhaps west-
south-west to clear the promontory of the city and the bank about 550
metres off the Church of St Andrew and the House of the Temple at its

[9] William of Tyre, *Historia rerum in partibus transmarinis gestarum*, in *R.H.C. Occ.*,
vol. 1 (Paris, 1844), XVII.8 (pp. 770–1).
[10] See below, pp. 36, 51–3.
[11] William of Tyre, *Historia*, XI.20 (p. 487).

head.[12] Moreover, in the Bay of Haifa the prevailing west to north-west winds found out to sea are reinforced by the diurnal sea breezes set in motion by the heating of the land during the day. These give rise to unusually strong west to south-west winds which set in around 1000 hours and which last until around 1600 hours.[13] No wonder that Ibn Jubayr's ship sailed before daybreak, when it might have received some assistance from the nocturnal land breeze while still close in to the coast as well as from the easterly prevailing winds once out to sea.

Five days out of Acre the wind swung to the west. Even though it must have been only a light head wind since 'the sea was calm and gentle', the impression given by Ibn Jubayr is that despite tacking the captain was hard put to make any headway at all. Because of the design of such ships this is readily believable.[14] The artemon (foremast) yard was broken by a sudden squall, which was a common occurrence with the lateen rig, the ship was becalmed, she made some progress before occasional northerly and easterly winds, and she eventually made landfall on 13 November, possibly at Rhodes, or more probably at Karpathos. She had been at sea without sight of land for 26 days.[15] Acre to Rhodes/Karpathos is approximately 500 miles as the crow flies. However, it is very probable that the Genoese captain initially laid a course for the south-east of Crete via Beirut and Cape Gata, Cyprus.[16] When the ship sailed, Ibn Jubayr and his companions were in fact left behind. Because the sailing had been delayed for some time by unfavourable winds, they had been sleeping ashore. They hired a four-oared rowing boat and set out in pursuit, catching up with the ship at sunset. If she had stood directly out to sea, it seems most improbable that they would have risked such a chase. But if she had headed north along the coast towards Beirut, five to ten miles offshore, then the risk was not so great since they could easily have returned to land.[17] The voyage via Beirut and Cape Gata to Rhodes/Karpathos is about 550 miles. The ship managed a grand total of about 20 miles a day headway, or three-quarters of a knot, in

[12] See D. Jacoby, 'Crusader Acre in the thirteenth century: urban layout and topography', *Studi medievali*, 3rd ser., 20 (1979), 1–45; here pp. 9–12 and fig. 4.; B. R. Motzo, ed., *Il Compasso di Navegare: opera italiana del metà di secolo XIII* (Cagliari, 1947), p. 62.
[13] Great Britain, Admiralty, Hydrographic Department, *Mediterranean pilot*, vol. 5, 4th edn (London, 1950), p. 214.
[14] See below, pp. 32–5   [15] Ibn Jubayr, *Travels*, pp. 327–30.
[16] This was the normal route to the West in the Crusader period. See below, pp. 95–7.
[17] Ibn Jubayr, *Travels*, p. 327.

what do not appear to have been exceptionally stormy conditions. Three hundred years later, in spite of improvements in ship design, similar experiences were still common. The Venetian great galley on which Pietro Casola made his pilgrimage in 1494 took 24 days for the voyage from Jaffa to Rhodes along the same route as Ibn Jubayr. The galley was constantly held in port, forced to drop anchor, and driven back at sea by contrary winds, even though there were no storms.[18] In worsening weather Ibn Jubayr's ship took another 25 days for the voyage from Rhodes/Karpathos to Messina via the south coast of Crete and Zante; an average headway of about 30 miles a day, or one knot.[19] Yet in favourable conditions with the wind astern or abeam she was capable of considerable speed. The run along the south coast of Crete was completed in two days even though 'the sea was agitated and the wind unfavourable'; an average headway of about 80 miles a day, or three knots.[20] At that time of the year the wind was probably strong, gusty, and blowing from the north to north-west, from the starboard beam of Ibn Jubayr's ship, making conditions uncomfortable for passengers like him, but also making for quite good passage times.

Every detail of Ibn Jubayr's adventures at sea suggest that in the twelfth century, just as in antiquity, the art of navigating sailing ships lay very much in utilizing seasonal variations in weather patterns and localized meteorological phenomena in order to sail as often as possible in moderate conditions with the wind abeam or astern. There is nothing surprising in that. It remained the rule for commercial shipping through to the end of the days of sail. Because of their keel and hull configuration in particular, and rigging and design in general, sailing ships of the twelfth and thirteenth centuries had great difficulty tacking into any sort of head wind. Although they could point into the wind, they made a great deal of leeway, even when the wind was merely abeam. These qualities are discussed in depth below.

Out to sea away from the coasts, the prevailing wind directions in the Mediterranean are from the north-west to the north-east across the entire length and breadth of the sea.[21] At the same time the counter-clockwise circulation of the currents and the geographically hostile and dangerous nature of the southern coasts meant that

---

[18] Pietro Casola, *Canon Pietro Casola's pilgrimage to Jerusalem in the year 1494*, trans. M. Newett (Manchester, 1907), pp. 291–305; esp. pp. 294, 296, 298–9, 301.
[19] Ibn Jubayr, *Travels*, pp. 330–8.   [20] Ibid., p. 330.
[21] See below, pp. 16–20.

voyages from east to west in particular could be made more safely and quickly along the northern coasts of the sea.[22] The technological limitations of ancient and medieval Mediterranean merchant ships, both sailing ships and oared galleys,[23] on the one hand, and the geographical and meteorological conditions of the sea on the other combined to produce a milieu in which from antiquity through to the sixteenth century the preferred routes for commercial shipping lay along the chain of islands and coasts in the north of the sea; as long as other factors were equal, of course.[24] For east–west voyages the main trunk routes ran from Alexandria to Tyre or Beirut, then either north to Antioch and west along the coast of Lycia or else west to the south coast of Cyprus, thence to Rhodes, Karpathos, and the south coast of Crete. From there they turned north into the Ionian Sea past Zante and Cephalonia, across the Straits of Otranto to Apulia, across the Gulf of Taranto to Calabria and the east coast of Sicily. From Sicily they diverged. Ships could turn north through the Straits of Messina into the Tyrrhenian Sea and then simply follow the mainland coasts around to the approaches to the Straits of Gibraltar. Alternatively, they could swing south-west past Malta into the Sicilian Channel north of Tunisia and then head north-west to the south coast of Sardinia and thence either north via the west coasts of Sardinia and Corsica to Provence or west across the open sea to the Balearics. From there all of the North African coast and the Gibraltar approaches were easily accessible. Even for west–east voyages, for which winds were more generally favourable and for which more variety of route was therefore possible, shipping still preferred to follow the island-hopping sea lanes along the north of the sea whenever possible. For voyages either north or south the east coast of Spain, the west coasts of Corsica and Sardinia, the west coast of Italy, the west coast of the Balkans, and the west coast of Asia Minor were usually preferable. The details of these major sea lanes or trunk routes are developed in more detail below.[25]

Scattered along the sea lanes were a string of crucial mainland and island naval bases and commercial ports which were used for their

---

[22] See below, pp. 12–13, 21–4.   [23] See below, pp. 32–9, 51–7.

[24] For antiquity see E. C. Semple, *The geography of the Mediterranean region: its relation to ancient history* (London, 1931), p. 599. For the Byzantine period see P. Schreiner, 'Zivilschiffart und Handelschiffahrt in Byzanz: Quellen und Probleme bezüglich der dort tätigen Personen', in R. Ragosta, ed., *Le genti del mare mediterraneo* (Naples, 1981), 9–25; here pp. 14–15.   [25] See below, ch. 3.

logistical facilities by war fleets and corsair ships and as trading entrepôts by commercial shipping; some of the more important being the Balearics, Almeria and Malaga, Bonifacio in Corsica and Cagliari in Sardinia, Sicily, Malta, the Ionian islands, Coron and Modon in the Peloponnesus, Naxos as well as Lesbos and Tenedos in the Aegean, Crete, Rhodes, Attalya and other Cilician ports, and Cyprus. Such islands and ports as these dominated the sea lanes, and possession of them was the key to sea power and control of maritime traffic throughout the Middle Ages. As a consequence, in the interminable naval struggle and *guerre de course* waged between Islam, Byzantium, and the Christian West over a thousand years the principal strike areas for both battle fleets and corsair ships of both faiths tended to be in certain zones along the trunk routes where commercial shipping agglomerated at certain times of the year: the quadrilateral bounded by Beirut, Tripoli (Syria), Famagusta, and Limassol; the Bay of Attalya and the channels around Rhodes, Karpathos, Crete, and Lesbos; the Dodecanese archipelago; the Balkan coast of the Ionian Sea; the Straits of Otranto; the southern Tyrrhenian north of Sicily; the Sicilian Channel between Cape Bon and the south coast of Sicily; the west coasts of Sardinia and Corsica; around the Balearics; and in the Gibraltar approaches. Almost invariably, when the battle fleets of Islam and Christendom clashed in major naval engagements, they did so as part of amphibious campaigns either to acquire or to defend possession of islands, bases, and ports astride the major sea lanes.

When these considerations are viewed in conjunction with an assessment of the logistical limitations of the main strike weapon used at sea by all belligerents up to the end of the sixteenth century, oared warships, or galleys in general parlance, it becomes apparent that a considerable advantage lay with the forces of Byzantium and the Christian West for most of the period. Galleys were extremely narrow and had little depth in hold. Their length to breadth ratio was often as high as ten or more to one and amidships they might have less than a metre of freeboard. Their provision- and water-carrying capacity was small and their large crews of oarsmen, sailors, and marines consumed great quantities of both, especially of water. Supply problems seriously limited their cruising range.[26] For most of the period, the major sea lanes lay within easy striking range of Christian

---

[26] See below, pp. 75–85.

naval forces but at the limit of the range of Muslim ones. These studies seek to explore the parameters of this advantage possessed by Christendom. While certainly *not* attempting to argue for technological or geographical determinism, they point to a series of factors and combinations of factors lying in the nexus between technology and geography which help to explain certain historical phenomena: the extreme seriousness of the Muslim naval and corsair assault on Christian maritime traffic mounted in the ninth and tenth centuries and the ultimate failure of that assault; the failure of Egypt to attempt to exterminate the Crusader states of Syria and Palestine in the twelfth and thirteenth centuries by means of attack on their essential supply and communications sea lanes to the West; the processes by which shipping of the Christian West came to predominate in trans-Mediterranean maritime traffic from the eleventh to the fifteenth centuries; the dimensions of the threat to that dominance posed by the Turkish *ghazi* emirates in the fourteenth century and the Ottoman sultanate in the fifteenth and sixteenth centuries and the advantages possessed by Turkish naval and corsair forces in this period as compared to the situation of other Muslim naval forces in the early and central Middle Ages; and finally, the inherent weakness of the Barbary corsairs in the sixteenth century.

Technological and geographical factors *do not*, of course, provide the sole, or even a sufficient, explanation of the ultimate Christian or European success at sea in the Mediterranean. These studies *do not* amount to a maritime history of the Mediterranean world in the period. A whole range of other factors, political, cultural, economic, religious, and logistical, also affected profoundly the course and outcome of the struggles between Islam, Byzantium, and the West. Many of these factors call for independent studies of their own which cannot be attempted here. Even given the pioneering studies of Lombard and others on the timber resources of the Mediterranean world,[27] there is a pressing need for a comprehensive study comparing the access of the Byzantines, the various Muslim powers, and the

---

[27] See M. Lombard, 'Arsenaux et bois de marine dans la Méditerranée musulmane: VIIe–XIe siècles', rpt. in his *Espaces et réseaux du haut moyen-âge* (Paris, 1972), 107–51; M. Lombard, 'Le bois dans la Méditerranée musulmane: VIIe–XIe siècles: un problème cartographié', rpt. in his *Espaces et réseaux*, 153–76; R. Meiggs, *Trees and timber in the ancient Mediterranean world* (Oxford, 1982). See also ch. 2, n. 214 below.

Christian West to essential supplies of materials for shipbuilding; not only timber but also iron, pitch, cotton and canvas for sails, and cordage for rigging. One suspects that such a study would show an integrated Mediterranean economy in these resources, with materials in great quantities crossing the 'frontiers' between Islam, Byzantium, and the West in spite of governmental and religious prohibitions against the export of strategic raw materials. So also there is a pressing need for a comparative study of the status and role of seamen in society in the three civilizations, of methods of recruitment and training, and of remuneration; in short, of the background factors to an assessment of the fighting qualities of the crews and the skills of the officers. Both of these two areas of inquiry call for major investigations beyond the scope of this work.

In addition to factors such as these, intra-civilizational conflicts amongst the various Muslim and Christian powers also affected the inter-civilizational struggle at sea. Even in the case of the Byzantine world, with its more impartible character, rebellions and antagonisms between periphery and centre were relevant at various times. In the cases of the Christian West and the Muslim world, in certain periods and in certain sectors of the Mediterranean, these intra-civilizational conflicts assumed greater importance than the inter-religious and inter-civilizational struggles. They had a direct and profound bearing on the course and outcome of these latter.[28] I *do not* pretend that the struggles between Islam, Byzantium, and the West were monolithic ones. On the contrary, they were multi-faceted. Again, investigation of the influence of intra-civilizational conflict on the course and outcome of inter-civilizational struggle is beyond the scope of this book; although it is canvassed to some degree in the case of maritime traffic and the *guerre de course*.

The book isolates a single aspect of the maritime history of the Mediterranean in the period: the nexus between geography and maritime technology, its influence on naval warfare and the *guerre de course*, and the influence of both of these on competition in maritime traffic. In my opinion, a consideration of the parameters of this nexus

---

[28] See the judicious comments of F. Braudel, *The Mediterranean and the Mediterranean world in the age of Philip II*, 2nd edn, trans. S. Reynolds (New York, 1973), vol. 2, pp. 842–4.

provides insights which have been under-emphasized even by those historians who have been most conscious of the influence of geography and technology on the course of Mediterranean maritime history.[29]

---

[29] In addition to Braudel see E. Eickhoff, *Seekrieg und Seepolitik zwischen Islam und Abendland: das Mittelmeer unter Byzantinischer und Arabischer Hegemonie (650– 1040)* (Berlin, 1966): J. F. Guilmartin, *Gunpowder and galleys: changing technology and Mediterranean warfare at sea in the sixteenth century* (Cambridge, 1975); A. R. Lewis, *Naval power and trade in the Mediterranean A.D.500–1100* (Princeton, 1951); W. L. Rodgers, *Naval warfare under oars, fourth to sixteenth centuries* (Annapolis, 1939).

1. *The sea*

For ancient and medieval man, the Mediterranean had a deserved reputation for benevolence. Compared to the Atlantic and the North Sea, it offers favourable conditions for navigation for many more months of the year. Clear skies, moderate winds, and slight seas can be expected across most of the sea from late March through to late October. Because of the small size of the sea, in world geographical and meteorological terms, the huge rollers which make Atlantic navigation so dangerous in storms are not to be found in the Mediterranean; although it is true that the short, steep chop raised by strong winds in some parts of the Mediterranean can be equally as hazardous as the Atlantic's rollers. Similarly, the tides, which so governed navigation in the North Sea as to affect the evolution of ship design, are virtually absent from the Mediterranean except in certain narrows. The many islands scattered throughout the northern half of the sea reduced the need to make long voyages out of sight of land and thus promoted maritime traffic in an age of small ships. The clear skies of summer nights facilitated navigation by the stars. But if the Mediterranean was particularly favourable to men's endeavours upon the sea by comparison to other waters, nevertheless geographical and meteorological factors still influenced profoundly matters such as ship design, the rhythms of seasonal voyaging, and the choice of routes. Navigation under oars and sail was always strongly influenced by, if not actually controlled by, the set of the currents and tides, the patterns of prevailing winds, the configuration of the coasts, and the contours of localized meteorological phenomena, particularly the diurnal land and sea breezes.

The main basin of the Mediterranean has few major rivers feeding into it; the Nile, Po, and Rhône being virtually the only rivers which provide any major water inflow. The contribution of smaller rivers such as the Orontes, Meander, Maritsa, Vardar, Tiber, Arno, and Ebro is insignificant. In the modern era, but before the building of the

Nile dams, all the rivers of the main Mediterranean basin compensated for only about 25% of the loss through evaporation above rainfall over the surface of the sea. The figure may have been a little higher in the Middle Ages because there was much less tapping of the rivers before they reached the sea, but not high enough to affect any conclusions to be reached about the circulation of the currents. The Russian rivers, the Don, Dneiper, and Dneister, together with the Danube, provide in the Black Sea a net water gain from rainfall and inflow above evaporation. This then sets up a current out through the Bosphorus and Dardanelles into the Aegean, a current which was famed throughout antiquity and the Middle Ages. Today this current compensates for a further 4% of the water loss in the Mediterranean. The remaining 71% of the loss has to be made up by a massive inflow from the Atlantic through the Straits of Gibraltar. Heavier, more saline, Mediterranean water flows out into the Atlantic in a deep, subsurface current while lighter, less saline, Atlantic water flows into the Mediterranean in a surface current which averages about six knots.[1] The power of this surface current influences the entire sea. Until very late in the Middle Ages, shipping had great difficulty making the exit from the Mediterranean to the Atlantic against this current, and it had a significant effect on the course of history.[2] The combined effects of the inflows from the Straits of Gibraltar, the Dardanelles, and the Nile, Po, and Rhône are to set up a general counter-clockwise current circulation throughout the whole sea (figure 2). Its strength varies from about six knots through the Straits of Gibraltar to three to six through the Sicilian Channel, two to three off the coasts of Egypt, Palestine, and Syria, about four through the Dardanelles, about two around Crete, up to six or more through the Straits of Messina (either intensified or decreased by the tides there), and about a half to one and a half along the coasts of Italy and France.

In the days when oars and sails powered shipping these currents were either formidable foes or very helpful allies. The Straits of Messina, with their whirlpools and tidal rips, *tagli*, gave rise in

[1] E. Bradford, *Mediterranean – portrait of a sea* (New York, 1971), p. 36; J. J. Branigan & H. R. Jarrett, *The Mediterranean lands* (London, 1969), p. 21; *Mediterranean pilot*, vol. 1, 8th edn (London, 1951), pp. 5–9; D. S. Walker, *The Mediterranean lands*, 3rd edn (London, 1965), p. 13.

[2] A. R. Lewis, 'Northern European sea power and the Straits of Gibraltar, 1031–1350 A.D.', in W. C. Jordan et al., eds., *Order and innovation in the Middle Ages: essays in honour of Joseph R. Strayer* (Princeton, 1976), 139–64.

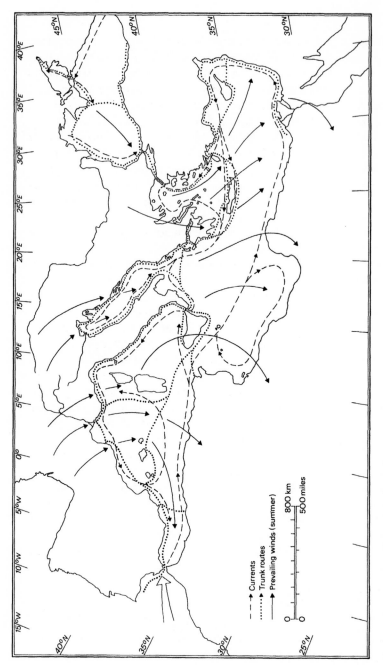

Figure 2 Currents, prevailing winds (summer), and trunk routes

antiquity to the legend of Scylla and Charybdis. Ibn Jubayr commented that: 'The sea in this strait, which runs between the mainland and the island of Sicily, pours through like the "bursting of the dam" and, from the intensity of the contraction and the pressure, boils like a cauldron. Difficult indeed is its passage for ships.'[3]

The network of currents around the sea was utilized for navigation both in antiquity and throughout the Middle Ages.[4] The assistance it could offer was particularly useful for voyages from east to west and south to north, which had to be made against the prevailing winds, and thus contributed considerably towards establishing the popularity of the trunk routes. Ships attempting to sail north or west against the winds could often claw their way along the coasts by using the currents setting in their favour as well as by taking advantage of the daily cycle of morning and evening sea and land breezes, which, close in to shore, predominated over the prevailing winds in some sectors.

The climatology of the Mediterranean region is extremely complex.[5] In the most general terms the climate may be said to be governed by the influences of external inter-continental pressure systems interacting with geographical features of the Mediterranean basin; particularly the mountain ranges, which surround the sea on all sides except the south-east, and the warm sea itself. The most important influences on meteorological conditions are exerted at various times of the year by four great inter-continental pressure systems: the Atlantic sub-tropical high-pressure system centred around 30° north latitude over the Azores; the North-Atlantic, sub-polar low-pressure system, which in winter moves south to about 65° north latitude between Iceland and Greenland; the Mongolian high pressure system, which in winter moves south to about 50° north latitude centred over Soviet central Asia and which ridges across the Ukraine into the Danubian basin; and the Indo-Persian, monsoonal low-pressure system, which in summer develops at about 30° north latitude over Pakistan and which also ridges west into both Asia

---

[3] Ibn Jubayr, *Travels*, p. 336.

[4] For antiquity see Semple, *Geography of the Mediterranean*, p. 582.

[5] For the following consult in general Branigan & Jarrett, *Mediterranean lands*, pp. 29–37; J. I. Clarke, ed., *An advanced geography of Africa* (Amersham, 1975), pp. 74–115; *Mediterranean pilot*, vol. 1, pp. 30–42; Great Britain, Admiralty, *Notes on climate and other subjects in Eastern Mediterranean and adjacent countries* (London, n.d.); R. A. Muller & T. M. Oberlander, *Physical geography today: a portrait of a planet*, 2nd edn (New York, 1974), pp. 117–43; Walker, *Mediterranean lands*, pp. 18–27; *Weather in the Mediterranean*.

Minor and across the Arabian peninsula into Saharan Africa. All of these systems generate successive waves of pressure cells and fronts which enter the Mediterranean basin through gaps in its surrounding mountains: the Biskra gap between Tunisia and the Atlas mountains, the Straits of Gibraltar, the Iberian plateau, the Carcassonne gap between the Pyrenees and the French Massif Central, the Rhône gap between the Massif Central and the Alps, the Trieste gap between the European Alps and the Dinaric Alps of Yugoslavia, the valleys of the rivers Vardar and Struma, the Bosphorus and Dardanelles, and the Gulf of Iskenderon (Alexandretta) between the Taurus mountains and the Lebanon. In general terms, the fronts and pressure cells track in a roughly easterly direction across the Mediterranean basin. Interacting with effects of the warm water of the sea and the cold highlands of the mountains surrounding it, their influences produce complex and variable localized weather systems. Winter and summer patterns are quite different, and the eastern and western basins are governed by different regimes. The Ionian Sea, over which the eastern and western regimes meet and interact, is subject to especially complex, changeable, and often inclement weather conditions.

In the winter the climate is dominated by the North Atlantic low and the Mongolian high (figure 3a). The Atlantic sub-tropical high is weak and located to the south and west beyond a position of influence at this time of the year. In winter it is really part of a continuous high-pressure belt running round the earth at about 20° north latitude, and any influence which it has on the Mediterranean is exerted by the Saharan anticyclone to the south of the Atlas. The Indo-Persian low does not really exist in winter at all. In the western basin of the Mediterranean, the North Atlantic low exerts the predominant influence in winter. Moving south, it generates depressions which track eastwards and set up a whole series of localized depressions. Maritime polar air enters the Mediterranean through the Carcassonne and Rhône gaps. In the eastern basin of the sea, the Mongolian high governs the winter weather. Moving south, it ridges west into the Danubian basin. Air masses from the Eurasian Arctic enter the Mediterranean basin through the Trieste gap, the valleys of the Vardar and the Struma, and the Bosphorus and Dardanelles. Because, in the northern hemisphere, winds spiral counter-clockwise in towards the centres of low-pressure systems and clockwise out from the centres of high-pressure systems, the effects of these two inter-

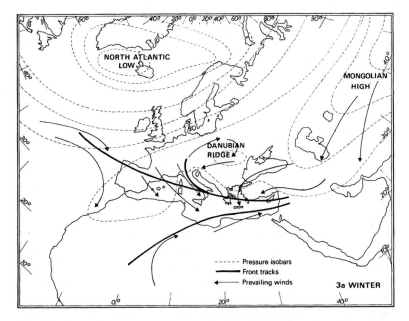

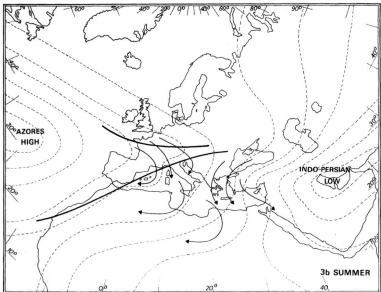

Figure 3a Winter – normal sea-level pressure systems, front tracks, and prevailing winds

Figure 3b Summer – normal sea-level pressure systems, front tracks, and prevailing winds

continental systems are to set up high winds varying from north-west to north-east across the entire Mediterranean.[6]

In the summer the North Atlantic low retreats north towards the pole and weakens (figure 3b). In its place the Atlantic, sub-tropical high intensifies and moves north and east to a position over the Azores, from where it exerts a powerful influence on the western basin of the Mediterranean. Maritime air from the Atlantic enters the Mediterranean through the Gibraltar gap, across the Iberian plateau, and through the Carcassonne gap. In the eastern basin of the sea, the Indo-Persian low governs the summer weather. The Mongolian high retreats north towards the north pole, just as does the North Atlantic low, and moves east into Siberia, losing influence over the Mediterranean. In its place the Indo-Persian, monsoonal low develops in April and May, reaching a peak of intensity over Pakistan in July, and extending west in two ridges into Asia Minor on the one hand and across the Arabian peninsula into Saharan Africa on the other. These ridges may intensify into separate cyclonic lows. Air masses associated with the system generally enter the Mediterranean in the northern Aegean through the Vardar/Struma and Bosphorus/Dardanelles gaps, and occasionally through the Gulf of Iskenderon. In the western basin, high-pressure systems and fronts generated by the Azores high bring prevailing north-west to north-easterly winds while in the eastern basin, winds spiralling anti-clockwise around the Indo-Persian low in towards its centre also set up prevailing northerlies.[7]

From autumn to spring the western basin of the sea is almost totally dominated by low-pressure systems formed generally in one or more of the following ways: depressions generated by the North Atlantic low and entering the Mediterranean through the Carcassonne and Rhône gaps; depressions actually generated within the Mediterranean basin itself either as a result of long-distance influences or else as a result of local geographical phenomena such as thermal contrasts between snow-covered mountains and the warm sea; and depressions created by cold fronts moving down from north-west Europe, piling up against the European Alps, and then bulging around through the Rhône or Trieste gaps into the Gulf of the Lion or the Adriatic, and

---

[6] *Weather in the Mediterranean*, vol. 1, pp. 8–17, fig. 1.1(a) (p. 6) and fig. 1.5(a) (p. 25). See also the 'Normal sea-level pressure' maps for November to February (pp. 60–1, 70–1) and April to September (pp. 63–8).

[7] Ibid., vol. 1, pp. 17–23, fig. 1.1(b) (p. 7) and fig. 1.5(b) (p. 26).

producing cyclonic lows in the lee of the Alps in the Po valley. At the same time the eastern basin of the sea is dominated by the Danubian ridge of the Mongolian high, although localized depressions generated in the central Mediterranean area over the Ionian Sea and moving eastwards also have significant influences.

The prevailing northerly winds of winter tend to be rain-laden in the western basin and cold and dry in the eastern. The famous *mistral* of Languedoc and Provence and *maestrale* of Liguria develop when depressions in the Gulf of the Lion or the Gulf of Genoa pull down masses of cold air from the Massif Central or the Alps through the Rhône gap. The *Golfe du Lion*, the Gulf of the Lion, not the Gulf of Lyons as it is so often translated into English, derives its name from the lion's roar of the *mistral*. Crossing Corsica and Sardinia into the Tyrrhenian, the wind sets more from the west, or even south-west, and is known as the *libeccio*. Similar conditions occurring at the head of the Adriatic produce the *bora*, which, when it crosses the Italian peninsula into the southern Tyrrhenian as a northerly, is known as the *tramontana*. Over Sicily and Malta, as a north-easterly, it is the *gregale*.[8] In the northern Aegean steep pressure gradients between depressions over the sea and the Danubian high produce the violent wind known as the *vardarac* which sweeps down the valleys of the Vardar and Struma rivers; the ancient Strymonian *boreas*. Depressions moving eastwards across the sea send westerly winds into Levantine waters.[9]

From spring through to autumn the western basin is dominated for the most part by high-pressure systems generated by the Azores high, entering the Mediterranean, and then tracking north and east towards the Gulf of Genoa and across northern Italy towards Trieste. Winds spiralling clockwise out from the centres of such systems produce prevailing north-west to north-easterly winds. In the far south-west of the sea, the Alboran Channel, the wind swings to the east and is known as the *levanter*.[10] In the eastern basin, the predominant influence in the summer is that of the Indo-Persian low. Winds spiralling anti-clockwise in towards the centres of this huge system and its Asia Minor and Arabian ridges produce prevailing north to

---

[8]   Ibid., vol. 1, pp. 72–82 and fig. 1.20 (p. 100); *Mediterranean pilot*, vol. 1, pp. 38–40.
[9]   *Weather in the Mediterranean*, vol. 1, pp. 77, 91–2 and fig. 1.20 (p. 100). See also Goldsmith & Sofer, 'Wave climatology', pp. 7–8.
[10] *Weather in the Mediterranean*, vol. 1, pp. 79–81, fig. 1.5(b) (p. 26) and fig. 1.20 (p. 100); *Mediterranean pilot*, vol. 1, p. 32.

north-westerly winds blowing out of the Aegean across the Mediterranean on to the coasts of Libya, Egypt, Palestine, and Syria. The *meltemi*, the famous Etesian winds of antiquity, which blows steadily from May to September, varying in direction from north-easterly in the northern Aegean to north-westerly in the southern Mediterranean, is produced by a combination of factors: high pressures in the western basin of the sea, the Indo-Persian low to the east of the sea, and low pressures over the eastern basin dragging down winds from high-pressure areas to the north of the sea.[11] The *meltemi* can blow so steadily that during the Roman period it was capable of bringing voyages from Egypt to Rome to a virtual halt for weeks on end.[12] At Iraklion (Candia) in Crete, its frequency at 1400 hours averages 75% from May to September, reaching a peak of 88% in July. At Rhodes the figures are 76.5% with a peak of 84% in August, and at Alexandria 83.5% with a peak of 90% in August and September.[13]

Virtually the only variation from the general pattern of prevailing northerlies is provided by the various forms of the *scirocco*. Particularly in the spring, but also again in the autumn, an increase of high pressure over the Mediterranean as a result of the influence of the Azores high can cause cyclonic, extremely low-pressure conditions to develop over the Sahara. The Saharan ridge of the Indo-Persian low can intensify into a separate cyclonic depression. When maritime air masses from the Atlantic flow into the rear of such depressions, they can induce a flow of Saharan air from the depression areas northwards. Hot winds of very great strength bring dust storms to the entire southern coast of the Mediterranean. Each region has its own name for these winds: the *shergui* in Morocco, the *leveche* in Algeria, the *scirocco* or *chili* in both Algeria and Tunisia, the *ghibli* in Libya, the *khamsin* in Egypt, and the *shlouq* in Palestine.[14] However, although the *scirocco* does break up the prevailing pattern of northerly winds, it is of little help to navigation because of the violent and dangerous nature of its winds.

For medieval ships, dependent upon human muscle and the force of

[11] *Weather in the Mediterranean*, vol. 1, pp. 20, 78–9, fig. 1.5(b) (p. 26) and fig. 1.20 (p. 100); *Mediterranean pilot*, vol. 3, 9th edn (London, 1970), p. 28. See also Goldsmith & Sofer, 'Wave climatology', p. 8.
[12] Semple, *Geography of the Mediterranean*, p. 580.
[13] *Weather in the Mediterranean*, vol. 2, pp. 55, 67, 78.
[14] Ibid., vol. 1, pp. 16, 22–3, 40–2, fig. 1.6 (p. 33) and fig. 1.20 (p. 100); *Mediterranean pilot*, vol. 1, pp. 40–1.

the wind for their motive power, prevailing winds from the north made the southern coasts of the Mediterranean a dangerous lee shore. Inadequacies in the performance capabilities of ships of the period, which are discussed below,[15] added their own dimensions to the natural hazards of the southern coasts.

The northern coasts of the Mediterranean were relatively kind to the mariner. The coastal profiles are high, providing good landmarks which can be seen easily from well out to sea. There are large numbers of bays and sheltered beaches where ships could take refuge in the lee of the land in inclement weather. The sea bottom generally drops away quickly, providing deep water and safe navigation while still close to land. To be sure, there are the omnipresent dangers of offshore reefs, shoals, islands, and sandbanks, as well as of stretches of cliff-lined coast, but nevertheless, the northern coasts presented a much more welcoming aspect in general to the ship powered by oars or sails than did the southern coasts.[16]

The North African coast of the Mediterranean has always been notorious for its treacherous character. From Ceuta eastwards to Tunisia the coast has shallows and islands miles off shore and reefs running far out to sea. The northern coast of Tunisia is characterized by rocky cliffs, offshore islands, and surrounding reefs all the way from the Algerian border to Cape Bon.[17] There are few natural anchorages providing safe, deep water, and most of the ports along this coast in the Middle Ages had been man-made.[18] The entire coast of the Maghreb, from Ceuta to Cape Bon, has been a graveyard for ships ever since antiquity.[19] In northerly storms the swell raised by the wind blowing out of the Gulf of the Lion across the breadth of the Mediterranean exacerbated the stock dangers of a lee shore.[20] Ludolph von Suchem, a fourteenth-century pilgrim, summed up the natural dangers of the Maghreb coast: 'no one dares to sail to the

---

[15] See below, pp. 32–9, 51–7.
[16] Cf. Guilmartin, *Gunpowder and galleys*, p. 64.
[17] *Mediterranean pilot*, vol. 1, *passim*, esp. pp. 286–8, 292, 301–3, 310–14, 318, 331–5, 346–7. Cf. Bradford, *Mediterranean*, p. 32; Braudel, *The Mediterranean*, pp. 133, 162; Guilmartin, *Gunpowder and galleys*, p. 64.
[18] J. L. Yarrison, *Force as an instrument of policy: European military incursions and trade in the Maghrib, 1000–1355*, Ph.D. thesis, Princeton University, 1982, pp. 21–3.
[19] Semple, *Geography of the Mediterranean*, p. 599.
[20] *Weather in the Mediterranean*, p. 184. Cf. S. Lane-Poole, *The Barbary corsairs* (London, 1890), p. 21.

south towards Barbary, for many rocks and shoals are to be found there covered by the water'.[21]

For voyages from the west to the east, the winds and currents at least are mostly favourable along this coast. However, even these could not be relied upon in the Middle Ages. In the Alboran Channel east to around Bougie, easterly *levanters* are frequent. Moreover, localized eddies in the main eastward-setting current can sweep ships back to the west. In 1248 this happened off Cape Bon to the ship carrying Jean de Joinville on the Sixth Crusade.[22] For voyages from the east to the west, both adverse currents and contrary prevailing winds could be expected along the entire coast.

The Gulf of Gabes and the Gulf of Sirte, from Cape Bon to Benghazi, are notorious for their low-lying coasts, which deny reliable landmarks and observations to shipping, and for sandbanks and quicksands which line the coasts, reaching up to 12 miles out to sea.[23] These banks were marked prominently on medieval portolan charts such as the *Carta Pisana* and were mentioned in the *Compasso de Navegare*.[24]

Similar conditions, a dangerous low-lying coast and shallows far out to sea, characterize the coasts of Libya and Egypt from the Nile delta to Ra's al-Tin.[25] Marino Sanudo Torsello said that for each mile out to sea the depth of water increased by only one *passus* (1.75 m) between Damietta and Alexandria.[26] In fact it varies quite a lot but, nevertheless, there are large extents of shallow banks. In 1249 the large transport ships of St Louis's fleet were stopped by the Damietta

---

[21] Ludolph von Suchem, *Description of the Holy Land and of the way thither, written in the year 1350*, trans. A. Stewart in *P.P.T.S.L.*, vol. 12, part 3 (London, 1897), p. 14.

[22] Joinville, *The life of St. Louis by John of Joinville*, trans. R. Hague (London, 1955), p. 56.

[23] *Mediterranean pilot*, vol. 1, pp. 355, 360–3, 368–74 and vol. 5, pp. 39, 53, 57, 59, 63–5. Cf. Lane-Poole, *Barbary corsairs*, p. 16; J. Rougé, *Recherches sur l'organization du commerce en Méditerranée sous l'empire romain* (Paris, 1966), p. 36; J. Rougé, 'Discussione', on the paper of Lewicki, 'Les voies maritimes', in *La navigazione mediterranea nell'alto medioevo* (Spoleto, 1978), vol. 2, 471–2; Semple, *Geography of the Mediterranean*, p. 583.

[24] Motzo, *Compasso di Navegare*, pp. 68–72; *Carta Pisana*, in K. Kretschmer, *Die italienischen Portolane des Mittelalters* (Berlin, 1909), endpiece.

[25] *Mediterranean pilot*, vol. 5, pp. 77–9, 82, 87–8, 94–5, 112, 117–18, 120. Cf. Semple, *Geography of the Mediterranean*, p. 591; A. Udovitch, 'Time, the sea and society: duration of commercial voyages on the southern shores of the Mediterranean during the High Middle Ages', in *La navigazione mediterranea nell'alto medioevo*, vol. 2, 503–46, here p. 544.

[26] Marino Sanudo Torsello, *Liber secretorum fidelium crucis super Terrae Sanctae recuperatione et conservatione* (Hanover, 1611), II.4.25 (p. 87).

Table 2. *The North African coast: average percentage frequency of unfavourable winds for east–west voyages, May to September*[27]

Place	Observation time	Unfavourable wind direction	Average percentage frequency of unfavourable winds, May to September
Alexandria	1400	W to N	94%
Salum	1400	W to NE	90%
Derna	1400	W to N	85.5%
Benghazi	1500	SW to N	79%
Sirte	1300	W to NE	88%
Misurata	1300	W to NE	62.5%
Tripoli (Libya)	1500	W to NE	79%
Gabes	1400	NW to E	77.5%
Sfax	1300	N to SE	70%
Sousse	Average	N to SE	58.5%
Tunis	1300	W to NE	92%
Bone	1400	W to NE	92%
Algiers	1300	W to NE	80%
Oran	1300	W to N	84.5%

banks, which in places have less than three metres of water over them, from approaching more than three leagues to the shore off Damietta.[28]

From Ra's al-Tin westwards to Benghazi, the coastal profile is more prominent and medieval shipping could move out to sea with greater confidence. Nevertheless, with the exception of Tobruk, there was no major haven along the coast from Alexandria to Tripoli (Libya) in the Middle Ages.[29] For ships caught in northerly storms, this coast also was implacably hostile. Whether generated by strengthening of the *meltemi* in summer or by the passage of depressions across the Ionian Sea in winter, by the time that such

[27] Compiled from statistics given in table 1: General climatic tables, of *Weather in the Mediterranean*, vol. 2, pp. 1–80. See also fig. 1.19(b) and fig. 1.19(c): Percentage frequency of wind direction and speed for March–May and June–August, in vol. 1, pp. 97–8.

[28] Jean Sarrasin, 'The letter of John Sarrasin', ed. A. E. Foulet (1924), trans. R. Hague in Joinville, *Life of St. Louis*, pp. 242–3. See also C. Cahen, 'Douanes et commerce dans les ports méditerranéens de l'Egypte médiévale d'après le *Minhādj* d'al-Makhzūmī', *Journal of the economic and social history of the Orient*, 7 (1964), 217–314, here p. 236.

[29] Udovitch, 'Time, the sea and society', pp. 535, 543–4. Cf. C. Courtois, 'Remarques sur le commerce maritime en Afrique au XIe siècle', in *Mélanges d'histoire et d'archéologie de l'Occident musulman* (Algiers, 1957), vol. 2, 51–9, here p. 53 n. 15.

storms reach the North African coast, the swell which they whip up is considerable.[30]

The configuration of the coasts, then, and particularly the unfriendly nature of the southern shores, added its own influence to those of the set of the currents and the direction of the prevailing winds to promote the popularity of sea lanes following the northern coasts. It is significant that in his analysis of the Cairo Geniza material, Goitein draws almost all his *exempla* evidence for the dangers of sea travel from the route to the Maghreb from Egypt, even though he does not suggest that the sea voyage was regarded as particularly dangerous at the time.[31] To these influences was added that of the geographical 'accident' that not too far off the northern coasts was a series of major islands which could provide refuge for shipping in bad weather, facilities for repairs, and trading opportunities: the Balearics, Corsica, Sardinia, Sicily, Corfu and the Ionian islands, Crete, Negropont (Evvoia), Naxos and the Aegean islands, Rhodes, and Cyprus. With the exception of the Balearics, Sardinia, and Sicily, which could also service the routes along the southern shores of the sea, the islands in the south of the Mediterranean, such as Alboran, Galite, Pantelleria, Lampedusa, Malta and Gozo, Kerkenna, and Djerba, were small, poorly populated, and could not offer shelter, facilities, or opportunities comparable to those which the northern islands could. That is not to say that they were never used as refuges and supply stations for, of course, they were.[32] Nevertheless, their qualities were obviously inferior to those of the northern islands.

---

[30] *Weather in the Mediterranean*, vol. 1, pp. 78–9, 92, 185, fig. 1.25 (p. 108), fig. 1.26 (p. 109).

[31] S. D. Goitein, *A Mediterranean society: the Jewish communities of the Arab world as portrayed in the documents of the Cairo Geniza. Volume I: economic foundations* (Berkeley, 1967), pp. 276–81, 319–23.

[32] Yarrison, *Force as an instrument of policy*, pp. 30, 101–6 and appendix B–39, 58.

2. The ships

It would, of course, be impossible to trace in detail here the entire history of ships and shipbuilding in the Mediterranean from the late Roman period to the sixteenth century.[1] Moreover, such a study would be unnecessary since we are concerned not so much with the naval architecture of ships for its own sake as with certain technological properties and performance characteristics of the major types of oared warships on the one hand and both oared and sailing merchant ships on the other. The parameters of those properties and characteristics are related to problems of performance and to logistical capabilities and limitations which affected the course and outcome of both the naval struggle at sea and also competition in maritime traffic.

COMMERCIAL SHIPPING

The early Middle Ages to the end of the thirteenth century

Information about early medieval shipping is meagre in the extreme. For wind-powered sailing ships it is only in the middle Byzantine

[1] In fact no scholarly work has ever been devoted solely to this subject and a modern, up-to-date study is sorely needed. Amongst the most useful works are the following: H. Ahrweiler, *Byzance et la mer: la marine de guerre, la politique et les institutions maritimes de Byzance au VIIe–XVe siècles* (Paris, 1966), pp. 408–39; R. C. Anderson, *Oared fighting ships: from classical times to the coming of steam* (Kings Langley, 1976); G. F. Bass, ed., *A history of seafaring based on underwater archaeology* (London, 1972); M. Bonino, *Archeologia e tradizione navale tra la Romagna e il Po* (Ravenna, 1978); A. M. Fahmy, *Muslim naval organization in the Eastern Mediterranean* (Cairo, 1966); B. M. Kreutz, 'Ships, shipping and the implications of change in the early medieval Mediterranean', *Viator*, 7 (1976), 79–109; B. Landstrom, *The ship: an illustrated history* (New York, 1961); F. C. Lane, *Venetian ships and shipbuilders of the Renaissance* (Baltimore, 1934); G. la Roerie & J. Vivielle, *Navires et marins de la rame à l'hélice* (Paris, 1930); U. Nebbia, *Arte navale italiana* (Bergamo, 1932); W. Unger, *The ship in the medieval economy 600–1600* (London, 1980). There is also much useful information in many contributions to *La navigazione mediterranea nell'alto medioevo* (Settimane di Studio del Centro italiano di studi sull'alto medioevo, XXV) (Spoleto, 1978).

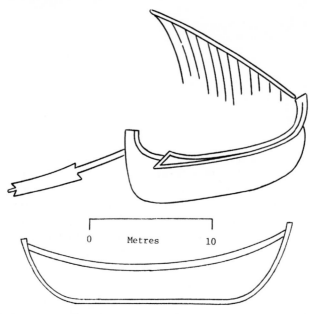

Figure 4 Merchant sailing ship of the middle Byzantine period, from the Sermons of St Gregory of Nazianzus, and longitudinal hull plan of the seventh-century Yassi Ada wreck

period that we begin to acquire a few details about ship construction. In recent years the work of nautical archaeologists has added immeasurably to the skeletal information which had been derived previously from written sources and art history.[2] By around the seventh century a number of important changes had occurred since the late Roman period. Ships had become much smaller, or at least the very large grain ships of the Roman empire had disappeared.[3] Also,

---

[2] See in particular G. F. Bass & F. H. van Doorninck jr, eds, *Yassi Ada. Volume I: a seventh-century Byzantine shipwreck* (College Station, 1982); J. R. Steffy, 'The reconstruction of the 11th-century Serçe Liman vessel: a preliminary report', *I.J.N.A.*, 11 (1982), 13–34.

[3] M. A. Bragadin, 'Le navi, loro strutture et attrezzature', in *La navigazione mediterranea nell'alto medioevo*, vol. 1, 389–407, here p. 403; Kreutz, 'Ships', p. 102; R. S. Lopez, 'The role of trade in the economic readjustment of Byzantium in the seventh century', *D.O.P.*, 13 (1959), 68–85, here pp. 71–2; Unger, *The ship*, p. 47; W. Unger, 'Warships and cargo ships in medieval Europe', *Technology and culture*, 22 (1981), 233–52, here pp. 236–7; F. van Doorninck jr, 'Byzantium, mistress of the sea: 330–641', in Bass, *History of seafaring*, 133–58, here p. 139.

shipwrights had begun to abandon the old technique, which had produced very strong ships but at great expense in terms of labour skill required and of construction time, of laboriously building up the hull planking first by fastening one plank to another with mortise and tenon joints and only afterwards inserting ribs for strengthening. Instead they began to build the ships' skeletons of ribs first and then to add the planks afterwards, nailing them to the ribs. This change was still in transition in the seventh century but had been completed by the eleventh.[4] In the same period, or perhaps even earlier, the square sails which had powered virtually all major sea-going ships in antiquity were replaced by triangular, fore-and-aft, lateen sails. In fact the lateen sail may have developed from the ancient square sail, which, unlike its modern equivalent, did not rotate around the mast in a single, horizontal plane, but rather could be peaked to one side.[5] Ninth-century representations of Byzantine sailing ships in a manuscript of the sermons of St Gregory of Nazianzus accord remarkably with the hull plan of the seventh-century Yassi Ada wreck[6] (figure 4). Ordinary merchantmen of the Byzantine empire from the seventh to eleventh centuries were small, of less than 250 tons deadweight tonnage, were powered by a single lateen sail, were steered by two steering oars on the stern quarters, had curved stemposts and sternposts giving the hull configuration a rounded look, and had no

[4] G. F. Bass & F. H. van Doorninck jr., 'An 11th-century shipwreck at Serçe Liman, Turkey', *I.J.N.A.*, 7 (1978) 119–32; Bass & van Doorninck, *Yassi Ada*, pp. 55–63; Kreutz, 'Ships', pp. 104–6: Steffy, 'Serçe Liman'; Unger, *The ship*, pp. 36–42; F. H. van Doorninck jr, *The seventh-century Byzantine ship at Yassi Ada: some contributions to the history of naval architecture*, Ph.D. thesis, University of Pennsylvania, 1967, pp. 100–6; van Doorninck, 'Byzantium', pp. 138, 143–4; L. White jr, 'Introduction: the reticences of the Middle Ages', in R. Berger, ed., *Scientific methods in medieval archaeology* (Berkeley, 1970), 3–14, here pp. 7–9.

[5] Kreutz, 'Ships', pp. 80–6 *et passim*; Unger, *The ship*, pp. 47–50; van Doorninck, 'Byzantium', pp. 134–5, 139. There is an enormous specialist literature on the origins and diffusion of the lateen sail. Two of the best articles are R. H. Dolley, 'The rig of early medieval warships', *M.M.*, 35 (1949), 51–5 and P. Adam, 'A propos des origines de la voile latine', in Mollat, *Méditerranée et Océan Indien* (VIème Colloque international d'histoire maritime, Venezia, 1962) (Paris, 1970), 203–28. On the characteristics of the ancient square sail and the possible development of the lateen sail from it, see P. Adam, 'Conclusions sur les développements des techniques nautiques médiévales', *Revue d'histoire économique et sociale*, 54 (1976), 560–7, here p. 561.

[6] Bib. Nat. Paris, MS. Grec 510. Note that some Byzantine art historians believe that the MS. Grec 510 illustrations are ninth-century copies of much older originals. See A. Graber, *Byzantine painting* (New York, 1953), p. 172; S. der Nersessian, 'The homilies of Gregory of Nazianzus', *D.O.P.*, 16 (1962), 197–228, here p. 227.

deep keel.[7] These characteristics remained the norm for all Mediterranean sailing ships to the end of the thirteenth century.

If there is a paucity of evidence for the construction of middle Byzantine shipping, there is a positive dearth for that of the early Muslim world. Probably as a result of early Muslim strictures against representations of the human form, there are few illustrations of Muslim ships before the thirteenth century.[8] Although it seems certain that shipping of the early Muslim world was, like that of the Byzantine, composed of a wide variety of types, there is no reason to suspect that it differed in any marked or general way from that of the Byzantines. After the first conquests, the Muslims predominantly used ships taken from, or modelled upon those of, indigenous seafaring peoples of the Mediterranean coasts; particularly the Byzantines.[9] The name of one widely used type, *qārib* or *carabi*, was certainly derived from the Greek κάραβος or καράβιον.[10] However, the Muslims may also have introduced into the Mediterranean some ship types brought from their own world of the Red Sea and Indian Ocean. The *tarida*, for example, known to the Byzantines as ταρίτα and to the Christian West as *tarida*, may have been derived from the *ṭarīda* or *ṭarrāda* of the Muslims, which was originally a reed canoe used in the Red Sea.[11] In the tenth to twelfth centuries, Muslim, and particularly Egyptian, merchantmen were largely sailing ships with lateen sails and were manoeuvred by steering oars.[12] That they were quite small is indicated by the fact that the *qārib* was often undecked.[13] The name of another of the types most commonly mentioned in the Cairo Geniza material, *khinzīra*, seems to suggest that its hull had a rounded configuration.[14] Currently being excavated off Serçe Liman, Turkey, is an eleventh-century ship with a markedly curved and rounded sternpost which may possibly be

[7] Landstrom, *The ship*, pp. 80–1; Lopez, 'Trade', pp. 71, 79; Unger, *The ship*, pp. 29, 47; van Doorninck, 'Byzantium', pp. 139, 146.
[8] Udovitch, 'Time, the sea and society', p. 516.
[9] Bragadin, 'Le navi', p. 390; Kreutz, 'Ships', pp. 94–5.
[10] V. Christides, 'Two parallel naval guides of the tenth century: Qudama's document and Leo VI's Naumachica: a study on Byzantine and Moslem naval preparedness', *Graeco-Arabica*, 1 (1982), 51–103; here p. 95.
[11] V. Christides, *The conquest of Crete by the Arabs (ca. 824): a turning point in the struggle between Byzantium and Crete* (Athens, 1984); p. 46.
[12] Goitein, *Mediterranean society*, pp. 305–6; Kreutz, 'Ships', pp. 86, 101–3; Udovitch, 'Time, the sea and society', p. 517; Unger, *The ship*, pp. 53–4.
[13] Goitein, *Mediterranean society*, p. 305.   [14] Ibid., p. 477 n. 13.

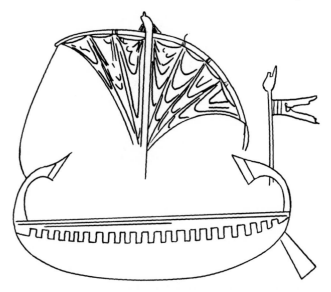

Figure 5 Thirteenth-century Muslim sailing ship, from the Damascus MS of Al-Hariri's *Maqamat*

Muslim. It is presumed that its stempost was also similarly curved.[15] Although they do have significant differences, nevertheless the similarities between the hull configuration of this ship and that of the seventh-century Yassi Ada ship are remarkable. The ship in the Bibliothèque Nationale manuscript of al-Hariri's *Maqamat* (figure 5), drawn in 1222 probably in Damascus or in the Jezireh, may have been intended by the artist to represent a Tigris or Euphrates river boat, but its general outlines seem very similar to those of Mediterranean ships of thirteenth-century Byzantium and the Christian West.[16]

From the middle of the twelfth century some detailed information about Italian sailing ships begins to appear. Later it does also for other seafaring regions of the Christian West. The size of ships began to increase amongst the Italians and may have done so also in Byzantium and in the Muslim world.[17] Figure 6 shows a rare

[15] Bass & van Doorninck, 'Serçe Liman', p. 131; Steffy, 'Serçe Liman', pp. 21, 31, fig. 13.

[16] Udovitch, 'Time, the sea and society', p. 517 n. 16 referring to E. Blochet, *Les enluminures des manuscrits orientaux – turcs, arabes, persans – de la Bibliothèque Nationale* (Paris, 1926), pp. 54–5 and plate V.

[17] Kreutz, 'Ships', p. 107; Unger, *The ship*, pp. 105, 122–3, 127–8.

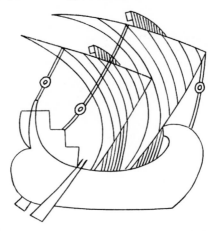

Figure 6 Byzantine? sailing ship of the thirteenth century, from a plate found at Corinth

depiction from a plate found at Corinth of what may have been a large, two-masted Byzantine sailing ship of the thirteenth century; although, admittedly, since the plate in question dates from a period in which Corinth was in Frankish hands, there is no way of knowing whether the artist's model was Western or Byzantine.[18] At the time of the First Crusade there is evidence that the Italians had taken at least a temporary lead both in the size and in the technological capabilities of their ships.[19] By the thirteenth century the shipyards of Venice, Genoa, Pisa, and other cities were producing large round ships which commonly had two decks and not infrequently had three.[20] Although

---

[18] H. Antoniadis-Bibicou, *Etudes d'histoire maritime de Byzance: à propos du 'Thème des Caravisiens'* (Paris, 1966), plate 4.

[19] Kreutz, 'Ships', pp. 101–3; J. H. Pryor, 'Transportation of horses by sea during the era of the Crusades: eighth century to 1285 A.D.', *M.M.*, 68 (1982), 9–27 and 103–25, here pp. 13–14.

[20] On the round ships of the Italian and other maritime cities see R. Bastard de Péré, 'Navires méditerrananéens du temps de Saint Louis', *Revue d'histoire économique et sociale*, 50 (1972), 327–56; J. E. Dotson, 'Jal's *Nef X* and Genoese naval architecture in the thirteenth century', *M.M.*, 59 (1973), 161–70; J. H. Pryor, 'The naval architecture of Crusader transport ships: a reconstruction of some archetypes for round-hulled sailing ships', *M.M.*, 70 (1984), 171–219, 275–92, and 363–86; Unger, *The ship*, pp. 120–7; Unger, 'Warships and cargo ships', p. 237. Also useful, although it rests on some outdated secondary works, is A. Gateau, 'Quelques observations sur l'intérêt du voyage d'Ibn Jubayr pour l'histoire de la navigation en Méditerranée au XIIᵉ siècle', *Hesperis*, 36 (1949), 289–312.

Figure 7 Pisan round ship of the thirteenth century, from the Leaning Tower of Pisa

Figure 8 Venetian three-masted round ship of the thirteenth century, from a mosaic in S. Marco, Venice

two masts were the norm, three-masted ships were mentioned as early as the turn of the eleventh and twelfth centuries by Anna Comnena, and there are thirteenth-century mosaics of such three-masted ships in S. Marco, Venice[21] (figures 1, 7 and 8). However, improvements in naval architecture in this period were made with respect to increase in size and to modifications to long-established designs rather than to any radically new features. If the ships became larger, their basic characteristics did not change. They still used only a single lateen sail on each mast, they were manoeuvred by steering oars on each stern quarter rather than by sternpost rudders, they did not have deep keels, and they had a rounded hull profile with curved stemposts and

[21] Anna Comnena, *The Alexiad*, trans. E. R. A. Sewter (Harmondsworth, 1969), X.8 (p. 315).

sternposts.[22] Regrettably, marine archaeologists have still not excavated scientifically in the modern period a ship which may be
identified positively as having had a provenance in the Christian West
during the twelfth or thirteenth centuries. The Contarina ships
excavated near Venice in 1898 dated from the very late thirteenth
century at the earliest, and were not excavated by the standards of
modern archaeology.[23] A wreck discovered recently near Marsala in
Sicily and dated to the second half of the twelfth century still awaits
proper excavation and reconstruction. It is possible that it was a
Western ship, but the evidence of its cargo may suggest a Maghrebin
provenance.[24]

Not all commercial shipping was driven by the wind alone. From
the Byzantine period right through to the sixteenth century, a variety
of oared vessels were also used for maritime traffic by all seafaring
peoples of the Mediterranean. Such ships ranged from true galleys
intended primarily to be propelled by oars with only occasional and
incidental use of sails, through a variety of hybrid types combining
features of both oared and sailing ships, to vessels which were
intended to be sailed for the most part but which carried some oars for
emergencies and for manoeuvring in confined waters. Such hybrid
commercial shipping included the Byzantine κατήνα and ταρίτα, the
Arab *qārib*, *ghurāb*, and *ṭarīda*, the Western *sagena* and *tarida*, and the
turkish *mavna*.[25]

The really important questions to be asked of all these round-hulled
sailing ships and merchant galleys, whether Byzantine, Muslim, or of
the Christian West, concern their sailing qualities and sea-keeping
capabilities. Kreutz has suggested with good sense that the small

---

[22] See also M. Bonino, 'Lateen-rigged medieval ships: new evidence from wrecks in
    the Po delta (Italy) and notes on pictorial and other documents', *I.J.N.A.*, 7 (1978),
    9–28 and his *Archeologia e tradizione navale*, pp. 62–4 on the first Contarina wreck,
    a small coaster of *c*. 1300 wrecked near Venice.
[23] Commissione eletta dalla R. Deputazione Veneta di storia patria, *Sulla scoperta di
    due barche antiche nel territorio del comune di Contarina in provincia di Rovigo nel
    gennaio 1898* (Venice, 1900); rpt. in *Miscellanea di storia veneta edita per cura della
    R. Dep. Ven. di storia patria*, ser. 2, 7 (1901), 3–64. See also Bonino, 'Lateen-rigged
    medieval ships', pp. 13–21.
[24] G. Purpura, 'Un relitto di età normanna a Marsala', *Bolletino d'arte*, ser. 6, 29
    (Jan.–Feb. 1985), 129–36.
[25] Ahrweiler, *Byzance et la mer*, pp. 414–15 and 420; Goitein, *Mediterranean society*,
    pp. 305–7; Kreutz, 'Ships', pp. 102–3; Pryor, 'Transportation of horses', p. 18;
    S. Soucek, 'Certain types of ships in Ottoman–Turkish terminology', *Turcica*, 7
    (1975), 233–49, here pp. 235–7; Unger, 'Warships and cargo ships', pp. 237–8.

coasting vessels of the middle Byzantine period, ships of the type of the seventh-century Yassi Ada ship and the Gregory of Nazianzus miniatures, which Lopez once characterized as 'fast blockade runners' by comparison to their Roman predecessors, were in fact 'graceless vessels by any modern standard'.[26] Both are probably correct. The evidence of Yassi Ada confirms that they were in fact 'tozze e panciute', squat and pot-bellied, as Bragadin thinks.[27] I see no reason to assume that Muslim merchantmen of the same period were any better. The evidence presented by Goitein and Udovitch from the Cairo Geniza for the eleventh and twelfth centuries would certainly not suggest so. It has already been pointed out that Ibn Jubayr indicated that the performance of twelfth-century Genoese merchantmen left much to be desired, and I have argued elsewhere that the Crusader transport ships built by Genoa, Venice, and Marseilles for St Louis in the thirteenth century were unwieldy and difficult to handle, having in particular poor upwind performance capabilities.[28]

Because lateen sails are rigged fore-and-aft, and because their leading edge is rigid along the yard, it is a commonplace that ships lateen rigged can point closer to the wind than could the same ships if square rigged. Or, at least it is a commonplace as far as post-medieval square rig is concerned. Adam has cast some doubt on the degree of superiority of the lateen rig over the ancient square rig in this respect, but his thesis remains to be proven.[29] Casson has calculated that Roman square-rigged merchantmen could probably point no closer to the wind than seven points: that is, 78.75°. In the nineteenth century, at the high point of refinement of the sailing ship, square riggers could manage only six points to the wind, or 67.5°.[30] Lateen-rigged Arab dhows, however, can manage five points, or a heading only 56.25° off the wind.[31] A figure of about 60° for medieval lateeners seems probable.[32] But even if a ship can point into the wind

[26] Kreutz, 'Ships', p. 207, discussing R. S. Lopez, 'East and West in the early Middle Ages; economic relations', in *Relazioni del X Congresso internazionale di scienze storiche*, vol. 3 (Florence, 1955), 113–63; here p. 131.

[27] Bragadin, 'Le navi', p. 402.   [28] Pryor, 'Naval architecture', pp. 378–83.

[29] Adam, 'Développements des techniques nautiques', pp. 561–2; Kreutz, 'Ships', pp. 81–2; Lane, *Venetian ships*, p. 38; D. Phillips-Birt, *A history of seamanship* (New York, 1971) p. 129; Unger, *The ship*, p. 49.

[30] L. Casson, *Ships and seamanship in the ancient world* (Princeton, 1971), p. 274 and n. 16.   [31] L. Dimmock, 'The lateen rig', *M.M.*, 32 (1946), 35–41; here p. 35.

[32] D. Phillips-Birt, *Fore and aft sailing craft and the development of the modern yacht* (London, 1962), p. 59; Pryor, 'Naval architecture', p. 379; Unger, *The ship*, p. 49.

effectively, its actual track through the water will be a product of its heading and the leeway made as it is pushed sideways through the water by wind, tide, and current. Thus the shape and configuration of the hull are very important in determining real ability to tack into the wind, or even to hold a course with the wind abeam.[33] The flat, wide floors and rounded bilges of early medieval Mediterranean sailing ships, their lack of deep keels, and their curved stem and sternposts and lack of a cutwater, all made their ability to resist leeway and thus to hold a course into the wind anything but startling.[34] In terms of performance to windward, the advantages derived from their lateen sails were very much mitigated by their hull design. Furthermore, imbalance in their sail plan cannot have helped. In the thirteenth century the foremast, or artemon mast, of two- and three-masted ships of the Christian West was stepped forward in the hull and raked forward at an angle of about thirteen to twenty degrees.[35] At least in so far as the Gregory of Nazianzus miniatures allow us to judge, the masts of single-masted ships of the earlier periods were also stepped quite far forward in the hull and also raked forward. Unfortunately, the archaeological evidence on this point is inconclusive. Unless a ship had a third mast at the stern, and most did not, the huge lateen sails of these ships were set almost entirely over the forward section of the ship. Because the aerodynamic effect of a lateen sail is to act as a sort of aerofoil, within which the air spirals upwards in an eddy,[36] the combination of mast and sail position with the aerodynamic qualities of lateen sails and the hull configuration almost certainly militated against the effectiveness of the steering oars at the extreme stern of the ship.[37] The steering oars themselves, it should be noted, are widely considered by modern scholars to have been highly efficient as steering mechanisms and to have had performance characteristics not markedly inferior to those of the later sternpost rudder.[38]

---

[33] See the comments of P. Gille on the paper of P. Adam, 'Voile latine', in *Méditerranée et Océan Indien*, pp. 215–18.

[34] Pryor, 'Naval architecture', pp. 379–80. For the same comment on round-hulled Roman merchantmen see J. Sottas, 'A model of the Portus ship', *M.M.*, 21 (1935), 145–52; here p. 152.

[35] Pryor, 'Naval architecture', pp. 284–5. See also figures 1, 7 and 8.

[36] Dimmock, 'Lateen rig', pp. 35–6; Phillips-Birt, *Fore and aft sailing craft*, p. 43. But see the judicious comments of Kreutz about not being overly enthusiastic about these qualities as far as early medieval ships are concerned. See Kreutz, 'Ships', p. 82.   [37] Pryor, 'Naval architecture', pp. 379–80.

[38] Amongst many others see the comments of P. Pomey on the paper of Bragadin, 'Le navi', in *La navigazione mediterranea nell'alto medioevo*, vol. 1, pp. 409–11.

My estimation, and it is only an estimation, even though one based on observation of a model built for the purpose and on the reading of many medieval accounts of voyages, is that early medieval round ships conceded as much ground in leeway as they gained through their ability to point into the wind. In other words, they could maintain a real course at 90° to the wind only with great difficulty, even when that wind was by no means of gale force. Such a calculation makes sense of Ibn Jubayr's comment that his Genoese captain was hard pressed not actually to lose ground to the light headwind from the west. It also accords well with the observations of many other medieval voyagers. With performance capabilities of that order, any lee shore was a master's nightmare.

In terms of the technological limitations of early medieval sailing ships, the use of oars by merchant galleys, either as a primary or as an auxiliary source of motive power, gave some advantages. Within the limitations of human strength, oars could be used to make headway against wind, current, and tide. However, the cruising speed that galleys under oars could sustain was no more than two to three knots. The technology of this point is discussed below in relation to war galleys.[39] Headwinds or adverse tides or currents of sufficient strength to drive a galley backwards at more than two or three knots would completely nullify any efforts that oarsmen might make except for very short bursts of less than half an hour or so. Adverse conditions of that order of magnitude were extremely common.

A second performance advantage held by galleys over round ships was that their much lower freeboard and higher length to breadth ratio decreased the amount of leeway made when tacking or when reaching with the wind abeam. However, this advantage was negated by their lower freeboard. For greatest mechanical efficiency, oars have to be as nearly parallel to the water as possible in order to put the blades in the water as far from the hull as possible. Consequently, throughout history oared ships always rode low in the water and had little freeboard. This made them extremely susceptible to being swamped in any sort of a sea and, particularly relevant to this context, decreased their ability to heel under sail. If a ship cannot heel very far, its ability to tack into the wind, or even to reach with the wind abeam, is much reduced. It must spill wind from its sails or set the sails in less than the most efficient setting in order to remain upright. Conse-

---

[39] See below, pp. 71–5.

quently, it will be unable to maintain its heading or will make increased leeway, and normally both.[40]

Conclusive testimony to the fact that both sailing round ships and oared merchant galleys of the early Middle Ages could not make their way to windward very effectively may be found in comparisons of the duration of voyages made before prevailing winds with those made against them. If we may believe the figures, the voyage made by the monk Bernard the Wise from Taranto to Alexandria in 867, apparently in a sailing ship, took 30 days, while his return from Jaffa to near Rome took 60 days.[41] The duration of voyages of eleventh- and twelfth-century ships compiled from the Egyptian Geniza materials suggests that those made against prevailing winds took a great deal longer than those made before the wind.[42] Three voyages from Alexandria to ports in the Maghreb and Spain (Almeria, Mahdia, and Tripoli of Libya) were conducted at an average speed of 1.05 knots, whereas seven voyages from Mahdia and Tripoli to Alexandria were conducted at an average speed of 1.7 knots. A voyage from Alexandria to Amalfi via Constantinople and Crete was conducted at 0.65 knots, whereas five voyages from Marseilles, Mazara, and Palermo to Alexandria were conducted at an average of 1.92 knots. On his outward voyage from Ceuta to Alexandria Ibn Jubayr's Genoese ship made the passage in 31 days before following winds. But on his return voyage against the winds another Genoese ship took 51 days to make Messina from Acre.[43] During the Sixth Crusade the fleet of St Louis reached Cyprus from Aigues Mortes in 24 days, but took 10 weeks for the return from Acre to Hyères.[44] Average upwind speed for these early medieval voyages was 1.16 knots, while downwind speed averaged 2.25 knots. Data from the early Middle Ages are predictably meagre, but the more abundant data from the fourteenth to sixteenth centuries, all of which point to similar conclusions,[45] support the indications of the earlier sources that voyages made against prevailing winds habitually took twice as long as those made with them.

[40] The technology of this point is discussed below in relation to war galleys. See pp. 71–3.
[41] Bernard the Wise, 'The voyage of Bernard the Wise: A.D. 867', ed. & trans. T. Wright, in *Early travels in Palestine* (London, 1848), 23–31; here pp. 24, 29.
[42] Udovitch, 'Time, the sea and society', pp. 510–12.
[43] Ibn Jubayr, *Travels*, pp. 26–9, 326–36.
[44] J. R. Strayer, 'The Crusades of Louis IX', in R. L. Wolff & H. W. Hazard, eds., *The later Crusades, 1189–1311* (vol. 2 of K. M. Setton, ed., *A history of the Crusades*) (Madison, 1969), 487–518, here p. 493; Joinville, *Life of St. Louis*, pp. 182–91.
[45] See below, pp. 51–3.

Until the fourteenth century, when innovations in design, construction, and navigational techniques combined to reduce at least the requirements of seamanship to do so, geographical and meteorological conditions operated with the technological limitations of the ships to promote certain narrow and well-defined major sea lanes for ships navigating the Mediterranean: the trunk routes along the chain of northern islands and coasts (figure 2). In the case of sailing ships, it was poor upwind performance, the fear of lee shores, and the need for refuge in inclement weather which were the critical considerations of navigation. If bound on voyages from east to west or south to north, they could overcome the obstacle of adverse prevailing winds on the open sea most easily by hugging the coasts, taking advantage of any favourable currents, and attempting to reach with the daily cycle of land and sea breezes on one or other beam. At the same time fear of a hostile lee shore discouraged voyages from east to west along the southern shores of the sea; except, of course, when other considerations overrode those of navigation. The large number of island and mainland bays and harbours along the northern trunk routes offered ships a degree of refuge in inclement weather, particularly towards the beginning and end of the sailing season, that the southern coasts could not emulate. For voyages from north to south or west to east, sailing ships had more freedom of action, since the prevailing winds were behind them and they did not have so great a need to utilize currents and land and sea breezes on the one hand and to fear lee shores on the other. As Roger of Hoveden pointed out in discussing the routes of Richard Coeur de Lion and Philip Augustus to Acre for the Third Crusade, routes which in both cases followed the trunk routes, for voyages from west to east a high seas route was sometimes preferable:

> And it should be understood that if the wind be favourable to those who wish to go from Marseilles to Acre, they may leave the island of Sardinia, and the island of Sicily, and the island of Crete off the left side of the ship. And if they hold a straight course, they will not see the land until they see the land of Syria. And that route is shorter and safer, but they should beware lest they fall off too far to the right of the ship because of Barbary and the many other islands in which live the pagans under the Emperor of Africa.[46]

At the same time, the particular technological limitations of galleys encouraged them also to navigate by the coastal routes: particularly

---

[46] Roger of Hoveden, *Chronica*, ed. W. Stubbs (Rerum Britannicarum medii aevi scriptores, 51) (London, 1870), vol. 3, p. 160. The translation is mine.

their lack of freeboard and susceptibility to being swamped (discussed in greater detail below in relation to war galleys), their inadequate space in hold for stowing provisions and water, necessitating frequent ports of call to resupply, and their own upwind performance limitations. In the case of galleys, the direction of the voyage was less relevant than it was in that of sailing ships, for the major fear was of being caught in the open in rising seas and being swamped. This could happen no matter in what direction bound. Roger of Hoveden added that:

> galleys cannot, nor dare not, go by that route [the open sea crossing from Marseilles to Acre] since, if a storm should arise, they may be swamped with ease. And therefore they ought always to proceed close to the land.[47]

As has already been emphasized, these studies examine only one aspect of the maritime history of the Mediterranean in the period. There were always many other factors at work in addition to the geographical and technological ones. *Of course*, economic and other considerations constantly induced ships to voyage away from the main trunk route sea lanes. In particular politico-religious considerations were instrumental in causing Muslim shipping to follow dangerous routes along the southern coasts throughout the period and to avoid Christian coasts altogether when hostilities intervened.[48] Not unnaturally, in the works of Muslim geographers of the ninth to eleventh centuries the routes along the southern coasts were the best documented of all Mediterranean maritime routes.[49] But nevertheless, shipping, particularly Christian shipping, preferred to follow the navigationally safer trunk routes whenever possible. One index of how preferable these routes were if other factors were equal is the fact that in the same Muslim geographical works, as well as in other Muslim sources, they appeared as a major alternative to the southern coastal routes in spite of the obvious dangers from Christian war fleets and corsairs to Muslim shipping using them.[50] In the eleventh century southern Italy was quite familiar to Muslim

---

[47] Ibid., p. 160.
[48] See in particular C. Courtois, 'Les rapports entre l'Afrique et la Gaule au début du moyen-âge', *Cahiers de Tunisie*, 2 (1954), 127–45, here pp. 138–42 and Courtois, 'Remarques', pp. 51, 55.
[49] T. Lewicki, 'Les voies maritimes de la Méditerranée dans le haut moyen-âge d'après les sources arabes', in *La navigazione mediterranea nell'alto medioevo*, vol. 2, 439–69; here pp. 443–7.
[50] Ibid., pp. 447–50.

cartographers.[51] In Boccaccio's tale of Alatiel, daughter of the sultan of Babylon (Egypt), betrothed to the king of Algarve (Morocco), her ship from Alexandria bound for Algarve passed by way of Sardinia and the Balearics.[52] Traselli regards this as an error on Boccaccio's part for the southern coastal route along the coast of the Maghreb.[53] But in fact Boccaccio was quite correct. He had lived in Naples and knew about ships and seamen. The route via Sardinia and the Balearics was the natural one from Cape Bon to the Straits of Gibraltar if politico-religious conditions permitted. In another tale, Gerbino, grandson of William II of Sicily, intercepted a ship carrying the daughter of the king of Tunis from Carthage to Granada off the coast of Sardinia 'knowing that the lady's ship must pass [that way]'.[54] Admittedly, Boccaccio's experience was based on knowledge of Christian rather than Muslim shipping in a period when Sicily, Sardinia, and the Balearics were in Christian hands. But his choice of route nevertheless reflected the natural one which would have been used by Muslim shipping in an earlier period when these islands were in Muslim hands.

The fourteenth to sixteenth centuries

A type of ship totally different from the Mediterranean round ship, the North European cog, characterized by a single mast and a square sail, a sternpost rudder, and a hull configuration remarkable for its straight stempost and sternpost, had been seen in the Mediterranean since at least as early as the Third Crusade. However, Mediterranean shipbuilders either proved slow to realize the advantages that this type of ship could offer or else, and more probably, when first seen it was still in its early stages of development and they declined to emulate it until later, when its own internal development had reached a stage where it was obviously superior to the traditional Mediterranean lateen-rigged round ship. Not until the fourteenth century is there definite evidence for Mediterranean shipbuilders building such

[51] C. Cahen, 'Commercial relations between the Near East and Western Europe from the VIIth to the XIth century', in K. I. Semaan, ed., *Islam and the medieval West: aspects of intercultural relations* (Albany, 1980), 1–25; here p. 15.

[52] Boccaccio, *Decameron*, ed. V. Branca (Florence, 1976), II.7 (p. 122).

[53] C. Trasselli, 'Naufragi, pirateria e doppio giuoco', in Ragosta, *Le genti del mare mediterraneo*, 499–510; here pp. 499–500.

[54] Boccaccio, *Decameron*, IV.4 (p. 292): 'avvisando quindi dovere la nave della donna passare'.

Figure 9 Fourteenth-century Mediterranean cog, from a Spanish MS of 1350

ships.[55] A Spanish miniature of *c.* 1350 showed clearly the original form of the cog (figure 9). Even in this simple form with a single mast and square sail, the cog plainly had some desirable features by comparison to traditional Mediterranean ships. Its hull was remarkably capacious for its size, its sternpost rudder offered some advantages, the cutwater formed by its straight stempost and sternpost should have reduced leeway considerably, and its square sail was undoubtedly easier to handle than the huge lateen sails of thirteenth-century Mediterranean round ships.[56] Most probably, on the other hand, early cogs could not point into the wind as well as the traditional Mediterranean lateen-rigged ships and therefore may not have tacked as well. With the eclectic ingenuity of their profession, Mediterranean seamen were quick to realize that a combination of some features of the old lateeners with the basic design of the new cogs would produce a ship with the best features of both. By 1367 Pizigani's portolan chart showed an important new ship type in which the lateen sail was reinstated on a mizzen mast at the stern and a curved stempost

[55] On the cog and its introduction into the Mediterranean see J.-C. Hocquet, *Le sel et la fortune de Venise. Volume 2: Voiliers et commerce en Méditerranée 1200–1650* (Lille, 1979), pp. 104–9; Landstrom, *The ship*, pp. 90–1; E. Scandurra, 'The maritime republics: medieval and Renaissance ships in Italy', in Bass, *History of seafaring*, 205–24, here p. 214; Unger, *The ship*, pp. 129, 183–8, 216–7; Unger, 'Warships and cargo ships', pp. 243–7. See also the papers by P. van der Merwe, 'Towards a three-masted ship', and I. Friel, 'England and the advent of the three-masted ship', and the comments by C. Villain-Gandossi, W. Unger, and W. A. Baker in 'Session VI: the three-masted ship', in *Proceedings of the Fourth international congress of maritime museums* (Paris, 1981), pp. 121–51.

[56] See below, pp. 42–3.

Figure 10 Fourteenth-century Mediterranean cog with a lateen sail on the mizzen mast and curved stempost, from a portolan chart of 1367 by Pizigani

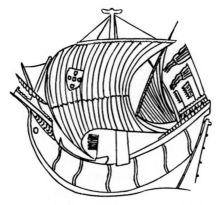

Figure 11 Early fifteenth-century carrack, from a plate of Moorish workmanship from Manises near Valencia

reintroduced. The sternpost remained straight to mount the rudder (figure 10). The purpose of the lateen mizzen sail was to improve bite on the helm and steering rather than to provide propulsion.[57] In the fifteenth century, a third mast with another square sail was added at the bow, thus establishing the characteristic features of the famous full-rigged carrack of Renaissance commerce in the Mediterranean and of the age of discoveries (figure 11). Virtually the only other major improvement to be made during the remainder of the period was the

[57] K. Djupedal, *The innovation and construction of the wooden sailing ship, 1150–1650*, M.A. thesis, University of Oregon, 1978, p. 17; Landstrom, *The ship*, p. 92; Phillips-Birt, *History of seamanship*, p. 184; Unger, *The ship*, p. 186.

addition of a topsail on the main mast, which permitted a significant expansion of sail area in the main drive section of the ship's sail plan without greatly increasing difficulty of handling. Other minor improvements included the addition of a spritsail at the bow, of a bonaventure mast with a second small lateen sail at the extreme stern, and significant refinements in rigging.[58]

There is no doubt that the Mediterranean carrack of the fifteenth and sixteenth centuries was a much handier vessel than had been her thirteenth-century predecessor, the lateen-rigged round ship. Tacking with lateen sails was a complicated and dangerous business. The ship had to fall off the wind, usually to wear ship by turning away from the wind and presenting her stern to the following seas, and then the yards had to be hauled to the vertical and transferred around the front of the masts to the other side. For small boats with small sails this manoeuvre was not a great problem. However, for the huge merchantmen of the thirteenth century, whose yards could be over 45 metres long and weigh up to seven metric tons,[59] it was a major one indeed.[60] In his account of his pilgrimage to Jerusalem in 1480, Felix Fabri gave a graphic description of the difficult and dangerous process of tacking with the lateen sails of a great galley.[61] By contrast, square sails could be simply forced around for a new tack by means of braces. When a foremast was added to the ship, the square sail at the bow helped to swing it across the wind on to the new tack, thus eliminating the dangerous process of wearing ship. A mizzen lateen sail gave the rudder bite as the helm was swung over. A full-rigged carrack could tack more often and more easily, had better balance and control in its sail plan, and a hull configuration which conceded less leeway than the traditional round ship. It could maintain a course at 80° to the wind and therefore claw off a lee shore,[62] except, of course, in gale-force conditions. Although I am not for a moment suggesting

---

[58] On the evolution of the carrack see Djupedal, *Wooden sailing ship, passim*; Hocquet, *Le sel: Voiliers*, pp. 109–12; Landstrom, *The ship*, pp. 92–105; Lane, *Venetian ships*, pp. 38–48; Unger, *The ship*, pp. 186–7, 216–18; Unger, 'Warships and cargo ships', p. 247. But see in particular the papers and comments of Van der Merwe et al., in 'Session VI: the three-masted ship'.

[59] Pryor, 'Naval architecture', p. 367 and n. 87.

[60] Dimmock, 'Lateen rig', pp. 36, 40–1; Djupedal, *Wooden sailing ship*, pp. 18–20; Landstrom, *The ship*, p. 83; Phillips-Birt, *History of seamanship*, pp. 126–7; Phillips-Birt, *Fore and aft sailing ship*, pp. 58–9.

[61] Felix Fabri, *The book of the wanderings of brother Felix Fabri*, trans. A. Stewart in *P.P.T.S.L.*, vols. 7–10 (London, 1896–7), vol. 1 (7), p. 172.

[62] Lane, *Venetian ships*, pp. 39, 42; Unger, *The ship*, pp. 186, 217–28.

Figure 12 Fifteenth-century great galley, from the commonplace book of Giorgio Timbotta of Modon, 1444

that the technological innovations embodied in the carrack had overcome completely the obstacles presented by geography and meteorology to the objectives for which men designed and built ships, for as we shall see carracks and other ships of the fourteenth to sixteenth centuries were still very imperfect as technological means of achieving men's needs and desires, nevertheless the implications of these innovations for at least reducing the tyranny of geography and meteorology over navigation are obvious.

At the same time as the cog and then carrack were gradually replacing the traditional round ship in the Mediterranean, other important improvements were made to the design of the traditional merchant galley. From the late thirteenth century, the Genoese, Venetians, and Florentines increased both the size and seaworthiness of their galleys, eventually developing the remarkable ship known as the 'great' galley (figure 12).[63] With a slightly lower length to breadth ratio than the war galley and the traditional merchant galley, it had a hull which rose at the bow to give greater ability to ride the waves, a much higher freeboard, and up to three masts, all of which originally had lateen sails. Later the sail on the mainmast was replaced in some

[63] On the great galley see J. E. Dotson, 'Merchant and naval influences on galley design at Venice and Genoa in the fourteenth century', in C. L. Symonds, ed., *New aspects of naval history: selected papers presented at the fourth naval history symposium* (Annapolis, 1979), 20–32; Landstrom, *The ship*, pp. 128–35; Lane, *Venetian ships*, pp. 15–26; M. E. Mallett, *The Florentine galleys in the fifteenth century* (Oxford, 1967), pp. 26–34; Scandurra, 'Maritime republics', p. 211; Unger, *The ship*, p. 176; Unger, 'Warships and cargo ships', p. 238.

cases by a square sail. Since it was designed primarily to be sailed rather than rowed, the oars of a great galley were intended to be used only for getting in and out of harbour and in emergencies. In 1494 Pietro Casola's Venetian great galley, the *Contarina*, could not put into Sebenico (Sibenik) to take refuge from contrary winds because: 'the galley was so large . . . that it could not be propelled by the oars'.[64] Casola was exaggerating, of course, but his comment reveals the essential truth of the fact that great galleys were primarily sailing ships. They were extremely seaworthy being used for voyages in the Atlantic to Flanders and England as well as for those to the Black Sea and Egypt and for the pilgrim traffic to the Holy Land. That such a ship was eventually made redundant in the sixteenth century by the improved handling of the full-rigged carrack is eloquent testimony to just how much had been achieved in the latter. The development of the great galley, like that of the carrack, also reduced the necessity imposed by technological limitations for merchant galleys to cling to the great trunk routes along the coasts. With their increased freeboard and redesigned hulls, great galleys had little fear of being swamped in a storm and were perfectly capable of open-sea crossings. Their increased hull capacity also meant that they could carry larger quantities of provisions and water and thus stay at sea for longer, so long as that increased capacity was not given over to loading more passengers or cargo; as was in fact normally the case.[65]

What of Muslim and Byzantine shipping during the later Middle Ages and the sixteenth century? Unfortunately there is a dearth of primary information, and I know of no secondary work on either subject. Up to the end of the thirteenth century there is nothing to suggest that the galleys or lateen-rigged round ships of the Muslims or Byzantines were in any way appreciably inferior to, or noticeably different from, those of the Christian West. It may be true that round ships of a size equal to those of the huge Crusader and pilgrim transports of Genoa and Venice in the thirteenth century were never built by Muslims and Byzantines, but that is probably as far as any differences may be stretched. In 1136 a Genoese squadron captured a 'great and rich' Muslim merchant ship off Bougie, from whose cargo each of the twelve attacking galleys received £700 in booty.[66] Also in the twelfth century, Usāmah ibn Munqidh reported a Muslim ship

---

[64] Casola, *Pilgrimage*, p. 169.   [65] See below, pp. 55, 83.
[66] Caffaro, *Annali genovesi de Caffaro e de'suoi continuatori*, vol. 1, ed. L. T. Belgrano (Genoa, 1890), p. 28.

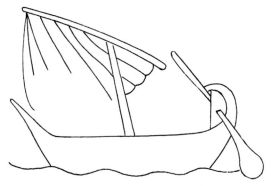

Figure 13 Early fourteenth-century Muslim sailing ship, from an Egyptian MS of Al-Hariri's *Maqamat*

from the Maghreb bound for Alexandria with 400 pilgrims for Mecca.[67] This ship must have been as large as most Western ships of the period. In 1191 Saladin sent a large relief ship from Beirut to Acre which impressed the Crusaders of Richard Coeur de Lion by its size and which was at first taken by them to be a Christian ship.[68] In fact *ruses de guerre* of this sort, which remained common throughout the entire period with which we are concerned, are perhaps the best indication that there were never any very noticeable differences between the ships of Islam, Byzantium, and the Christian West. A ship in a fourteenth-century Egyptian manuscript of the *Maqamat* of al-Hariri was very similar indeed to the style of thirteenth-century lateen-rigged round ships of the West (figure 13).[69]

From the middle of the fourteenth century, when cogs, carracks, and great galleys came into widespread use in the merchant marines of the Christian West, it may have happened that for a time at least the commercial shipping of Byzantium and the Muslim world was smaller than that of the West and inferior in performance. However, if this was the case, it is a case which still remains to be proven by further research. Whether and when the cog ever became emulated in the Muslim world appears to be unknown. The word *kuka* is first cited from an Arabic verse of 1206, but was used there with reference to a

[67] Usāmah ibn Munqidh, *Memoirs of an Arab–Syrian gentleman or an Arab knight in the Crusades*, trans. P. K. Hitti (Beirut, 1964), p. 110.
[68] Ambroise, *L'estoire de la guerre sainte*, ed. G. Paris (Paris, 1897), coll. 58–9 and pp. 358–9.
[69] D. Haldane, *Mamluk painting* (Warminster, 1978), pl. 68, p. 102.

type of river craft and obviously had nothing to do with the European cog.[70] According to Soucek, the cog was never used by the Turks.[71] This may well have been true, for when *kuka* did appear in Ottoman terminology from the late fifteenth century, it referred to much more complex ship types than the simple, single-masted, square-rigged cog.[72] In the fifteenth century the Turks knew both the carrack and the great galley but built few of them, probably because they were not well suited to the needs of their own commerce. Those that did appear in the sources did so mostly in a military, naval capacity as transports and flagships (figure 14).[73] On the other hand, the *barça*, a large sailing ship of a carrack type, emulated from the Venetian *barza*, was used by the Turks both as a merchantman and as a naval transport.[74] So also was the small, lateen-rigged *gripar* or *iğribār*, which was used by the *ghazi* emirs in the fourteenth century and which may have been developed from the Venetian *grippo*.[75] In the far western Mediterranean, the commercial and war fleets of the Nasrid sultanate of Granada in the first half of the fourteenth century were composed, according to Christian sources, of *naves*, *galeote*, *carrace*, and *saetie*; that is, of types of ships precisely similar to those used by contemporary Christian maritime powers.[76] In the Catalan–Moroccan war of 1337–43 we meet another incident involving a *ruse de guerre* which suggests that Muslim and Christian ships could not be easily differentiated.[77] What the situation was in the rest of the Muslim Mediterranean world appears to be unknown (figure 15).

So also does it in the Byzantine world. The specific history of ships and shipping in the late Byzantine empire and in ex-Byzantine territories progressively lost to the Turks remains unwritten. Works

---

[70] H. & R. Kahane & A. Tietze, *The lingua franca in the Levant: Turkish nautical terms of Italian and Greek origin* (Urbana, 1958), pp. 171–3.

[71] Soucek, 'Ships in Ottoman–Turkish terminology', p. 239.

[72] C. H. Imber, 'The navy of Süleyman the Magnificent', *Archivum Ottomanicum*, 6 (1980), 211–82, here p. 213; Kahane, *Lingua franca*, pp. 171–3.

[73] Imber, 'Navy of Süleyman the Magnificent', pp. 211–14; Kahane, *Lingua franca*, pp. 147–8; Soucek, 'Ships in Ottoman–Turkish terminology', pp. 235–7.

[74] Hocquet, *Le sel: Voiliers*, p. 113; Imber, 'Navy of Süleyman the Magnificent', p. 212; Kahane, *Lingua franca*, pp. 98–9; Soucek, 'Ships in Ottoman–Turkish terminology', p. 242.

[75] Hocquet, *Le sel: Voiliers*, p. 97; Imber, 'Navy of Süleyman the Magnificent', pp. 212–3. See also below, p. 169.

[76] C. T. Delgado, 'El Mediterráneo Nazarí. Diplomacia y piratería. Siglos XIII–XIV', *A.E.M.*, 10 (1980), 227–36; here p. 230.

[77] J. A. Robson, 'The Catalan fleet and Moorish sea power (1337–1344)', *English Historical Review*, 74 (1959), 386–408; here p. 392.

Figure 14 Sixteenth-century carrack, from an Ottoman Turkish MS

Figure 15 Muslim carrack? of the late Mamluk period, from a plate from Egypt

dealing with the general history of late Byzantine trade and commerce, a study itself in its infancy, are insufficiently precise in their terminology for ship types to permit of any meaningful formulations.[78] About all that can be said with any confidence is that it is highly improbable that more than a handful of Byzantines or Greeks owned and operated ships of the largest size or of the latest types. Being confined in their maritime activities largely to the eastern Mediterranean and the Black Sea,[79] they may have had little need of ships such as carracks and great galleys. What evidence there is suggests that their ships were mainly coasting vessels, probably of the traditional Mediterranean lateen-rigged type for the most part, and that there was a significant contrast between them and the ships of Italians plying the waters of the Aegean and the Black Sea in the fourteenth and fifteenth centuries.[80] So also would there have been, however, before too hasty conclusions are drawn from this point, between coastal shipping along the Italian coasts and the ships used by Italians for trans-Mediterranean traffic. There are references to Byzantine shipmasters visiting places such as Venice, Dubrovnik, Chios, Crete, Egypt, and even Genoa in the period, and in some cases they were operating on a large scale, even as agents for the Byzantine emperor himelf.[81] Some of these Byzantines had large ships which may have been of the new cog or carrack types, though whether bought from Italians or built by Byzantines remains unknown. Graffiti from the Theseion in Athens dating from the late Middle Ages show ships which were similar to the accustomed types of the light galley, possibly the great galley (figure 16), a lateen-rigged hybrid ship with a small square topsail on the main mast and a stern rudder, and a full-rigged carrack (figure 17).[82] It is true, of course, that these graffiti do not necessarily represent Byzantine or Greek ships. As with the Corinth plate, they may have been executed from Western models in a period in which Athens was in Frankish hands. However, from the inscriptions which accompany some of them, they

---

[78] See in particular A. E. Laiou-Thomadakis, 'The Byzantine economy in the Mediterranean trade system: thirteenth–fifteenth centuries', *D.O.P.*, 34–5 (1980–1), 177–222; N. Oikonomides, *Hommes d'affaires Grecs et Latins à Constantinople (XIIIᵉ–XVᵉ siècles)* (Montreal, 1979).   [79] See below, pp. 145–6, 148–52.

[80] M. Balard, *La Romanie Génoise (XIIᵉ – début du XVᵉ siècle)* (Genoa, 1978), pp. 337–8; Laiou-Thomadakis, 'Byzantine economy', pp. 196, 210, 217–18.

[81] See below, pp. 148–52.

[82] M. Goudas, 'Μεσλιωνικὰ καράγματα πλοίων ἐπὶ τοῦ Θησείου', *Byzantis*, 2 (1910), 329–57, esp. *exempla* 2, 4, 14, 15, 17, 19, 20.

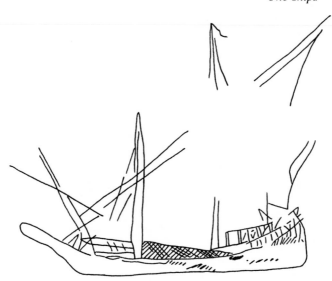

Figure 16 Byzantine great galley? of the late medieval period, from a graffito in the Theseion, Athens

Figure 17 Byzantine carrack? of the late medieval period, from a graffito in the Theseion, Athens

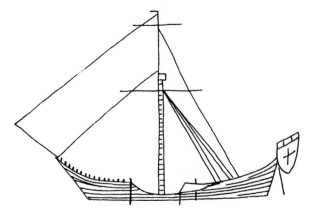

Figure 18 Genoese cog of the late Middle Ages, from a graffito in Hagia Sophia, Trebizond

were clearly inscribed by Greeks. Similar graffiti of cogs or carracks, and possibly of great galleys, are to be found in the church of Hagia Sophia in Trebizond. Some of these, however, were definitely meant to represent Genoese ships, for some of the graffiti bear the cross of St George of Genoa (figure 18).[83]

In the fourteenth, fifteenth, and sixteenth centuries, at least until the development of the Ottoman merchant marine, it was really only the ships of the Christian West which plied the trans-Mediterranean sea lanes in any large numbers.[84] We may limit ourselves, therefore, to evidence from the West for the degree to which technological innovation in the development of new ship types and refinements of those types facilitated a departure from the previous situation in which trans-Mediterranean traffic had been closely confined to the major sea lanes or trunk routes. In fact, it will be argued, in spite of innovations in design, rigging, and navigational techniques, the trunk routes were in the sixteenth century much the same, and almost as predominant, as they had been in the days of the Roman empire. On the one hand, some of the innovations can be shown not to have

[83] A. Bryer, 'Shipping in the empire of Trebizond', *M.M.*, 52 (1966), 3–12; here pp. 5–9 and figs. 1–6. Bryer believes that the graffiti of figs. 1–2 represent Western *naves bucii* or Byzantine *katerga*, the latter of which he believes were, by the late Byzantine period, sailing ships like the Western *naves bucii*. To my eye, however, graffiti 1–2 are clearly galleys, and possibly great galleys. They fit an understanding of *katerga* in their original sense as galleys.   [84] See below, pp. 135–52.

increased measurably the capabilities of the ships to overcome the obstacles presented by geography and meteorology. On the other hand, where they can in fact be shown to have done so, other factors then became operational to perpetuate adherence to the trunk routes.[85] Consistent evidence from a wide variety of sources for both sailing cogs and carracks and also great galleys indicates that the upwind performance of these ships was little better than that of the old lateen-rigged round ships and light galleys of the twelfth and thirteenth centuries. Travelling in a cog in 1384, three Tuscan pilgrims took 23 days for the voyage from Venice to Alexandria but 42 for the return to Venice from Beirut.[86] On board a Venetian great galley in 1395, Ogier VIII d'Anglure took 32 days to reach Jaffa but over five months for the return to Venice.[87] The galley on which Felix Fabri travelled in 1480 took 43 days to make Jaffa from Venice but 70 for the return voyage. In his journal Fabri lamented constantly that the galley was held up by contrary winds.[88] In fact this was an experience common to many voyagers in the late Middle Ages. Casola, de Clavijo, and others referred continuously to galleys in particular, but also to sailing ships, being held in port, forced to anchor in the shelter of the land, or being blown back at sea by contrary winds.[89] Casola

[85] Braudel, *Mediterranean*, pp. 104–7. In 'Time, the sea and society', pp. 508–9, Udovitch makes a similar point for an earlier period about improvements in maritime technology failing to produce any noticeable increase in average speeds for voyages. In discussion of Udovitch's paper, Kedar uses the evidence supplied by Balard in 'Escales génoises sur les routes de l'Orient méditerranéen au XIVe siècle', in *Les grandes escales. Première partie: antiquité et moyen-âge* (Recueils de la Société Jean Bodin, XXXII) (Brussels, 1974), 243–64 to reiterate that technological advance did little to change the practice of coastal navigation by galleys in the later Middle Ages. See B. Z. Kedar, 'Discussione' on the paper of Udovitch 'Time, the sea and society', in *La navigazione mediterranea nell'alto medioevo*, vol. 2, 558–9.

[86] T. Bellorini & E. Hoade, eds. & trans., *Visit to the holy places of Egypt, Sinai, Palestine and Syria in 1384 by Frescobaldi, Gucci and Sigoli* (Jerusalem, 1948), pp. 159–60, 185.

[87] F. Bonnardot & A. Longnon, eds., *Le saint voyage de Jherusalem du seigneur d'Anglure* (Paris, 1878), pp. 5–11, 79–98.

[88] Felix Fabri, *Wanderings*, vol. I (7), pp. 13–23, 24–44. Fabri did not give the duration of his voyages, but they were given by his fellow traveller the anonymous French pilgrim. See C. Schefer, ed., *Le voyage de la saincte cyté de Hierusalem* (Paris, 1882), pp. 29–57, 101–16.

[89] See, for example, Casola, *Pilgrimage*, pp. 168–70, 294, 296, 298–9, 301 *et passim*; Ruy Gonzalez de Clavijo, *Narrative of the embassy of Ruy Gonzalez de Clavijo to the court of Timour, at Samarcand, A.D. 1403–6*, trans. C. R. Markham (Hakluyt Soc. Works. First series, 26) (London, 1859), pp. 19–28.

reached Jaffa from Venice in 37 days, but took 66 to return.[90] Hyde's computations of the durations of six fifteenth-century galley voyages from Venice to Jaffa and return, all made on the same ships and including Casola's voyages, produce average durations of 36.6 days for the outward voyage and 64 days for the return; a ratio of 1:1.75.[91] Data for Genoese commercial voyages in the fifteenth century on sailing ships give not dissimilar results. Voyages by the same ship from Chios to Pera in 1453 took 20 days, while the return took only three days.[92] For these voyages the adverse conditions created by the prevailing winds on the outward voyage were exacerbated by the contrary currents in the Bosphorus and Dardanelles. In the same year another Genoese ship took 55 days to reach Ancona from Chios, but only 20 days to make the return.[93] Two spring voyages from Genoa to Alexandria in 1379 and 1391 took 24 days and 35 days respectively, whereas a late autumn voyage from Beirut to Genoa in 1396 took 53 days.[94] It is, of course, extremely hazardous to conclude too much from data for voyage durations because raw times usually included many days lost in ports of call. Lay-over time may not have been equal for both outward and return voyages. Masters were usually more concerned to press on quickly when going in one direction than in the other. However, the data are sufficiently consistent to conclude that any improvements in ability to point into the wind and to resist leeway had not increased upwind performance at all measurably. Surviving accounts suggest that the difference between the amount of time required for upwind voyages and that required for downwind voyages was still of much the same order in the fourteenth and fifteenth centuries as it had been earlier. The data from these late medieval voyages give an average upwind speed of 1.0 knot and a downwind speed of 1.85 knots. Perhaps the last word should be left to Ludolph von Suchem:

[90] Casola, *Pilgrimage*, pp. 166–221, 291–336.
[91] J. K. Hyde, 'Navigation of the Eastern Mediterranean in the fourteenth and fifteenth centuries according to pilgrims' books' in H. McK. Blake et al., eds., *Papers in Italian archaeology I: The Lancaster Seminar. Recent research in prehistoric, classical, and medieval archaeology*, part 2 (British Archaeological Reports Supplementary series, 41(2)) (Oxford, 1978), 521–40; here p. 526 and table 31.1 (p. 537).
[92] J. Heers *Gênes au XVe siècle: activité économique et problèmes sociaux* (Paris, 1961), p. 297.
[93] Ibid., p. 297.
[94] J. Heers, 'Il commercio nel Mediterraneo alla fine del sec. XIV e nei primi anni del XV', *Archivio storico italiano*, 113 (1955), 157–209; here pp. 170–2.

in general men sailing from the West to the East are wont to make provision of food for fifty days, though when sailing from the East to the West they are wont to provide food for one hundred days, because the ship always flies as it were from west to east with a fair wind.[95]

Von Suchem reduced the question to a simple formula: voyages against prevailing winds took twice as long as those made with them because of poor upwind performance capabilities of ships of all types. For east–west and south–north voyages at least, the attractions of the coastal trunk routes with their helpful currents and daily cycle of land and sea breezes were no fewer in this later period than they had been in the earlier.

Development of new types of ships with better handling qualities in the fourteenth and fifteenth centuries was accompanied by extremely important innovations in navigational techniques. The adoption and diffusion of the ship's compass, portolan sailing directions, and accurate charts reduced the necessity to navigate by coastal landmarks.[96] There can be no doubt of that. Navigation out of sight of land undoubtedly became much easier than it had been previously. But the determination and establishment of the major coastal sea lanes or trunk routes in antiquity and the early Middle Ages had never been due so much to inadequate navigational techniques as it had been to the nexus between geographical and meteorological factors and ship design. Navigation out of sight of land without a compass had never been very difficult in the Mediterranean.[97] Even after the compass was well known and widely available, shipping continued to navigate the Mediterranean without it for a very long time simply because it was not really essential there.[98] One can accept with Lane that the use of the compass and its associated charts and sailing

[95] Ludolph von Suchem, *Description of the Holy Land*, p. 12.
[96] On improvements in navigation techniques see Kretschmer, *Italienischen Portolane*; F. C. Lane, 'The economic meaning of the invention of the compass', *American Historical Review*, 68 (1963), rpt. in his *Venice and history* (Baltimore, 1966), pp. 331–44; Motzo, *Compasso di Navegare*; E. G. R. Taylor, *The haven-finding art: a history of navigation from Odysseus to Captain Cook* (London, 1956), pp. 89–121.
[97] On navigation in the Mediterranean before the compass see *La navigation dans l'Antiquité* (Dossiers de l'Archéologie, 29 (July/August 1978); P. Pomey, 'Comment naviguait-on dans la Méditerranée romaine', *L'histoire*, 36 (July/August 1981), 96–101; Rougé, *Recherches*, pp. 81–3; J. Vernet, 'La navegación en la alta edad media', in *La navigazione mediterranea nell'alto medioevo*, vol. 1, 323–81.
[98] Braudel, *Mediterranean*, pp. 103–8.

directions facilitated navigation in overcast conditions and thus helped both to lengthen the sailing season back into early spring and forward into late autumn, and also to reduce dependence upon coastal landmarks for navigation.[99] Yet in both these respects improvements in ship design were as, if not more, important than those in navigational techniques. A decision of the Great Council of Venice of 1292, relating to new partnership regulations as a result of the recently acquired ability of ships to make two round trips per year, referred not to the adoption of the compass but rather to the development of the great galley, which could hold the winter seas longer.[100] Similarly in the case of navigation out of sight of land. If the combination of improvements in navigational techniques and those in ship design certainly made it possible for shipmasters to voyage by open-sea crossings with much greater ease and safety, other evidence suggests that the attractions of the coastal routes in the Mediterranean continued to persuade them not to take advantage of the new possibilities. The full importance of the compass was not to be realized until the era of trans-oceanic navigation.

Similarly, the development of the great galley, with its ability to hold the sea in bad weather and thus to make open-sea crossings in safety, did not alter fundamentally the popularity of the coastal trunk routes for commercial galley voyages. *Of course*, the great galleys were capable of open-sea crossings, and they did make them with regularity when it was convenient and advantageous to do so: from Crete and Rhodes to Alexandria, from the Bosphorus to Caffa and Tana, from Genoa to the Balearics, and from Galicia to Brittany across the Bay of Biscay. However, whenever coastal routes offered a reasonable alternative, the galleys continued to follow them. Virtually every pilgrim to the Holy Land travelling on Venetian great galleys in the fourteenth and fifteenth centuries went by way of the coasts of the Balkans, Crete, Rhodes, and Cyprus. Such galleys were technologically capable of crossing directly from the Ionian to Jaffa, but they did not do so. In the final centuries of the period, it was not now so much technological, geographical, and meteorological considerations as others which determined that merchant galleys should continue to follow the trunk routes. The same desiderata explain why, by and large, the compass did not radically alter the routes followed by sailing ships on commercial voyages. In the case of galleys, the need

---

[99] Lane, 'Invention of the compass'.   [100] Ibid., p. 341.

for frequent watering and provisioning imposed by their large crews and passenger complements, as well as by the space in hold turned over to cargo, meant that of necessity their routes remained largely coastal in the Mediterranean. As commercial vessels, the great galleys sacrificed space in hold for provisions and water in the interests of loading passengers and cargo. They did not normally carry provisions and water for more than a week or so, especially water.[101] In Felix Fabri's account of his pilgrimage voyages from Venice to Jaffa in 1480 and 1483, he referred constantly to the need to provision and water the galley. On the first voyage the captain put in to Parenza (Piran), Zara (Zadar), Lesina (Hvar), Curzola, Ragusa (Dubrovnik), Corfu, Modon, Limassol, and Larnaca.[102] Other ports of call on this route used frequently by the galley captains included Pula, Sibenik, Trogir, Cephalonia, Zante, Coron, Candia (Iraklion), Rhodes, Paphos, and Famagusta. In Fabri's case, as in that of others also, the reasons for so many ports of call were not related solely to the needs of provisioning and watering. The captain's need for news, intelligence, and diplomatic assistance was another. Turkish squadrons were at sea. So also was the passengers' need for recreation. Casola's galley put in to Ragusa only five days after leaving Zara, yet he wrote that: 'all the pilgrims went ashore . . . with a great longing to refresh themselves'.[103] The need for frequent reprovisioning, and especially for watering, always remained, however, one of the major considerations for masters of galleys of any type.

Sailing ships, with their smaller crews and much greater stowage capacity, were not governed by these demands to anything like the same extent. Yet they also continued to follow the coastal, island-hopping, trunk routes. By the fourteenth century, most of the great trading ports at which ships would want to call to trade lay along these routes. Unless a ship was bound specifically for a particular port or ports for some special purpose and these happened to lie off the main sea lanes, as, for example, in the case of the fifteenth-century galley caravans to the coast of the Maghreb, the *galee de trafego*, then the *modus operandi* of maritime traffic in the late Middle Ages and the sixteenth century remained as it had always been: coastal voyaging from one port to another, accumulating cargoes and profits as the

---

[101] See below, p. 83.
[102] Felix Fabri, *Wanderings*, vol. I (7), pp. 13–23. The return voyage in 1480 followed a similar route, and so also did the outward voyage in 1483. Ibid., pp. 24–44, 164–207.   [103] Casola, *Pilgrimage*, p. 172. See also p. 164.

voyage progressed.[104] Much more so was this the case for voyages of small ships and of privately owned ships than it was for the galley caravans of Genoa, Venice, and Florence.[105] Voyages of the latter usually had more purpose. Reaching their ultimate destinations and then returning to their home ports was always kept firmly to the forefront of their considerations. But even the galleys of Venice made a series of stopovers in Corfu, Patras, Modon or Coron, and Candia, no matter whether they were bound for Beirut, Egypt, or 'Romania'. If bound for Beirut, Famagusta was also a port of call. If bound for Romania, Monemvasia and Negropont (Chalkis) were.[106] The map of Venetian galley caravan routes in the fifteenth century compiled by Lane makes the point extremely well.[107] Even Genoese shipping to the Levant and Romania, more normally sailing ships than merchant galleys, usually put in along the way to trade wherever possible.[108] Genoese ships avoided ports of call in Venetian Romania for obvious political reasons,[109] but they still stopped wherever they could to trade. Famagusta on the route to Beirut, Chios on that to Constantinople, and Rhodes on that to Alexandria were normal ports of call for Genoese ships.[110] In the western Mediterranean, the ships of Barcelona and Catalonia frequented ports of call in Corsica and Sardinia and, when they ventured east into Levantine waters, also touched at ports such as Naples, Palermo, Messina, Syracuse, and Rhodes.[111] Florentine galleys bound for England and Flanders in the

---

[104] Braudel, *Mediterranean*, pp. 106–8. For the Middle Ages see the important chapter on the structure of Genoese trade with Sicily in D. Abulafia, *The two Italies: economic relations between the Norman Kingdom of Sicily and the northern communes* (Cambridge, 1977), pp. 217–54. See also C. Carrère, *Barcelone: centre économique à l'époque des difficultés 1360–1462* (Paris, 1967), pp. 270–2.

[105] Heers, 'Commercio nel Mediterraneo', pp. 173–4.

[106] F. Thiriet, *La Romanie Vénitienne au moyen-âge: le développement et l'exploitation du domaine colonial vénitien (XIIe–XVe siècles)* (Paris, 1959), pp. 328–9, 424–6; F. Thiriet, 'Les itineraires des vaisseaux vénitiens et le rôle des agents consulaires en Romanie Greco-Vénitienne aux XIV–XV siècles', in Ragosta, *Le genti del mare mediterraneo*, 587–608, here pp. 591–2. See also P. Racine, 'Note sur le trafic Veneto-Chypriote à la fin du moyen-âge', *Byzantinische Forschungen*, 5 (1977), 307–29.

[107] F. C. Lane, *Venice: a maritime republic* (Baltimore, 1973), map 9, p. 341. See also Heers, 'Commercio nel Mediterraneo', pp. 167, 169.

[108] Balard, *Romanie Génoise*, pp. 568–9, 576–8, 585–7, 849–68; Balard, 'Escales génoises', *passim*; Heers, *Gênes*, p. 297; Heers, 'Commercio nel Mediterraneo', pp. 170–3.

[109] Balard, 'Escales génoises', p. 249 and diagram; Heers, *Gênes*, p. 418.

[110] Heers, *Gênes*, pp. 375, 388, 396–400, 401–2.

[111] Carrère, *Barcelone*, p. 236; A. Unali, *Marinai, pirati e corsari catalani nel basso medioevo* (Bologna, 1983), p. 115.

fifteenth century followed coastal routes to the Straits of Gibraltar even though they were quite capable of making the open crossing direct from Pisa to the Alboran Channel and in fact did so in reverse on the return voyage. The 'log' of Luca di Maso degli Albizzi makes it quite clear that coastal routes were chosen for the outward voyage not because of inability to hold the sea but rather because of the commercial and provisioning attractions of the series of coastal ports.

In the eastern Mediterranean, official ports of call for the Florentine great galleys on the Alexandria run, published in 1447, included Gaeta, Naples, Salerno, Palermo, Messina, Syracuse, Modon, Rhodes, Alexandria, Jaffa, Beirut, Cyprus, Chios, and Crete (Candia).[112] As many authorities have emphasized,[113] coastal routes still offered significant attractions to maritime traffic in the late Middle Ages and the sixteenth century; refuge in calm water during bad weather, an avenue of escape from the omnipresent corsairs and pirates, the opportunity to lay over at night and to avoid dangerous nocturnal navigation, ease of navigation by coastal landmarks, an endless series of trading opportunities, assured supplies of provisions and water, facilities to make repairs and particularly to caulk the ships, and the opportunity to break the monotonous tedium of slow sea travel at frequent intervals. Improvements in navigational techniques and in ship design may have made it easier and safer to navigate away from the coasts, but they never made the attractions of those coasts any the less attractive.

WARSHIPS

Throughout the Middle Ages and to the end of the sixteenth century, the main offensive weapon of all contending powers at sea in the Mediterranean was the light war galley. The principal war craft of the imperial navy throughout the later centuries of the Roman empire, the liburnian galley, had been a small, fast, two-banked galley with a main mast carrying a square sail, a small artemon mast and sail

[112] Mallett, *Florentine galleys*, pp. 31–3, 65, 83–98, map 2, and the 'diary' of Luca di Maso degli Albizzi, pp. 207–75. See also the ports of call for the Constantinople galleys (p. 67), the Barbary galleys (p. 73), and the Catalonia–Sicily galleys (p. 78).

[113] Balard, 'Escales génoises', pp. 245–6, 255; Braudel, *Mediterranean*, pp. 106–7; E. Fasano-Guarini, 'Au XVIᵉ siècle: comment naviguent les galères', *Annales: E.S.C.*, 16 (1961), 279–96, here pp. 289, 291, 293; U. Tucci, 'Sur la pratique vénitienne de la navigation au XVIᵉ siècle', *Annales: E.S.C.*, 13 (1958), 72–86.

58   *Geography, technology, and war*

Figure 19 Byzantine dromon of the twelfth century, from a MS of the Sermons of St Gregory of Nazianzus in the monastery of the Panteleimon, Mount Athos

forward, a ram below water at the prow, and sometimes a fighting castle amidships.[114] During the early Byzantine period fundamental changes were made to produce the dromon, which was really an entirely new type of ship (figure 19). There were, of course, several different types of oared warships in use with Byzantine fleets at various times. As well as the dromon (δρόμων) per se, there was the chelandion (χελάνδιον), the pamphylos (πάμφυλος), and the galley (γαλέα), as well as other types. I use 'dromon' generically since, in terms of the characteristics under discussion, there does not appear to have been a great deal of difference between the types, and the various names were probably used without a great deal of discrimination.[115]

Procopius, who first mentioned the dromon in the sixth century, said that it had a single bank of oars, but by the ninth century Leo VI referred to two banks of oars for the dromon in his *Naumachica*.[116] At

---

[114] On the liburnian galley see Casson, *Ships and seamanship*, pp. 141–7.

[115] See Bragadin, 'Le navi', p. 397. On Byzantine warships see Ahrweiler, *Byzance et la mer*, pp. 408–18; Bragadin, 'Le navi', pp. 392–4; Casson, *Ships and seamanship*, pp. 148–54; Christides, *Conquest of Crete*, pp. 42–6; V. Christides, 'Naval warfare in the Eastern Mediterranean (6th–14th centuries): an Arabic translation of Leo VI's Naumachica', *Graeco-Arabica*, 3 (1984), 137–48, here p. 140; Christides, 'Naval guides', p. 60; R. H. Dolley, 'The warships of the later Roman empire', *Journal of Roman Studies*, 38 (1948), 47–53; Eickhoff, *Seekrieg* pp. 133–51; Kreutz, 'Ships', pp. 83–6. Anderson suggests that Byzantine dromons may have had outriggers for the oars, and Bonino appears to be convinced that they had beaks rather than rams as early as the sixth century. Anderson, *Oared fighting ships*, pp. 36–41; Bonino, *Archaeologia*, pp. 44–6 and fig. 8.

[116] Procopius, *History of the wars: book III. The Vandalic war*, trans. H. B. Dewing, in *Procopius*, vol. 2 (London, 1953), III.xi.15–16 (pp. 104–5). Christides, *Conquest of*

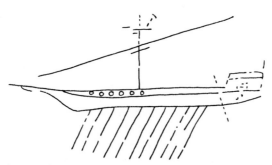

Figure 20 Byzantine dromon of the later Middle Ages, from a graffito in the church of St Luke of Stiris

some time, possibly as late as the tenth century, the ram, *rostrum*, was replaced by a beak, *calcar*, a projection at the bow well above the water line and raked upwards. It was intended not for ramming but to provide a bridge across which marines could board enemy ships. According to Christides, the *Naumachica* dedicated to the *patricius* Basil mentioned rams on Byzantine dromons in the tenth century.[117] However, this may be a reference to an above-water beak rather than to a below-water ram. Other Byzantine sources indicate that the bow projection on Byzantine dromons was used not to hole the hull of an enemy ship below the water line and thus to sink it, as the ancient *rostrum* was, but rather to damage it above the water line and immobilize it by smashing its oars and upper hull.[118] Graffiti from the church of St Luke of Stiris, a church built in the twelfth century, but from which, of course, the graffiti may date from a later period, from the twelfth-century church of Christ the Saviour in Megara, and from the church of St Nicholas of Mavrika, clearly show dromons with beaks at the prow at the level of the gunwale (figure 20).[119]

The objective of naval engagement changed from sinking ships to boarding and capturing them. This was to remain the case until the end of oared warfare in the Mediterranean. By the seventh century the main attack weapon of dromons of the imperial fleet at Constantinople, not of the provincial fleets, was Greek Fire, an inflammable substance of some kind whose composition is much

Crete, p. 44 and Christides, 'Naval guides', p. 61 referring to A. Dain, *Naumachica partim ad hunc inedita* (Paris, 1943), 1.9, 3–5. Dain was unavailable to me.
[117] Christides, 'Naval guides', p. 61, referring to Dain, *Naumachica*, p. 66, par. 15, unavailable to me. [118] Christides, *Conquest of Crete*, p. 44.
[119] Christides, *Conquest of Crete*, fig. 5; Christides, 'Naval guides', figs. 5(1) and 7(1).

debated, projected through a siphon (σίφων) at the prow.[120] At the same time the square sail was replaced by a lateen sail and larger dromons began to have more than one mast. The dromon as it developed in the middle Byzantine period embodied almost all of the features which were to be common on light galleys of all maritime powers from the twelfth century onwards, with the exception that the Byzantine sources, to the best of my knowledge, made no mention of an outrigger, an *apostis* as it was to become, for the oars.

Christides has argued that both Byzantines and Muslims made the transition from two steering oars on the stern quarters to a single sternpost rudder.[121] However, the argument is really pressed beyond any point that the sources adduced will sustain. That the plural πηδάλια in the *Naumachica* to Basil refers to two stern-quarter steering oars while the singular πηδάλιον in the same work and in a passage of Eustathios of Thessalonica refers to a sternpost rudder seems an unjustifiable conclusion.[122] Why cannot texts refer to only one of two stern-quarter steering oars, or, alternatively, is it not possible that some Mediterranean ship types employed only one stern-quarter steering oar, as did Scandinavian ships? The same objections may be made to an interpretation of the use of plural and singular versions of the same word for a steering mechanism in the *Al-Ahkām* of Ibn al-Manqali as referring to dual stern-quarter steering oars on the one hand and to a sternpost rudder on the other for Muslim ships.[123] As far as the iconographic evidence is concerned none of the Byzantine graffiti adduced as evidence for the use of a sternpost rudder can be dated definitely to a period prior to the fourteenth century, when the sternpost rudder was introduced into the Mediterranean with the cog. That they are found in twelfth-century churches proves nothing, for church walls contain graffiti from many periods subsequent to that in which they were built. One particular graffito, from the twelfth century church of Christ the Saviour of Megara, looks extremely similar to drawings of galleys with sternpost rudders found in fifteenth-century Venetian treatises on naval architecture such as the

[120] On Greek Fire see Christides, *Conquest of Crete*, pp. 62–77; H. R. E. Davidson, 'The secret weapon of Byzantium', *Byzantinische Zeitschrift*, 66 (1973), 66–74; J. Haldon & M. Byrne, 'A possible solution to the problem of Greek fire', *Byzantinische Zeitschrift*, 70 (1977), 91–9; M. Mercier, *Le feu grégois* (Paris, 1952).
[121] Christides, *Conquest of Crete*, pp. 45–6; Christides, 'Naval guides', pp. 65–6.
[122] Christides, *Conquest of Crete*, p. 46; Christides, 'Naval guides', p. 66.
[123] Christides, *Conquest of Crete*, p. 46.

Figure 21 Byzantine galley? of the later Middle Ages with a stern rudder, from a graffito in the church of Christ the Saviour in Megara, and a fifteenth-century galley with both stern rudder and quarter steering oars, from the Venetian *Fabbrica di galere*

Fabbrica di galere (figure 21).[124] The same is true of all the Muslim iconography adduced as evidence for Muslim use of the sternpost rudder. None of it, with the exception of the famous illustration of a merchant ship from the Baghdad manuscript of al-Hariri's *Maqamat*, which has a Persian Gulf provenance, can be dated to before the fourteenth century.[125]

---

[124] Christides, 'Naval guides', fig. 5(3). Cf. Biblioteca Nazionale Firenze, Magliabecchiana, MS. Classe 19, palco 7, *Fabbrica di galere*, fols 7v, 11v, 18r, 24r.
[125] Christides, *Conquest of Crete*, figs. 14, 16, 17; Christides, 'Naval guides', figs. 17, 18, 23, 25–7.

Nothing at all is known about the construction of early Muslim warships, although there are some references in Byzantine sources to some Muslim ships having been slower and larger than the dromons of the imperial fleets.[126] As is the case with Muslim sailing ships, there are no representations of Muslim galleys before the fourteenth century. On the grounds that the Arabs are presumed to have taken over the ships and ship-building techniques of conquered peoples around the Mediterranean coasts, that they are known to have pressed some of them and their ships into Muslim service, and on the basis of some certain, some probable, and some possible Arabic adoptions of Byzantine names for ship types, it is generally agreed that although there were undoubtedly some differences, Muslim warships were not greatly dissimilar to Byzantine ones; certainly, that they were not technologically inferior.[127] The Arabic *dromonaria* or *adrumūnun* was certainly derived from δρόμων, *sanadīl* probably from σανδάλιον, *acatia* and *acatenaria* from κατήνα, *shalandī* from χελάνδιον, and *safīna* possibly from σαγήνη.[128] In the tenth and eleventh centuries the Fatimid navy used warships, *asātīl* and *markab ḥarbi*, and galleys, *shīnī*, and in the twelfth century the Egyptian navy of Saladin consisted of galleys, *shīnī*, of two different types: *ghurāb* and *musaṭṭah*. Such galleys could have crews of up to 140 oarsmen as well as marines, sailors, and officers but no doubt many were smaller than that.[129] As with the indiscriminate use of δρόμων and χελάνδιον in the Greek sources, *shīnī* and *shalandī* were probably used virtually interchangeably in the Arabic.[130] The Crusader chronicler Fulcher of

[126] Christides, 'Naval guides', p. 88; Eickhoff, *Seekrieg*, pp. 151–7, esp. n. 73; Kreutz, 'Ships', pp. 95–6.

[127] Christides, 'Naval guides', p. 92.

[128] On Muslim warships and possible Byzantine inspiration see Ahrweiler, *Byzance et la mer*, pp. 408–18; V. Christides, 'The raids of the Moslems of Crete in the Aegean Sea: piracy and conquest', *Byzantion*, 51 (1981), 76–111, here p. 80; Christides, 'Naval warfare', p. 140; Christides, *Conquest of Crete*, pp. 43–50; Christides, 'Naval guides', pp. 61, 95; Eickhoff, *Seekrieg*, pp. 151–7; Fahmy, *Muslim naval organization*, pp. 149–66 *et passim*; Kreutz, 'Ships', pp. 94–103; A. N. Stratos, 'The naval engagement at Phoenix', in A. E. Laiou-Thomadakis, ed., *Charanis studies: essays in honour of Peter Charanis* (New Brunswick, 1980), 229–47, here pp. 231–2; Unger, 'Warships and cargo ships', p. 237.

[129] Christides, *Conquest of Crete*, pp. 43–4; A. Ehrenkreutz, 'The place of Saladin in the naval history of the Mediterranean Sea in the Middle Ages', *Journal of the American Oriental Society*, 75 (1955), 100–16, here p. 106 n. 66; Y. Lev, 'The Fātimid navy, Byzantium and the Mediterranean Sea 909–1036 C.E./297–427 A.H.', *Byzantion*, 54 (1984), 220–52, here pp. 247–8.

[130] Christides, 'Naval warfare', p. 140; Christides, *Conquest of Crete*, pp. 43–4.

Chartres informs us that Egyptian galleys had beaks, although he used the classical word *rostrum* for the beak (*naves rostratae*). However, his use of the same phrase for the galleys of the Italian maritime republics of the same period, which are known to have had above-water beaks rather than below-water rams, indicates that he meant beak rather than ram.[131] According to Ibn al-Manqalī, an Egyptian writing in the fourteenth century who made a translation of the *Tactica* of Leo VI, Muslim *shīnī* had two banks of oars, as did the Byzantine δρόμων.[132] However, the evidence of a fourteenth-century Muslim translating the work of a ninth-century Byzantine hardly constitutes conclusive evidence for ninth- and tenth-century Muslim practice, or for fourteenth-century Muslim practice, for that matter. As mentioned above, Procopius specified that Byzantine dromons of the sixth century had only one bank of oars. One suspects that Muslim *shīnī* of the early period may have had only one bank of oars also.

From the end of the eleventh century, and then more abundantly in the twelfth, evidence about the nature of the war galleys of the Italian maritime cities begins to accumulate. Kreutz has argued that the *sagena* of eleventh-century Amalfi was a superior type of craft, probably modelled on Islamic predecessors, employing both oars and sails and particularly suited to corsair requirements.[133] The derivation of *sagena* from the Arabic *safīna*, or possibly *suqiyya*, still seems forced by comparison to the more obvious derivation from the Byzantine σαγήνη, although it is certainly possible that the Arabic terms were intermediary between the Byzantine and Amalfitan ones. Although a great variety of terms for various types of oared warships came to be used in the medieval Christian West, that which predominated was *galea*, galley. The Genoese fleet which sailed for the First Crusade in 1098 consisted of twelve *galee* and one hybrid oared and sailing fleet supply ship, a *sandanum*.[134] Dating from the second half of the twelfth century, the first manuscript drawings of such galleys occur in the Bibliothèque Nationale manuscript of the *Annales januenses* of Caffaro and his continuators (figure 22). Their typical construction by that time is quite clear. With an extremely high

131 Fulcher of Chartres, *Historia Hierosolymitana (1095–1127)*, ed. H. Hagenmeyer (Heidelberg, 1913); II.53.4 (p. 585). Cf. II.8.1 (p. 394), II.25.1 (p. 462), II.40.1 (p. 528).   132 Christides, *Conquest of Crete*, p. 44.
133 Kreutz, 'Ships', pp. 101–3.
134 Caffaro, *De liberatione civitatum Orientis liber*, ed. L. T. Belgrano, in *Annali genovesi di Caffaro e de'suoi continuatori* (Genoa, 1890), vol. 1, p. 102.

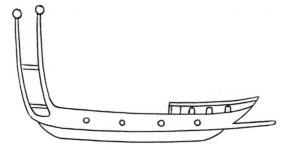

Figure 22 Genoese galley to illustrate an attack on a Pisan galley in 1175, from the continuation of Caffaro's *Annales januenses*

length to breadth ratio, they carried one mast with a single lateen sail. At the bow they had a beak rather than a ram. The oarsmen were seated in a single bank with two oarsmen per bench, each rowing a separate oar. The oars were not pivoted through oar ports in the hull but rather at tholes on an outrigger, an *apostis* or *telaro*, which carried the deck out over the hull. Such light galleys, *galee sottili*, formed the main strike forces of all Christian maritime powers of the West during the twelfth, thirteenth, and fourteenth centuries.[135] Only two major innovations or improvements were made, the addition of a second mast in the thirteenth century, and the use of three oarsmen per bench towards the end of that century and in the fourteenth.[136]

The earliest detailed statistics for the dimensions of such galleys anywhere in the Mediterranean world derive from the now destroyed Angevin archives of Naples. Since they have never been used in histories of shipping and naval warfare, I give the main details here. The document from which they are taken was an order of 18 February 1275 from King Charles I of Anjou, king of Sicily, to the justiciar of the *Terra d'Otranto* for the construction of an unspecified number of

---

[135] The literature on the medieval galleys of the Italian republics is enormous. Amongst the most useful is Anderson, *Oared fighting ships*, pp. 52–6; M. (A.) Bragadin, *Histoire des républiques maritimes italiennes: Venise – Amalfi – Pise – Gênes* (Paris, 1955), pp. 37–45; Bragadin, 'Le navi', pp. 398–401; Lane, *Venetian ships*, pp. 3–13; C. Manfroni, *Storia della marina italiana dalle invasioni barbariche al trattato di Ninfeo (anni di C. 400–1261)* (Livorno, 1899), appendice, pp. 451–76; Rodgers, *Naval warfare*, pp. 53–8, 109–13; Unger, *The ship*, pp. 121–2; Unger, 'Warships and cargo ships', p. 238.

[136] Marino Sanudo, *Liber secretorum*, p. 57. See also J. H. Pryor, 'The naval battles of Roger of Lauria', *Journal of medieval history*, 9 (1983), 179–216; here p. 187.

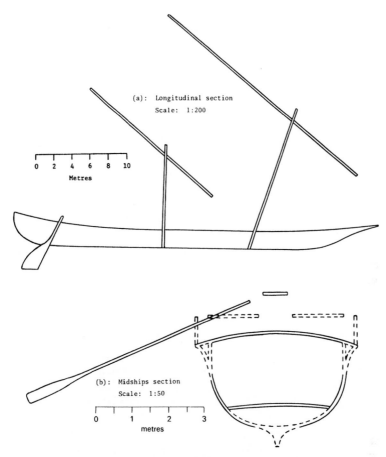

(a): Longitudinal section
Scale: 1:200

0 2 4 6 8 10
Metres

(b): Midships section
Scale: 1:50

0   1   2   3
metres

Figure 23 Schematic drawing of galleys of Charles I of Anjou, 1275:
(a) Longitudinal section (b) Midships section

galleys according to the dimensions of a certain red galley built in Provence.[137]

The reconstruction of these war galleys (figure 23) shows clearly that they were really huge rowing shells. The ratio of overall length to

---

[137] R. Filangieri, ed., *I registri della cancelleria angioina*, 33 vols. (Naples, 1950–81), vol. 12 (1959), pp. 126–9. There are many construction details and specifications included in this document. I hope to publish the full text with translation and reconstruction of the galleys in the near future.

Table 3. *Dimensions of galleys of Charles I of Anjou, 1275*[138]

Overall length from stempost to sternpost: 18 *cannae*, 6 *palmi*	39.30 m
Keel: 13 *cannae*, 3 *palmi*	28.03 m
Width on floor: 11.25 *palmi*	2.95m
Width of hull from bulwark to bulwark: 14 *palmi*	3.67 m
Width of the *apostis*: 17 *palmi*	4.45 m
Height of the sternpost: 13⅔ *palmi*	3.58 m
Height of the stempost: 11⅓ *palmi*	2.97 m
Height amidships: 7.75 *palmi*	2.03 m
Width of the *cursia*, gangway: 2.5 *palmi*	0.655m
Height of the foremast: 23 *gubiti*	16.08 m
Length of the foremast yard: 34 *gubiti*	26.72 m
Height of the middle mast: 14 *gubiti*	11.00 m
Length of the middle mast yard: 22 *gubiti*	17.29 m
Length of the two steering oars: 23 *palmi*	6.03 m
Number of oars: 108	
Length of the oars: 26 *palmi*	6.81 m
except for some at the bow and stern of: 30 *palmi*	7.86 m
Approximate deadweight tonnage:	80 metric tons

beam in the hull amidships was 10.7:1. Amidships, with a gunwale height of only 2.03 metres above the keel, the *apostis* can scarcely have been more than a metre or so above the water line. They were obviously designed to be driven primarily by oars rather than by sails and to cut through the water rather than to ride the waves. Such ships would have been dwarfed by the larger round ships of the period, which could have a deadweight tonnage of over 800 metric tons.[139]

In the later Middle Ages war galleys on all sides of the Mediterranean diversified into a number of different types. The fleets of Genoa, Venice, the Papacy, the Hospitallers, the Kingdom of Sicily, Aragon and Castile, later of united Spain, which came to comprise the main strike forces of the Christian West, were generally speaking composed of two main types of galleys. The light galleys, *galee sottili*, of much the same dimensions as those of the galleys of Charles I of Anjou, continued in use everywhere. When rowed with three oarsmen per bench, they were called, misleadingly, *triremi*. Occasional experi-

---

[138] The three major measurements used in the Angevin chancery orders were the *canna, gubitus,* and *palmus*. A *canna* equalled eight *palmi*, and a *gubitus* three *palmi*. The Neapolitan *palmus* of the thirteenth century was equal to approximately 0.262 metres. See H. Doursther, *Dictionnaire universel des poids et mesures anciens et modernes* (Brussels, 1840), p. 375.

[139] For discussion of the method of calculating deadweight tonnage used here see Pryor, 'Naval architecture', pp. 373–4.

ments were made with light galleys with four or even five oarsmen to a bench, but their lack of success demonstrated that the pinnacle of the art form for the light galley had been reached with two or three oarsmen per bench.[140] These were *galee alla sensile*, galleys of the simple form.[141] They formed the main body of all major war fleets and as *galiotte*, smaller versions with fewer rowing benches, were the favoured craft of corsairs everywhere until the seventeenth century.[142] Only in the sixteenth century was the merchant great galley adapted for war. At the same time a move was made away from the *alla sensile* system of having one oarsman per oar to the *al scaloccio* system of having multiple oarsmen pulling on a single oar. This permitted an increase in the size of oars and an improvement in the speed of galleys.[143] At Lepanto the fleets of Venice and the Holy League included six great galleys, *galeazze*, which played a crucial role in the battle.[144]

What of Muslim war galleys in the later Middle Ages and the sixteenth century? In the Ottoman sources *kaliyota* or *kalita*, a Turkicization of the Italian *galiotta*, was used for a galley of a size smaller than the norm. It was a favoured craft of the Turkish *ghazi* emirs in the fourteenth century and of Muslim corsairs in general throughout the Mediterranean in the late Middle Ages and sixteenth century.[145] So also was the *gripar* or *iġribār*.[146] The *kadīrga*, from the Byzantine Greek κάτεργον for fleet and men of the fleet, was the normal Ottoman war galley, the equivalent of the *galea sottile* (figure 24).[147] The *mavna* was the equivalent of the great galley, the

---

[140] Anderson, *Oared fighting ships*, pp. 56–8; Lane, *Venetian ships*, pp. 64–8.

[141] Anderson, *Oared fighting ships*, pp. 52–60; Lane, *Venetian ships*, pp. 9–13 *et passim*; Rodgers, *Naval warfare*, pp. 110–12; Scandurra, 'Maritime republics', pp. 206–10.

[142] Braudel, *Mediterranean*, pp. 865–91; P. Earle, *Corsairs of Malta and Barbary* (London, 1970), pp. 48, 134; Guilmartin, *Gunpowder and galleys*, *passim*; Lane-Poole, *Barbary corsairs*, pp. 205, 218–20; Soucek, 'Ships in Ottoman–Turkish terminology', p. 234.

[143] Anderson, *Oared fighting ships*, pp. 67–73; Guilmartin, *Gunpowder and galleys*, pp. 226–8; Imber, 'Navy of Süleyman the Magnificent', p. 217; Lane, *Venetian ships*, pp. 31–3.

[144] On the battle of Lepanto see, above all, Guilmartin, *Gunpowder and galleys*, pp. 221–52.

[145] Lane-Poole, *Barbary corsairs*, pp. 218–20; Soucek, 'Ships in Ottoman–Turkish terminology', p. 234; C. Villain–Gandossi, 'Notes sur la terminologie turque de la course', in *Course et piraterie* (XVᵉ Colloque international d'histoire maritime, San Francisco, 1975) (Paris, 1975), vol. 1, 137–45, here p. 140.

[146] Imber, 'Navy of Süleyman the Magnificent', pp. 212–13.

[147] L. Basch, 'A galley in Istanbul; the *kadīrga*', *M.M.*, 60 (1974), 133–5; Imber, 'Navy of Süleyman the Magnificent', pp. 214–15; Kahane, *Lingua franca*, pp. 523–6; Soucek, 'Ships in Ottoman–Turkish terminology', pp. 234–5.

Figure 24 Sixteenth-century Ottoman galley to illustrate the siege of Malta, from a MS of a *History of Sultan Suleiman* by Luqmān

galeazza.[148] In addition, the Ottomans used a *bastarda*, a galley larger than the normal *kadīrga* but smaller and lower in the water than the *mavna*, for an admiral's flagship.[149] They also had specialized artillery ships and horse transports and, in the sixteenth century, sailing galleons.[150] However, the main fighting strength of Turkish war fleets always remained, until the seventeenth century, the light galley, the *kadīrga*. Corsairs preferred the smaller and faster *kalita*. Of the ships which comprised the naval forces of other late medieval Muslim powers, the Mamluks of Egypt and the various Maghrebin rulers, little seems to be known. The Nasrids of Granada in the fourteenth century used *galeote*, as did the Barbary corsairs of Tunisia in the sixteenth.[151] Although little information is available, it seems highly probable that the preponderant division into the two classes of light galleys and galliots, which prevailed in the Christian West and amongst the Turks, characterized the naval forces of other Muslim powers also. It would appear that the light galleys of all Muslim naval forces in the sixteenth century had a reputation for being smaller, lower in the water, and faster under sail but slower under oars than the standard light galley of the Christian West.[152]

Following the Byzantine recapture of their capital city from the Latins in 1261, Michael VIII Palaeologus rebuilt the Byzantine fleet to a point where it became a significant force in the Aegean.[153] However,

[148] Souček, 'Ships in Ottoman–Turkish terminology', pp. 235–7.
[149] Imber, 'Navy of Süleyman the Magnificent', p. 214; Kahane, *Lingua franca*, pp. 100–2; Souček, 'Ships in Ottoman–Turkish terminology', pp. 237–8.
[150] Imber, 'Navy of Süleyman the Magnificent', pp. 212–14.
[151] Delgado, 'Mediterráneo Nazarí', p. 230; Earle, *Corsairs*, p. 48; Lane-Poole, *Barbary corsairs*, pp. 205, 218–20; A. Tenenti, *Piracy and the decline of Venice 1580–1615* (Berkeley, 1967), pp. 19–26.
[152] Guilmartin, *Gunpowder and galleys*, pp. 205–7; Lane, *Venetian ships*, p. 13.
[153] Ahrweiler, *Byzance et la mer*, pp. 336–73.

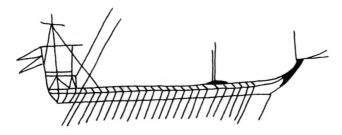

Figure 25 Late medieval graffito of a Trapezuntine? galley, from Hagia Sophia, Trebizond

his work was allowed to disintegrate under his successor Andronicus II, and from then on, with the exception of a brief attempt by John VI Cantacuzenus in 1347–9 to reconstitute a Byzantine fleet, Byzantine imperial fleets ceased to be a serious factor in maritime affairs in the Mediterranean.[154] Byzantine subjects and Greeks from former Byzantine territories now fallen under Turkish control continued to operate as corsairs, but the era of Byzantine sea power was over. Although, yet again, no work has been done on the specific question of the types of ships used in late Byzantine fleets and by Byzantine or Greek Ottoman corsairs, there seems little reason to suspect that they differed in any marked way from Western and Turkish galleys and galliots of the period. Graffiti of the late Middle Ages from the Theseion in Athens and Hagia Sophia in Trebizond show galleys very similar to Ottoman and Western galleys of the fourteenth and fifteenth centuries (figure 25).[155] Once again, these graffiti may admittedly have been intended to represent either Western or Ottoman galleys as well as Greek ones. However, Trapezuntine sources definitely refer to *katerga* and *gryparia* as warships in the fleets of Trebizond.[156]

These light galleys and galliots of the battle fleets and corsair flotillas had serious logistical limitations. Because of their low freeboard, they were extremely susceptible to being swamped in any

---

[154] Ibid., pp. 374–88; C. P. Kyrris, 'John Cantacuzenus and the Genoese 1321–1348', in *Miscellanea storica ligure, III* (Milan, 1963), 9–48: Oikonomides, *Hommes d'affaires*, pp. 46–9.

[155] Bryer, 'Shipping in the empire of Trebizond', figs. 1–2, 7; Goudas, 'Μεσλιωνικὰ καράγματα', figs. 6, 17, 19, 20.

[156] Bryer, 'Shipping in the empire of Trebizond', pp. 5–7, 11.

sort of a sea. Discussing his project to cripple Egypt by cutting off her maritime commerce, Marino Sanudo Torsello wrote that: 'by surveillance of the sea alone, it cannot be completely prevented that anyone be able to cross by sea to the lands subject to the Sultan. The reason for which is this: that armed galleys cannot stay out to sea in winter time, and even in calm weather they are ill advised to be found out of port at night time in winter'.[157]

As we saw above, Roger of Hoveden in the twelfth century commented on the perils to galleys of making crossings of the open sea because of the danger to them of being swamped. Both Hoveden's advice and Sanudo's analysis were based on experience and were accurate. The history of naval warfare in the Mediterranean is replete with instances of the virtual elimination of galley fleets caught out to sea by heavy weather. Four examples, chosen at random, may serve by way of illustration. In 1025 a Tunisian fleet was destroyed by a storm on its way to Sicily.[158] A Byzantine fleet was overwhelmed while returning home from Damietta in 1169.[159] The highly professional Argonese–Sicilian fleet under Roger of Lauria was severely mauled by a storm between the Balearics and Sardinia while returning to Sicily after its victory over the French at Las Hormigas in 1285.[160] And, finally, the Sicilian–Spanish fleet of Juan de Mendoza was eliminated as an active force by a storm in Herradura Bay in 1562.[161]

This inability of light galleys to hold the open sea necessitated their routes being invariably coastal and indirect. The routes of the galley fleets of the Third Crusade and that of Frederick II are instructive. Even though these voyages were made before the prevailing winds and therefore the geographical and meteorological factors discussed above were not important in these cases, the fleets hugged the coasts all the way to the Holy Land. In 1191 Richard Coeur de Lion's fleet sailed from Marseilles for Acre via the west coasts of Corsica and Sardinia, Messina, the south coast of Crete, Rhodes, the south coast of Cyprus, and Tyre.[162] Philip Augustus sailed from Genoa via the

[157] Marino Sanudo, *Liber secretorum*, I.4.2 (p. 28).
[158] Lewis, *Naval power*, p. 194.
[159] S. Runciman, *A history of the Crusades* (Harmondsworth, 1971), vol. 2, p. 388.
[160] C. Manfroni, *Storia della marina italiana dal trattato di Ninfeo alla caduta di Constantinopoli (1261–1453)* (Livorno, 1902), pp. 156–7.
[161] Braudel, *Mediterranean*, p. 995.
[162] *Itinerarium peregrinorum et gesta regis Ricardi*, ed. W. Stubbs (Rerum Britannicarum medii aevi scriptores, 38) (London, 1864), pp. 177–88; S. Painter, 'The Third Crusade: Richard the Lionhearted and Philip Augustus', in Wolff & Hazard, *The later Crusades*, 45–85, here pp. 58–62.

west coast of Italy, Messina, and then the same route as Richard. In 1228 Frederick II took his fleet from Brindisi to Acre via Corfu, Cephalonia, Crete, Rhodes, and Limassol.[163] Because the routes used by galleys were almost invariably coastal and indirect, the cruises from their home bases which were necessary for corsairs to reach the strategic areas along the trunk routes where they might hope to wreak havoc amongst agglomerated merchant shipping, or for battle fleets to make contact with their enemies, were greatly extended.[164] Thus inherent problems of their striking range were further exacerbated by their inability to keep the sea and to reach their destinations by the shortest routes available; unless, of course, provisioning and watering facilities were available en route.

Estimating the striking range of galleys is fraught with difficulties for an almost infinite number of variables demand consideration. However, the two primary variables were cruising speed on the one hand and stowage capacity for provisions, and especially water, on the other.

There is no doubt that for short bursts, up to 20 minutes or so, galleys could achieve quite remarkable speeds under oars: perhaps from seven to ten knots.[165] But cruising speeds under oars maintained continuously throughout daylight hours seem to have averaged out at about three knots when varying weather conditions are taken into account.[166] Calculated continuously over full 24-hour periods, therefore, cruising speeds under oars are unlikely to have much exceeded one and a half knots.

Galleys used their sails to rest their oarsmen whenever possible and,

[163] *Breve Chronicon de rebus Siculis a Roberti Guiscardi temporibus ad annum 1250*, in Philip de Novare, *The wars of Frederick II against the Ibelins in Syria and Cyprus*, trans. J. L. La Monte (New York, 1936), pp. 201–3. See also T. C. van Cleve, 'The Crusade of Frederick II', in Wolff & Hazard, *The later Crusades*, 429–62; here p. 451.

[164] Cf. M. Aymard, 'Chiourmes et galères dans la Méditerranée du XVIe siècle', in *Mélanges en l'honneur de Fernand Braudel* (Toulouse, 1973), vol. 1, 49–64, here p. 50; l'abbé Garnier, 'Galères et galeasses à la fin du moyen-âge', in M. Mollat, ed., *Le navire et l'économie maritime du moyen-âge au XVIIIe siècle, principalement en Méditerranée* (Deuxième Colloque international d'histoire maritime, Paris, 1957) (Paris, 1958), 37–51, here p. 38.

[165] Guilmartin, *Gunpowder and galleys*, p. 62. See also the debate on the speed of galleys under oars conducted in the pages of *Mariner's mirror*, 64 (1978) to 67 (1981).

[166] Rodgers, *Naval warfare*, p. 169; Guilmartin, *Gunpowder and galleys*, pp. 62 and esp. 197–8, where he refers to a document of the late 1560s attributed to Don Garcia de Toledo entitled 'Discourse on what a galley needs to navigate well armed, both with *ciurma* and with other people' (*Coleccion Navarrete*, Museo Naval, Madrid, vol. XII, dto. 83, fol. 310).

in fact, galley captains attempted to sail before favourable prevailing winds just as much as did the masters of sailing ships. Under sail and with the wind astern, galleys could make considerably more than three knots and maintain that speed as long as the wind remained favourable. But whether they could do so when the wind was ahead or abeam and they had to heel under sail seems very questionable. Being designed primarily to be rowed, galleys were notoriously poor sailers. A glance at the reconstruction of the galleys of Charles I of Anjou (figure 23) should suggest why immediately. Because of their low freeboard amidships and their *apostis* projecting out beyond the hull, they could heel under sail to only a small degree before the *apostis* became awash. I have attempted to compute a maximum angle of heel from the midship section of these galleys and, although there are too many imponderables and unknown quantities to permit any reliable figure to be adduced, a sound estimate would be between 10° and 15°. When the *apostis* became awash, galleys must have become dangerously unmanageable. Both Niccolò da Poggibonsi in 1346 and Gabriele Capodilista in 1458 referred to the alarming nature of galleys heeling under sail when tacking against unfavourable winds.[167] Admittedly both were landlubbers and may well have been terrified if the ship heeled even a few degrees. But, on the other hand, both were travelling on Venetian great galleys, which were much better sailing craft than light galleys. In order to remain within a safe angle of heel and thus to avoid being swamped, light galleys must have had to spill wind from their sails continuously. That would have meant that they would have had difficulty maintaining a heading into the wind on a tack and probably even reaching with the wind abeam. Spilling wind, either by letting the sheets fly, or by setting the sails in less than the most efficient position, would both slow the galleys down and also cause them to make greater leeway. Bearing in mind that they were designed to cut through the water rather than to ride the waves, in any sort of an adverse wind at all they were forced to run before it, to resort to oars, or to be content with minimal progress. Their safest recourse was to run for the shelter of the land and to anchor, if that was possible. Bragadin is convinced that in the Byzantine period dromons used their sails only when the wind was astern. Somewhat pessimistically perhaps, he affirms that it was not until *c.* 1400 that seamen learnt to sail galleys into the wind.[168] In absolute terms this was

---

[167] Hyde, 'Navigation', p. 526.   [168] Bragadin, 'Le navi', pp. 393–4.

undoubtedly not the case, but the general sentiment is certainly accurate. From the 'log' of Luca di Maso degli Albizzi it is clear that even the great galleys of Florence in the fifteenth century had serious limitations in tacking against head winds. On his voyage to Flanders and England in 1429–30, his galleys were constantly forced back to shore, delayed in port, or driven back at sea by contrary winds.[169] As we have already seen, similar experiences were the lot of Felix Fabri and Pietro Casola in the same period.[170] In fact they were to remain common for all galley voyages through into the sixteenth century. In those of the sixteenth century examined by Fasano-Guarini, although galleys reached 12 or 13 Venetian miles per hour (approximately 8.5 knots) on occasions in favourable conditions, delays caused by contrary winds reduced cruising speeds to about two or three knots when averaged out.[171] An estimate of this order is, indeed, a realistic one for the entire Middle Ages as well as for the sixteenth century. Because of problems consequent upon their design, the cruising speed of galleys under sail in all conditions was no greater than the two to three knots which they could manage under oars.[172]

There is support for these estimates in surviving records of the duration of voyages made by galley fleets; no doubt in all cases using both oars and sails according to conditions. Casson's compilation of durations of fleet voyages from ancient and early Byzantine sources would indicate that although weather conditions caused great variations, an average of two to three knots was usual.[173] Eickhoff has estimated that the cruising speed of Arab war fleets in the early Middle Ages was about four knots and that of Byzantine fleets of dromons about five.[174] However, although he cites some evidence for the speed of Arab fleets, he does not do so to substantiate the estimate of the speed of Byzantine ones. His estimates are probably too high. Belisarius's fleet of both oared and sailing ships averaged about 1.35 knots at sea on its 1250-mile cruise from Constantinople to Vandal Africa in AD 533.[175] An average speed of about two knots has been computed by Courtois for eleventh-century Maghrebin ships, whether oared or sailing is not specified, from al-Bakrī's *Description*

[169] Mallett, *Florentine galleys*, pp. 207–75 *passim*.   [170] See above, p. 51.
[171] Fasano-Guarini, 'Comment naviguent les galères', pp. 287, 289, 293–6.
[172] Cf. Guilmartin, *Gunpowder and galleys*, pp. 205–7.
[173] Casson, *Ships and seamanship*, pp. 292–6.
[174] Eickhoff, *Seekrieg*, pp. 146–7 and n. 44, 153 and n. 73.
[175] Rodgers, *Naval warfare*, pp. 9–12.

of North Africa.[176] In 1191 the fleet of Richard Coeur de Lion made the voyage from Messina to Limassol via Crete and Rhodes, a trip of about 1075 miles, in 30 days at sea; an average of about 1.36 knots.[177] That of Philip Augustus made somewhat better time, taking 22 days for the 1325-mile trip from Messina to Acre at an average speed of about 2.3 knots.[178] Frederick II's all galley fleet of 1228 left Brindisi on 28 June and entered Limassol 1075 miles away on 21 July; an average of 1.70 knots.[179] In 1285 the superb Catalan–Sicilian galley fleet of Roger of Lauria took about 30 days for the 1120-mile voyage from Messina to Barcelona via Tunisia, Sardinia, and Iviza; an average of about 1.4 knots.[180] In 1571 Don John of Austria brought the Spanish fleet for Lepanto from Barcelona to Messina in 35 days.[181] In 1351 a Genoese galley under Simone Leccavello, bearing news of war with Venice, took 35 days to reach Chios from Genoa, a voyage of about 1550 miles. Three days were lost when a Venetian ship was captured and the galley turned back to take her prize in tow; an average speed of about 1.85 knots. Later the same galley made a dash from Cape Skyllaion to Chios, a distance of about 200 miles, in some 28 hours at an average speed of 6.25 knots. The galley was capable of speeds of this magnitude when conditions were favourable, the need was pressing, and the distance involved was not too long. However, average cruising speeds over long distances were an entirely different matter.[182] A voyage made in 1557 by a squadron of Barbary corsairs under Jafer Re'is from Algiers to Corfu in 22 days at an average speed of just under two knots was regarded by Cristoforo da Canal as exceptionally fast.[183] In 1552 a fleet under the prince of Salerno reached Corfu from Marseilles without touching land en route in two weeks at an average speed of about three knots, and in 1557 an Algerian *fusta* made a non-stop voyage from Algiers to Santa

---

[176] Courtois, 'Remarques', p. 57. Al-Bakrī's data is tabulated by Yarrison, *Force as an instrument of policy*, appendix D-6.

[177] Painter, 'The Third Crusade', pp. 61–3.   [178] Ibid., pp. 61, 66.

[179] Van Cleve, 'Crusade of Frederick II', p. 451.

[180] Pryor, 'Roger of Lauria', pp. 195–6; Rodgers, *Naval warfare*, pp. 136–7.

[181] Guilmartin, *Gunpowder and galleys*, p. 237.

[182] M. Balard, 'A propos de la bataille du Bosphore: l'expédition génoise de Paganino Doria à Constantinople (1351–1352)', *Travaux et mémoires du Centre de recherche d'histoire et de civilization byzantines*, 4 (1970), 431–69, here pp. 461–3; J. E. Dotson, 'The voyage of Simone Leccavello: a Genoese naval expedition of 1351', in *Saggi e documenti*, VI (Genoa, 1985), 269–82, esp. p. 277.

[183] A. Tenenti, *Cristoforo da Canal: la marine vénitienne avant Lépante* (Paris, 1962), p. 43.

Maura/Levkas in 18 days at an average speed of approximately 2.5 knots.[184] Both of these voyages were also regarded as being unusually fast. The famous dash made in the winter of 1571 by Marc Antonio Querini from Candia to the relief of Famagusta, a distance of about 550 miles, was made before the prevailing winds in eight days at an average speed of about 2.60 knots.[185]

Examples could be multiplied, but there is little point in doing so. The figures are sufficiently consistent. For short periods galleys under oars could reach speeds of seven to ten knots, but only at the expense of exhausting the oarsmen after 20 minutes or so. Under oars they could maintain a speed of two to three knots throughout a day's passage, but the oarsmen would then need to be rested through the night. By using oarsmen in two shifts a continuous progress over 24 hours could be maintained, but then the speed would drop to about one and a half knots.[186] Using sails in favourable conditions quite high speeds of between six and ten knots could be reached, but there is no evidence to suggest that the use of sails enabled galley fleets to improve their general cruising speed over long distances beyond about two knots over continuous 24-hour periods. Speeds when running before favourable winds were much higher than when making way upwind, of course, but for a round trip in which a fleet had to return to its port of departure, which is the type of voyage which most concerns this book, the overall average of two knots is sound. This consideration is crucial to the argument which follows, for cruising speed was one of the two major variables which determined the striking range of galleys.

The other major variable was the stowage capacity of galleys for munitions, naval supplies, provisions, and above all fresh water. As Marino Sanudo Torsello said: 'in the summer time [galleys] are not able to stay at sea for many days without that they frequently put in to land to take on drinking water'.[187] Sanudo advised that Venetians especially skilled at finding water supplies be engaged for his projected Crusader fleet.[188] The need to water their galleys was a constant preoccupation of fleet commanders. In 533 Belisarius took on maximum supplies of water at Zante to make the crossing of the

[184] Ibid., p. 43.
[185] Guilmartin, *Gunpowder and galleys*, pp. 212–13. See also Garnier, 'Galères et galeasses', p. 39.
[186] Guilmartin, *Gunpowder and galleys*, fig. 10, p. 199.
[187] Marino Sanudo, *Liber secretorum*, I.4.2 (p. 28).   [188] Ibid., II.1.2 (p. 35).

Ionian to Sicily, even though he had just spent three weeks at Modon refitting and reprovisioning his fleet. The crossing from Zante to Sicily took sixteen days, and in that time the heat of midsummer spoiled the fleet's water.[189] In 1123 a Venetian expedition to the Holy Land was forced to stop frequently along the way to water, although its problems were probably exacerbated by the fact that it was carrying large numbers of horses.[190] Three years later a new Fatimid fleet from Alexandria sent to raid the coasts of the Kingdom of Jerusalem ran out of water off Beirut, was forced to put ashore, and was severely mauled.[191] During the war of Meloria a Genoese squadron blockading the Pisan fleet in Porto Pisano was forced to withdraw to replenish its water even though it had been at sea for little more than a week.[192] At the siege of Malta in 1565 the Ottoman fleet was sent off to get water less than two weeks after its arrival at Marsasirocco inlet because there was little water there.[193]

Guilmartin has estimated that a minimum daily water requirement for crews labouring through a long, hot Mediterranean summer's day was two quarts, or half a gallon, per man. This seems to be a reasonable and perhaps even conservative estimate, given that crews had not only to be kept alive but also to be maintained in good physical condition. Nothing saps man's ability to work hard as quickly as dehydration. Before the use of slaves and convicts as oarsmen became common in the West in the sixteenth century, that is throughout the Middle Ages in the West, where oarsmen were invariably free volunteers, they would have insisted upon adequate water supplies. In the Muslim and Byzantine world, where oarsmen were often low-class conscripts in the former case and legally obligated subjects from the maritime themes in the latter, their ability to insist was no doubt less than it was in the Latin West.[194] A typical light galley of the sixteenth century, with a crew of 144 oarsmen and 30 to 40 marines, sailors, and officers needed about 90 gallons of water per day. For a cruise of 20 days a galley of this size and complement

[189] Procopius, *History of the wars*, III.xiii.9–24 (pp. 120–5); Rodgers, *Naval warfare*, p. 11.   [190] Pryor, 'Transportation of horses', pp. 14–15.
[191] See below, pp. 115–16.   [192] Rodgers, *Naval warfare*, p. 129.
[193] Guilmartin, *Gunpowder and galleys*, p. 186.
[194] D. Ayalon, 'The Mamluks and naval power: a phase of the struggle between Islam and Christian Europe', *Proceedings of the Israel Academy of Sciences and Humanities*, 1 (1965), 1–12, here p. 4; Christides, *Conquest of Crete*, pp. 50–5; Christides, 'Naval guides', pp. 78–83; Ehrenkreutz, 'Place of Saladin', p. 111; Lev, 'The Fātimid navy', *passim*.

would require about 1800 gallons of water; one hundred 18-gallon barrels.[195] In the Middle Ages, up to the fourteenth century, when galleys normally used only two oarsmen per bench, the requirement would have been somewhat smaller. However, the galleys of this earlier period were also somewhat smaller.[196] Those of the early Middle Ages, the Muslim and Byzantine galleys of the pre-Crusade era, were certainly smaller in general, although there were undoubtedly some Byzantine dromons and Muslim *shīnī* of dimensions comparable to those of late medieval galleys.

It is worth noting that the galleys proposed by Marino Sanudo Torsello in the early fourteenth century for his projected Crusader squadron were approximately the same size as those of Charles of Anjou of 1275. Their overall length was to be 40.72 metres as opposed to the 39.30 metres of the latter.[197] Yet their proposed crew was 250 men, of which 120 were oarsmen.[198] Perhaps the larger numbers of crossbowmen, sailors, marines, and officers on these galleys would not have needed as much water as the oarsmen. Yet there can be little doubt that overall their crews' water requirements would have been greater than those calculated by Guilmartin. Unless they had the capacity to stow larger amounts of water than sixteenth-century galleys, which seems highly unlikely, the period for which they could stay at sea must have been considerably less than it was in the sixteenth century.

Guilmartin's estimate is theoretical and hypothetical. But data from fourteenth- and fifteenth-century sources, although they are fragmentary and difficult to interpret, would suggest that his estimate is not far off the mark and that water supplies carried by galleys in this period were in the range of approximately 800 to 1500 gallons. The inventories of two galleys from Barcelona of 1452 and 1462 mention 40 and 72 water barrels respectively.[199] The *Liber Gazarie* of Genoa of 1330 specified that the galleys of Romania and Syria should carry one or two *vegetes* or *butes* of a total capacity of twelve *metretes* or

---

[195] Guilmartin, *Gunpowder and galleys*, pp. 62–3.

[196] The dimensions of sixteenth-century Venetian light galleys given by Lane are on average a little greater in overall length and beam of the hull than those of the galleys of Charles of Anjou of 1275. Lane, *Venetian ships*, table B, p. 236. Expressed in metres, the formula – overall length plus floor plus depth amidships plus beam of the hull, all divided by four – gives 13.0 metres for the sixteenth-century galleys and 12.02 metres for those of 1275.

[197] Marino Sanudo, *Liber secretorum*, II.4.11 (p. 65).

[198] Ibid., II.4.20 (p. 75).   [199] Unali, *Marinai*, pp. 84–5.

mezarole for water.[200] An inventory for the galley of Simone Leccavello of Genoa in 1351 mentioned 54 water barrels.[201] Another for the galley of Georgio Ritto of Genoa in 1402 mentioned 70 barrels and one *veges*.[202] Two other Genoese inventories, for the galley of Leonardo de Oddone in 1400 and for that of Nicolao de Monelia in 1402, mentioned 72 and 48 barrels respectively.[203] A Venetian text of 1377 for public auctions of galleys for the Alexandria galley caravans mentioned 12 *botti* of water per galley.[204] Finally, a curious text for the equipping of a fleet at Savona in 1476 specified 998 water barrels for ten galleys being completed in the arsenal at Savona.[205]

The Venetian *botte* was equivalent to 648 litres (142.624 gallons).[206] This would mean that the Venetian Alexandria galleys carried in the region of 1722 gallons of fresh water. These were great galleys, and their total complement of crews and travelling merchants were well in excess of the 174 on which Guilmartin's estimates are based. But even if their complement reached 250–300 men, their water supplies should still have been good for some two weeks at least. The Genoese *mezarola* was equivalent to 148.86 litres (32.675 gallons).[207] Therefore, according to the *Liber Gazarie*, around 1330 Genoese Romania and Syria galleys carried only about 392 gallons of fresh water. Even though these were only light galleys, this figure was still far too low. In all probability the *Liber Gazarie* was specifying only a bare minimum or essential reserve of fresh water. Or, possibly, passengers and crew were expected to take aboard their own personal water supplies. The inventories for the various Genoese galleys suggest that they carried much more water than this. A barrel (*barrilium*) was half a *mezarola* or 74.23 litres (16.337 gallons), which would mean that the galley of Simone Leccavello carried 882 gallons, that of Georgio Ritto 1535 gallons, that of Leonardo de Oddone 1176 gallons, and that of Nicolao de Monelia 784 gallons. Savona had long

---

200   V. Vitale, ed., *Le fonti del diritto marittimo ligure* (Genoa, 1951), p. 94. I owe this and the following references to the kind auspices of M. le Professeur M. Balard.

201   Archivio di Stato di Genova, Antico Comune, Galearum introytus et exitus, No. 690.

202   G. G. Musso, 'Armamento e navigazione a Genova tra il Tre e il Quattrocento', in *Guerra e commercio nell'evoluzione della marina genovese tra XV e XVIII secolo* (Genoa, 1973), vol. 2, 6–77; here pp. 39–41, 41–3, 71–6.

203   Ibid., pp. 43–6, 59–60.

204   Archivio di Stato di Venezia, Senato Misti, Regestro 36, fol. 36v.

205   C. Varaldo, 'Inventario ed armamento di una flotta di galee a Savona nel 1476', *Atti e memorie della Società savonese di storia patria*, n.s. 14 (1980), 85–96; here p. 91.   206   Doursther, *Dictionnaire*, pp. 69, 432.   207   Ibid., p. 277.

been part of the territory of Genoa, and the maritime economies of the two cities were closely integrated. The *barrilo* of Savona can be presumed to have been the same as that of Genoa, and consequently each of the ten Savonese galleys of 1476 would have carried approximately 99.8 barrels, or 1630 gallons. These were war galleys, as opposed to the other galleys of Genoa and Venice, which were merchant galleys, and therefore the data for them are perhaps most pertinent. They may be presumed to have been outfitted to carry maximum water supplies if the need to do so arose. Similarly in the case of the two galleys of Barcelona of 1452 and 1462, which were corsair galleys. If the barrel of Barcelona was approximately equal to that of Genoa (I have been unable to determine its actual capacity),[208] then these two galleys of 1452 and 1462 carried approximately 653 gallons and 1176 gallons of fresh water respectively.

Quantities of water taken on board obviously varied according to the size and complement of the galley and also to the nature of the voyage to be undertaken. War galleys and corsair galleys could be expected to take on board water for longer periods than would merchant galleys. On the one hand they had no need to maximize space in hold for cargo and passengers, and on the other they were not as welcome everywhere should they need to rewater. The reverse of the coin, however, was that they were almost always light galleys or galliots with much less stowage space than great galleys. They also needed to occupy stowage space with war materials and to keep their decks clear for combat. Merchant galleys stowed cargo on the decks and along the *corsia*, which no corsair or war galley could afford to do. Moreover, they also carried many more crew proportionate to tonnage than did merchant galleys, or at least they attempted to do so whenever possible. These fourteenth- and fifteenth-century data are therefore subject to many qualifications in their interpretation. Nevertheless, there is nothing in them to suggest that supplies of water

---

[208] I am informed by Sr F. Foerster that, according to A. Torrent, *Balanza métrica* (Valencia, 1867), a work unavailable to me, the *barril* of Barcelona was 30.35 litres but that there were various *barriles*, one of which, the *carga*, was equivalent to four *barriles* or 121.4 litres. Possibly the *carga* was used as a *barril* on board ship and the small *barriles* were used to bring water on board to fill the *cargas*. Using the small *barril* would give water supplies of 267 and 481 gallons respectively for the two galleys of Barcelona of 1452 and 1462. Using the larger *carga* would give 1070 and 1925.5 gallons respectively. The larger *carga* would therefore give water supplies seemingly more appropriate to galleys being fitted out for corsair cruises but, since my information is so uncertain, I have preferred to leave the question open.

carried in this period were greater to any marked degree than those calculated by Guilmartin for the sixteenth century.

Evidence from the Western sources may be complemented for the sixteenth century from the fascinating Ottoman accounts for the campaign of Khair-ed-din Barbarossa in 1539 against Herceg Novi (Castelnuovo). According to Haji Khalifeh (Kâtip Çelebi), Barbarossa had 150 ships for the campaign.[209] In fact the campaign accounts show that he had 58 *bastardas*, 82 galleys (*kadīrge*), 11 galliots (*kalite*), and 4 artillery ships; a total of 155.[210] Barbarossa bought for the campaign 25 428 water barrels (*wārīl*); an average of 164 per ship.[211] The larger *bastardas* would have obviously shipped more barrels aboard than the smaller *kadīrge* and still smaller *kalite*. Perhaps an assumption of around 140 barrels for the *kadīrge* would not be far from the truth. I have been unable to obtain data on the size of the *wārīl* used in Ottoman fleets, but the word was adopted from the Venetian *baril*,[212] and assuming that it was roughly equivalent in size to the latter, that is, to 64.387 litres,[213] the water supply of a *kadīrga* ought to have been roughly in the order of 9000 litres or 2000 gallons. This would have been a maximum water load carried by a ship engaged on extended operations well beyond its bases of supply. By Guilmartin's calculations it would have given an operational period of approximately three weeks.

The Turkish occupation of Anatolia in the thirteenth and fourteenth centuries gave them access to plentiful timber supplies with which to build ships and also to make barrels for carrying water supplies. But what of the rest of the Muslim world? It is widely accepted that throughout the Middle Ages the Muslim world in general was starved of timber and that this had serious consequences for its naval and maritime capacities.[214] In antiquity amphorae had

---

[209] Haji Khalifeh, *The history of the maritime wars of the Turks*, trans. J. Mitchell (London, 1831), p. 67.

[210] Imber, 'Navy of Süleyman the Magnificent', p. 214.

[211] C. H. Imber, 'The costs of naval warfare: the accounts of Hayreddin Barbarossa's Herceg Novi campaign in 1539', *Archivum Ottomanicum*, 4 (1972), 203–16; here p. 216.   [212] Kahane, *Lingua franca*, pp. 96–7.

[213] Lane, *Venetian ships*, p. 245.

[214] See Eickhoff, *Seekrieg*, pp. 155–6; Lev, 'The Fātimid navy', p. 245; Lombard, 'Arsenaux', *passim*; Lombard, 'Le bois', *passim*. Meiggs, *Trees and timber*, ch. 5, 'Forests and fleets', has a great deal of information which remains relevant for the Middle Ages. For an opinion stressing the adequacy of Muslim timber resources, or at least emphasizing that Muslim timber shortcomings did not create for them a strategic disadvantage, see Christides, *Conquest of Crete*, p. 49 and 'Naval guides', pp. 57–60.

been used for transporting liquids of all kinds, including water. Barrels succeeded amphorae in the early medieval West, but did they do so in Byzantium and the Muslim Near East and North Africa? The seventh-century Byzantine Yassi Ada ship used a globular amphora for its water supply and so also, probably, did the eleventh-century Muslim ship from Serçe Liman.[215] Not at all surprisingly, so also did the post-tenth-century Naamah-South ship and the eighteenth-century Sharm-el-Sheikh ship found in the Red Sea.[216] In the Mediterranean it seems to me probable that non-Turkish Muslim shipping also used amphorae throughout the Middle Ages and into the sixteenth century. It is highly improbable that in timber-starved Egypt and North Africa wooden barrels would have been used. The only other possible alternative container would have been skins. Goitein has in fact suggested that in Egypt of the tenth to twelfth centuries skins had replaced amphorae as containers in Muslim maritime transport. He cites evidence from the Cairo Geniza documents for the use of both skins and earthenware vessels for transporting liquids such as oil, wine, vinegar, honey, and mercury and solids such as indigo and soap.[217] However, none of his evidence relates to ships' water supplies, and any conclusion from his evidence for cargo commodities that skins were used for water supplies also appears to be contradicted by the archaeological evidence. One incident from the Crusader period suggests to me that Egyptian galleys of the twelfth century were probably using amphorae. In 1126, when a Fatimid fleet ran out of water off Beirut, the Latin chronicler Fulcher of Chartres recorded that the Egyptians came ashore and tried to fill not their barrels or skins but their 'buckets' (*situle*) from a stream.[218] Fulcher of Chartres was perfectly familiar with the use of both barrels and skins for transporting water. He had grown up in France before the First Crusade, where he would have been used to

[215] Bass and van Doorninck, *Yassi Ada*, pp. 186–8, 315, 316; Bass and van Doorninck, 'Serçe Liman', p. 126 and also the wreck plan in figure 2 showing globular amphorae found towards the stern of the vessel near the living quarters.

[216] A. Raban, 'The mercury carrier from the Red Sea', *Sefunim*, 4 (1972), 28–32, here p. 30; A. Raban, 'The 'Naamah-South' expedition 1973', *Sefunim*, 4 (1972), 33–41, here p. 37; A. Raban. 'The shipwreck off Sharm-el-Sheikh', *Archaeology*, 24 (1971), 146–55, here p. 150. In a recent letter Professor Raban informs me that in no Arab wreck investigated by the Center for Maritime Studies of the University of Haifa has any trace of water barrels been found, yet in all of them large globular jars, presumably for water, have been found.

[217] Goitein, *Mediterranean society*, p. 334 and nn. 7 and 8.

[218] Fulcher of Chartres, *Historia Hierosolymitana*, III.56 (p. 804).

barrels, and he had lived in the Kingdom of Jerusalem since its conquest in 1099, where he would have been accustomed to the Arab use of skins for transporting water on land caravans. His deliberate use of the word *situla* suggests that the water containers on the Egyptian galleys could not be offloaded easily and filled directly from the stream, as would have been the case with both barrels and goat, sheep, or cattle skins. The Egyptians came ashore with buckets and then carried them full back to the ships to fill whatever containers they were using. This suggests amphorae, which, because of their weight and fragility, could not be manhandled easily off and on to the ships beached near the stream. But admittedly, it is also possible that if very large skins, such as camel skins, were in use on the ships, they may have been too heavy when full of water to be carried back to the ships, and therefore buckets may have been used to fill them.

Since amphorae were far more globular in shape than barrels, since because of their fragility they had to be stowed apart with dunnage between them, and since they had to be stowed upright, ships using them would have been able to carry much less water than the same ships using barrels. The difference in payload between liquids carried in amphorae and that in barrels has been estimated to be as high as 30%.[219] Until the advent of the Turks in the fourteenth century, this factor very probably meant that the striking range of Muslim galleys was inferior to that of the Christian West; although it is not possible to quantify that inferiority.

I know of no evidence in the Byzantine sources concerning replacement of amphorae by barrels for water supplies. As we saw, the seventh-century Yassi Ada ship used an amphora for its water. Goitein cites a letter from the Cairo Geniza, unfortunately undated by him, which refers to buckets used for bailing a Muslim ship holding 'half a Byzantine barrel'.[220] Apparently, by the eleventh or twelfth centuries at the latest the Byzantines were using barrels for some purposes, and those may have included water supplies. However, in a recent letter Professor Christides informs me that Greek ships used

[219] See P. Gille, 'Jauge et tonnage des navires', in M. Mollat, ed., *Le navire et l'économie maritime du XVe au XVIIIe siècle* (Première Colloque international d'histoire maritime, Paris, 1956) (Paris, 1957), 85–103, here pp. 87–8; F. C. Lane, 'Progrès technologiques et productivité dans les transports maritimes de la fin du moyen-âge au début des temps modernes', *Revue historique*, 251 (1974), 277–302, here p. 278; Unger, *The ship*, pp. 51–2.

[220] Goitein, *Mediterranean society*, p. 321.

special amphorae with flat bottoms (πλατεῖς πυθμένες), different from those used for wine, for water supplies through to the nineteenth century. The question clearly requires further research and must remain open at this stage.

I also know of no evidence from either the Latin West or the Byzantine or Muslim world in the Middle Ages to suggest that medieval ships of any type used the highly efficient single large water tanks of up to 20 000 gallons which were apparently used on some very large ancient ships.[221] Guilmartin's estimate is that the supply of water carried by the typical sixteenth-century Western light galley would last for no more than two weeks.[222] Rodgers' estimate for all galleys of the entire medieval and early modern periods is 20 days.[223] My own assessment of all the evidence which I have examined inclines me towards the lower figure rather than the higher. Although they are not strictly apposite since, as mentioned above, great galleys of the fifteenth century carried less than maximum water supplies in the interests of maximizing cargo payloads, nevertheless the data provided by Luca di Maso degli Albizzi on the duration of water supplies are relevant. They are fragmentary but consistent. His galleys took on water at Villa Gioiosa on 10 October 1429 and by the 16th off Almeria were running dry, although they did manage to last to Malaga on the 18th. By the 23rd they needed to water again at Cape Canpo, east of Cadiz. On the return voyage they left Southampton on 23 February 1430 and seem to have sailed without making port until 2 March when, because of contrary winds, they could not round Cape St Vincent and had to put back to Lisbon for water and supplies. On 10 March they left Silves with maximum water supplies ('essendo l'aqua piene'), but by the 16th off Cartagena they were again in need of water, although they lasted to reach Sciabbia on the 17th. The maximum time that these galleys could spend at sea without watering seems to have been only about eight or nine days.[224] Almost exactly comparable durations for water supplies were indicated by Pietro Casola and the anonymous French pilgrim of 1480 for the Venetian pilgrim galleys to Jaffa.[225]

[221] Casson, *Ships and seamanship*, pp. 177 nn. 177 and 197.
[222] Guilmartin, *Gunpowder and galleys*, pp. 62–3.
[223] Rodgers, *Naval warfare*, p. 232.
[224] Mallett, *Florentine galleys*, pp. 220–1, 223, 265–6, 268–71, 221 n. 3.
[225] Casola, *Pilgrimage*, pp. 184, 213–19, 293, 296, 311; Schefer, *Voyage de la saincte cyté*, pp. 109–13.

While I reiterate that such commercial and passenger galleys did not attempt to carry the full water supplies that war and corsair galleys would have done when engaged on extended operations, nevertheless these data support the calculations of Guilmartin and Rodgers on the one hand and the evidence for the duration of water supplies of war fleets cited above on the other,[226] that the maximum duration of the water supply of a normal light galley or galliot was between two and three weeks.

One further explanation of the limited duration of water supplies may be related to the problem of spoilage, or putrefaction, in the heat of the Mediterranean summer. During Belisarius' sixteen-day crossing from Zante to Sicily in the summer of 533, the fleet's water supply putrefied or 'spoiled' ($\delta\iota\alpha\phi\theta\alpha\rho\hat{\eta}\nu\alpha\iota$). Only a supply sealed in glass jars by Belisarius's wife and buried in sand in the hold of his ship remained unaffected ($\dot{\alpha}\pi\alpha\theta\grave{\epsilon}s$).[227] This is, however, the only reference known to me for water supplies putrefying, as opposed to running out. Many known crossings took a great deal longer than sixteen days out of sight of land – those of Ibn Jubayr for instance – yet the sources make no reference to the water supplies putrefying. Nevertheless, it is at least possible that problems of putrefaction in the heat of the Mediterranean summer induced, or added to the inducement for, ships' masters to carry water supplies for a limited duration only. Jacques de Vitry, bishop of Acre from 1216 to 1228, in a letter describing his voyage from Genoa to Acre to assume his office, wrote that the Genoese: '. . . have very sturdy ships of a great size, as a consequence of which they are used to crossing the sea in winter, for the reason that in that season the victuals aboard ship do not go bad easily nor the water putrefy as [it does] aboard ship in the summer season. . .'[228] In the absence, however, of further evidence on the subject, or alternatively of experimentation to determine how long water in wooden barrels, amphorae, and skins will stay drinkable in the Mediterranean summer, the question of the duration of water before putrefaction must remain open. Sixteen days, or any period between two and three

[226] See above, pp. 75–80.
[227] Procopius, *Vandalic war*, III.13.23–4 (pp. 124–5).
[228] Jacques de Vitry, *Lettres de Jacques de Vitry (1160/1170–1240) évêque de Saint-Jean d'Acre*, ed. R. B. C. Huygens (Leiden, 1960); I.174–7 (pp. 77–8): 'naves habent fortissimas et magne quantitatis, unde tempore hiemali consueverunt transfretare eo, quod tali tempore victualia in navi non facile corrumpuntur nec aqua sicut estivo tempore in navi putrescit'.

weeks, seems an unbelievably short time for water properly stowed and looked after to putrefy.

Although, as stated above, my own reading of the available evidence inclines me to Guilmartin's lower estimate of the duration of water supplies rather than to Rodgers' higher one, for the purposes of these studies I have used the higher figure. Even using the higher estimate, it can still be demonstrated that the cruising range of galleys was extremely limited, even given the highest possible estimate of the duration of water supplies. If Guilmartin's lower estimate, or some other figure near it, were to be accepted and used, then the arguments in this book which are consequent upon the limited cruising range of galleys would be strengthened even further.

With Rodgers' figure of 20 days' supply, and the estimated cruising speed of galley squadrons, a maximum of two knots when maintained continuously, a cruising range of approximately 960 nautical miles or 1100 standard imperial miles is obtained. The range of Muslim galleys using amphorae may have been considerably less, as also may have been that of Byzantine galleys of at least the early Byzantine period and that of Western galleys of the sixteenth century if Guilmartin's estimate of two weeks' water supply is correct for that period. It must be stressed that the figure of 1100 miles cannot be taken as any sort of absolute limitation, since it was subject to many variables, such as the availability of watering facilities en route, of course. Nevertheless it is an extremely useful calculation in attempting to quantify that limitation on the radius of action of galley fleets to which Lev has called attention for the Fatimid navy of the tenth and early eleventh centuries, Ehrenkreutz for the Ayyubid navy of the twelfth century, Imber for the Ottoman navy of the fifteenth and sixteenth centuries, and Guilmartin for galley warfare in general in the sixteenth century.[229]

One question which still remains open is why fleet commanders did not use sailing ships as fleet tenders to accompany galleys with extra water to extend their range. Eighteen hundred gallons of water would weigh about 8.6 metric tons, exclusive of containers. If the weight of barrels or amphorae brought it up to about 10 metric tons (in this context any exact figure does not matter), then a single large sailing

[229] Ehrenkreutz, 'Place of Saladin', pp. 102, 108; Guilmartin, *Gunpowder and galleys*, pp. 96–108; Imber, 'Navy of Süleyman the Magnificent', pp. 216–17; Lev, 'The Fātimid navy', p. 241.

ship of the mid thirteenth century, capable of carrying up to 800 metric tons of cargo,[230] ought to have been able to more than double the range of a fleet of 50 galleys. Use of fleet tenders seems such an obvious answer to the problem of the limited range of galleys that it almost passes belief that it was never thought of. The reason cannot have been that the speed of sailing ships was less than that of galleys and that fleet tenders could not keep up with galley fleets since, as we have seen, the data for voyage durations of sailing ships and their average speeds are quite similar to those for galleys and galley fleets.[231] Yet I know of no source throughout the entire period which specifically identifies supply ships accompanying a galley fleet as carrying extra water to resupply the galleys. To the best of my knowledge the solution was never attempted.

[230] Pryor, 'Naval architecture', pp. 373-4.   [231] See above, pp. 36, 52, 71–5.

3. Navigation: the routes and their implications

Because of the storms and dangerous squally conditions created in winter by localized meteorological phenomena, because of the strong northerly winds prevailing in that season, and because of the hazards caused by reduced visibility to coastal and celestial navigation as a result of overcast skies and fogs, commercial shipping generally avoided navigation in the winter whenever possible. This remained true from antiquity through to the sixteenth century. Naval warfare and piracy or privateering, the *guerre de course*, were also normally suspended. However, this suspension of maritime activity in winter was certainly never absolute. Neither did the degree to which seafaring was suspended remain uniform across the centuries. As a result of improvements in both ship design and in navigation techniques, particularly in the thirteenth to fifteenth centuries, the sailing season extended gradually back into early spring and forward into late autumn. By the sixteenth century it was far longer than it had been in the Roman, Byzantine, and Crusader periods.

In Boeotia of the eighth century BC, Hesiod, admittedly a landlubber, limited the safe sailing season to a mere 50 days in mid summer after the summer solstice; that is, from *c*. 21 June to *c*. 10 August, although he did admit a short but dangerous sailing season in early spring.[1] Several decrees of various Roman emperors addressed the subject of limitations on winter navigation,[2] and one of these, a decree of Gratian of AD 380, prohibited navigation for the ships of the Africa–Rome grain trade only from the Ides (15th) of October to the Kalends (1st) of April.[3] In the fifth century, Vegetius extended

---

[1] Hesiod, *Works and days*, in *Hesiod, the Homeric hymns and Homerica*, ed. and trans. H. G. Evelyn-White (London, 1959), ll. 646–94.

[2] *The Theodosian Code and Novels and the Sirmondian Constitutions*, trans. C. Pharr (New York, 1969); 13.5.26, 13.5.27, 13.9.3.3; *Codex Iustinianus*, in *Corpus iuris civilis*, ed. T. Mommsen, P. Krueger, R. Schoell & W. Kroll, vol. II, 15th edn (1877), rpt. (Dublin/Zurich, 1970), 1.40.6, 11.6.3.

[3] *Theodosian Code*, 13.9.3.3 (p. 399). Cf. *Codex Iustinianus*, 11.6.3.

the sailing season somewhat beyond even this. From 11 November to 10 March the sea was closed, he said. From 10 March to 15 May navigation could be resumed, but only at great risk. From 27 May to 24 September the sea became quite safe, but from then until 11 November it again became dangerous and risky.[4] Generally speaking, the Greeks and Romans left their commercial shipping in port from October to April:[5] although it was always true, no doubt, as Rougé has pointed out, that for the bold or imprudent the winter closure was shorter than that or did not exist in any absolute sense at all.[6] In Muslim Egypt of the eleventh and twelfth centuries, the sea was still closed from November to March.[7] The practice of the Christian West at this time was probably very similar to that of the Muslim world, for by *c.* 1160 at Pisa it was only from 1 November to 1 March that a captain who brought his ship into the port was prevented from leaving.[8]

In the late thirteenth and in the fourteenth and fifteenth centuries, the diffusion of the mariner's compass and the development of the cog and carrack ended finally whatever closing of the seas in winter there had ever been in absolute terms.[9] Genoese shipping to the Aegean and Black Seas could, and did, sail in winter.[10] The great galleys of Florence in the fifteenth century braved winter seas with regularity.[11] So also did sailing ships of the Venetian salt trade and Venetian galley caravans to the Levant.[12] However, if the seas were certainly no longer closed by the onset of winter in the late Middle Ages and in the sixteenth century, there was still, nevertheless, a marked decrease in navigation during the winter by comparison to the summer. Genoese shipping slowed down considerably from December to February, and there were many references to the dangers of winter navigation.[13]

---

[4] Vegetius, *Epitoma rei militaris*, ed. C. Lang (Stuttgart, 1872), IV.39 (pp. 158–60).

[5] L. Casson, *The ancient mariners: seafarers and sea fighters of the Mediterranean in ancient times* (New York, 1959), pp. 39, 234; E. de Saint-Denis, 'Mare clausum', *Revue des études latines*, 25 (1947), 196–214; J. Rougé, 'La navigation hivernale sous l'empire romain', *Revue des études anciennes*, 54 (1952), 316–325.

[6] Rougé, 'Navigation hivernale', p. 321.

[7] Goitein, *Mediterranean society*, pp. 316–17.

[8] Pisa, *Constitutum usus*, ed. F. Bonaini in *Statuti inediti della città di Pisa dal XII al XIV secolo* (Florence, 1854–70), c. XXVIII (vol. 2, p. 919).

[9] Cf. Lane, 'Invention of the compass', pp. 333–7.   [11] Mallett, *Florentine galleys*, p. 33.

[10] Balard, *Romanie Génoise*, pp. 578–80.

[12] Hocquet, *Le sel: Voiliers*, pp. 172–5; Heers, 'Commercio nel Mediterraneo', pp. 166–7.

[13] Balard, *Romanie Génoise*, p. 579.

Accounts by pilgrims of voyages which extended into the winter months reveal clearly how dangerous winter navigation remained.[14] Even in the sixteenth century, improvements in navigational techniques and in ship design had by no means defeated the elements and much maritime traffic still ceased in the winter unless there were strong incentives to take the risks.[15] Smaller ships were naturally more likely to lie over for the winter than the large cogs and carracks and state-of-the-art great galleys.[16] But, of course, circumstances dictated exceptions to the rule. Daring captains constantly braved winter voyages in the hope of high profits. Single ships on important military and diplomatic missions always ventured to sea in winter. In spite of the fact that the large war fleets were normally laid up for the winter,[17] naval expeditions also were occasionally launched in winter when strategic objectives outweighed the risks; sometimes with disastrous consequences.[18] Winter voyages were nevertheless the exception to the rule and the vast majority of shipping, both commercial and naval, sailed from spring to autumn under conditions dominated by summer meteorological patterns.

In the analysis which follows, therefore, summer weather patterns only have been considered unless specifically stated otherwise. It should be said, however, that since the direction of the prevailing winds was quite similar in winter to that of summer, though for different reasons, the conclusions to be drawn would not be affected by consideration of winter weather patterns.

Prevailing winds varying from north-west to north-east over the entire Mediterranean made voyages from north to south or west to east comparatively simple and fast. From Marseilles the Gulf of the Lion lay open towards the Balearics, Sardinia, and the Maghreb. From Genoa and Pisa, Sicily was easily accessible. From Venice it was a straight-forward run down the Adriatic to the Peloponnesus. From Constantinople both the currents and prevailing winds facilitated voyages down the Bosphorus and the Dardanelles to Crete, Rhodes, and Cyprus. From the Ionian Sea or Crete both Egypt and Palestine could be reached easily before the *meltemi*. Ships bound for the Holy

---

[14] Hyde, 'Navigation', pp. 531–2.
[15] Braudel, *Mediterranean*, pp. 248–55; Tucci, 'Pratique vénitienne de la navigation', *passim*.
[16] Braudel, *Mediterranean*, pp. 249–55; Heers, *Gênes*, pp. 299–300.
[17] Cf. Imber, 'Navy of Süleyman the Magnificent', p. 216.
[18] Braudel, *Mediterranean*, pp. 249, 251–3, 995 *et passim*.

Land could count on having winds from astern or from the port stern quarter all the way from Provence or Italy to their destinations. Voyages from south to north, or from east to west, were, however, much more difficult. Against the *meltemi* they could be simply impossible. Alternative routes had to be found. In fact the easiest and most navigationally logical route from Alexandria to the west or north began by clawing around the coasts of Palestine, Syria, Cilicia, and Lycia with the assistance of the currents and land and sea breezes. Voyages from Rhodes, Crete, and the Peloponnesus north through the Aegean to Constantinople had to be made into the teeth of the *meltemi*. Whether a ship followed the western, Greek coasts or the eastern, Anatolian coasts, the dangers of rocky, reef-strewn coasts and of offshore islands were exacerbated by contrary winds and choppy seas. The current also became a formidable obstacle from the Dardanelles on. From Crete to Sicily winds on the starboard beam facilitating an easier passage might be expected, but they could swing very easily to the west and drive a ship back on her path, as Ibn Jubayr discovered in 1184.[19] If a ship turned north into the Ionian towards the Straits of Otranto or attempted the haul up the Adriatic to Venice, frustrating delays and slow progress could be expected. In the western Mediterranean the passage through the Sicilian Channel had to be made against both current and prevailing winds. The voyage around the south-west tip of Sardinia and then north through the Gulf of the Lion to Marseilles could be hard and long. In fact a better route, once the initial difficulty of the passage of the Straits of Messina had been overcome, was that north along the coast of Italy and then west to Provence. At least here a ship might use the slight current and the daily land and sea breezes.

We are not concerned here with the navigational difficulties of the routes themselves. I have discussed those elsewhere.[20] Rather we are concerned with the implications of these routes for the agglomeration of maritime traffic in certain crucial sectors along them and with the implications of that for the prosecution of the *guerre de course*. We are also concerned with the implications of possession of the strategic ports and islands, which dominated these sectors of the routes because of their near proximity to them, for the larger struggle at sea between the competing maritime powers.

---

[19] Ibn Jubayr, *Travels*, pp. 330–8.
[20] J. H. Pryor, 'Winds, waves, and rocks: the routes and the perils along them', forthcoming at the International Congress of historical sciences, Stuttgart, 1985.

In the western basin of the sea the routes tended to be somewhat more diversified than they were in the eastern. Larger numbers of important ports scattered all around the northern coasts and islands, and also the larger numbers of ports along the coast of the Maghreb than along the Egyptian and Libyan coasts in the east, tended to diversify shipping lanes.[21] In addition, the prevailing winds in the western basin posed fewer difficulties for east–west and south–north passages than did the frustratingly consistent *meltemi* in the eastern basin. Consequently, the routes in the western basin were not confined so exclusively to certain narrow sea lanes where those difficulties could be most easily overcome. Nevertheless, coastal navigation along certain well-defined routes still very much predominated in the western basin whenever political and religious conditions permitted.[22]

From Catalonia, the Languedoc, and Provence voyages to the Sicilian Channel and Tunisia followed the age-old route known as the *route des îles*; down the west coasts of Corsica and Sardinia. In the early Middle Ages, except when politico-religious hostilities made one or other of the routes too dangerous, shipping between Africa and Gaul went either by way of Sicily and the Italian coast, or by way of the Spanish coast, or by the *route des îles*.[23] These routes all remained popular throughout the entire period. However, it was the Balearics which were the real key to maritime control in the western Mediterranean.[24] In Muslim hands from 902 to 1229, they permitted Muslim shipping to operate freely in the southern sector of the sea and enabled Muslim corsairs to range north to the Gulf of the Lion.[25] Following their conquest by the Aragonese they provided an essential way station for Christian shipping crossing from Catalonia and the Languedoc south to the Maghreb or east to Sardinia.[26] Transverse routes in the western basin centred around the crossings from the

---

[21] On Maghrebin ports see Yarrison, *Force as an instrument of policy*, pp. 21–3.
[22] C. Carrère, 'Marseille, Aigues Mortes, Barcelone, et la competition en Méditerranée occidentale au XIIIᵉ siècle', *A.E.M.*, 10 (1980), 161–72, here pp. 162–3; A. Santamaría Arández, 'La reconquista de las vías marítimas', *A.E.M.*, 10 (1980), 41–134, here pp. 50–1; Unali, *Marinai*, pp. 115–16.
[23] Courtois, 'Rapports', pp. 138–42; Courtois, 'Remarques', pp. 51, 55; Yarrison, *Force as an instrument of policy*, pp. 32–3.
[24] F. S. Colom, 'Navegaciones mediterraneas (s. XI–XVI): valor del puerto de Mallorca', in Ragosta, *Navigazioni mediterranee*, 15–74; Yarrison, *Force as an instrument of policy*, pp. 32–3, 60, 94.
[25] Colom, 'Navegaciones mediterraneas', pp. 19–23.
[26] Ibid., pp. 24, 61, 68; Yarrison, *Force as an instrument of policy*, pp. 32–3, 60, 94.

Gibraltar approaches to the Balearics, to Cape Teulada at the south-west of Sardinia, and from there to the west coast of Sicily. Christian ships avoided the coast of the Maghreb not only for fear of Muslim corsairs but also because of navigational considerations.[27] In 1185 Ibn Jubayr made the voyage from Trapani to Cartagena on a Genoese ship via Cape Teulada and Iviza.[28] In 1285 Roger of Lauria brought the Aragonese–Sicilian battle fleet to Barcelona from Sicily by this route.[29] It was in fact the natural transverse route across the western Mediterranean, as Boccaccio indicated in his tales of Alatiel and Gerbino,[30] although political considerations could, of course, influence shipping of one or the other faith to avoid it and to use navigationally less attractive routes in periods when it was infested by enemy fleets and corsairs.[31] Again, possession of the Balearics was the key to the situation. In the fourteenth and fifteenth centuries, Majorca became a regular way station for Genoese and Venetian galleys on their way to the Straits of Gibraltar and the English Channel and many Italian companies established branches on the island.[32]

From Liguria and Tuscany the run down the coast of Italy to the Straits of Messina was an easy one. Shipping hugged the coasts, utilizing the land and sea breezes, no matter whether bound north or south. The straits themselves, however, were probably the most difficult passage anywhere in the Mediterranean except for the Bosphorus, Dardanelles, and Negropont. The strong tides and currents, the whirlpools and tidal rips, *tagli*, and the strong winds channelled between the mountains on either side were formidable obstacles. We have already seen Ibn Jubayr comment on them.[33] Medieval ships had to wait off the approaches to the Straits of Messina for a combination of favourable tide and following wind. In the later Middle Ages, at least, according to Ludolph von Suchem and others, local pilots were used: 'between Calabria and Sicily . . . the sea runs so hard that no sailor dares to sail through without a special pilot'.[34]

From the Sicilian Channel or the Straits of Messina, ships could

---

[27] See above, pp. 21–2.   [28] Ibn Jubayr, *Travels*, pp. 361–5.
[29] Ramon Muntaner, *The chronicle of Muntaner* (Hakluyt Soc. Works. Second series, 47 & 50) (London, 1920–1), vol. 1, pp. 344–5.
[30] See above, p. 39.   [31] Cf. Courtois, 'Remarques', p. 55.
[32] Colom, 'Navegaciones mediterraneas', pp. 35–8, 58.   [33] See above, p. 14–15.
[34] Ludolph von Suchem, *Description of the Holy Land*, p. 11. See also *Portolan Parma-Magliabecchi*, in Kretschmer, *Italienischen Portolane*, p. 308.

either cross the Ionian Sea directly to Modon or Crete or alternatively follow the coasts of Sicily, Calabria, Apulia, and the Balkans. For east–west voyages the same choice was available in reverse. For west–east voyages the choice of route was fairly open because the prevailing winds from the north-west were astern and the choice could therefore be made according to the nature of the ship and its business and whether the Ionian was entered from the Sicilian Channel or the Straits of Messina. All of the major Crusader fleets which entered the Ionian from the Sicilian Channel crossed directly to the south coast of Crete. But Genoese galleys bound for the Levant or Romania and entering from the Straits of Messina almost always took the coastal route.[35] In fact galleys of all persuasions would normally have taken the coastal route, because even in summer the weather in the Ionian is unpredictable. Depressions moving east across the Mediterranean tend to linger there, and others are actually generated over the Ionian. Squalls whipped up by either the *bora* or the *scirocco* can be very violent, and the west coast of the Peloponnesus is hardly welcoming.[36] About 30 miles south-south-west of Zante, 30 miles off the coast, and only about 30 miles north of the direct lines between the Straits of Messina, the Sicilian Channel, and Modon, lie the notorious Strofadhes islands with their connecting reef. Arpia island in the group was the famous Harpy rock of the ancients. For east–west voyages the prevailing winds were badly adverse and therefore the attractions of the favourable currents and offshore and onshore breezes close in to the coasts were considerable for shipping of all types. But the run up from Crete to Corfu could always be difficult. In 1184 Ibn Jubayr's ship had great difficulty breaking away from Crete and making Zante.[37]

To and from Venice, voyages both up and down the Adriatic were made invariably along the Balkan coast unless a ship had business in one of the Italian ports. The prevailing winds generally make the Italian coast the lee shore, and in any case it is an unwelcoming one. There are few natural safe refuges, it is not backed by high mountains which would assist coastal navigation by landmarks, there are few offshore islands to provide shelter in bad weather, the holding ground

[35] Balard, 'Escales génoises', p. 248.
[36] *Weather in the Mediterranean*, vol. 1, p. 184, fig. 1.5(b) (p. 26), fig. 1.19(b) and (c) (pp. 97–8). See also Braudel, *Mediterranean*, pp. 133–4, 1118.
[37] Ibn Jubayr, *Travels*, pp. 330–2.

is generally poor, and there are large extents of dangerous shallows. The Balkan coast, by contrast, has a large number of islands and ports for refuge and supplies, is backed by high mountains, and is usually not the lee shore.[38] For the Venetians the many islands and ports possessed or dominated by the city in the lagoons on the Balkan coast from the eleventh century provided secure shelter and logistical facilities for their shipping. By the late Middle Ages they operated systems of pilots from Venice to Parenza and from Parenza to Modon.[39] As far south as Dubrovnik, the route lay amongst the islands and channels very close in to the mainland, often in extremely confined waters.[40] South of the Straits of Otranto, it lay inshore of Corfu, Cephalonia, and Zante, all of which had their main medieval harbours on their east coasts. The approaches to Modon were protected by the Oinousai islands, the largest of which was Sapienza.

From a navigational point of view, Crete was the key to the eastern Mediterranean. Its geographical importance in the east was on a par with that of the Balearics in the west and Sicily in the central Mediterranean. During the period in which the island was in Muslim hands (*c.* 824–961) it became the gateway to the Maghreb for Muslim shipping. The geographer Yāqūt ibn 'Abd Allāh al-Ḥamawī (*c.* 1179–1229) called the waters around Crete the *Baḥr al-Maghrib* (Sea of the Maghreb).[41] This was an exceedingly perspicacious perception for, as long as political circumstances permitted, the natural navigational route from Egypt or Syria to the Maghreb was via Crete. Not surprisingly the change in status of Crete from a backwater province of the empire under the Byzantines to an independent political entity under the Muslims resulted in a flourishing of the island's economy and to its assumption of a position as a centre of trans-Mediterranean trade and commerce.[42] The island could be passed either to the north or to the south. On the one hand, the major Crusader fleets all sailed for the Holy Land via the south of the island but, on the other, after the Venetian occupation of Crete early in the thirteenth century Venetian ships invariably headed for Candia on the north coast before continuing. Except in rare periods of peace between Genoa and

---

[38] J. Tadić, 'La côte occidentale des Balkans et ses liaisons maritimes et continentales (XIᵉ–XVIᵉ siècles)', in Ragosta, *Navigazioni mediterranee*, 99–110; here pp. 103–4.

[39] Casola, *Pilgrimage*, p. 170.

[40] Ibid., pp. 164–81. See also Louis de Rochechouart, 'Journal de voyage de Louis de Rochechouart évêque de Saintes', ed. C. Couderc in *Revue de l'Orient latin*, 1 (1893), 168–274; here pp. 228–30.   [41] Christides, *Conquest of Crete*, pp. 116–17.

[42] Christides, *Conquest of Crete*, pp. 116–21; Christides, 'Naval guides', p. 59.

Venice, Genoese ships avoided Crete and sailed either to its south or to its north through the Cyclades.[43] But whether a ship went north or south of Crete, the *meltemi* blew almost directly from the north, and ships could usually reach along either coast in either direction without great difficulty unless the wind veered or strengthened. On the north coast a master would have to be wary of being caught on a lee shore if the *meltemi* intensified into a gale, and on the south coast he would have to be extremely watchful for the notorious squalls generated by air currents descending suddenly from the Cretan mountains.[44]

East of Crete the main route to the Holy Land lay north-east to Rhodes and then to the Bay of Attalya, south-east to Cyprus, and then across to the coast around Tripoli or Beirut before coasting down to Acre or Jaffa. Ships bound for Egypt could, of course, cross directly to Alexandria from Crete or Rhodes before the following *meltemi*. In the late Middle Ages the pilgrim galleys to Jaffa also used this wind to cross directly south-south-east from Cyprus to Jaffa. However, during the lifetime of the Crusader states it was normal to cross from Cyprus to the Syrian coast around Tripoli or Beirut. Coast watchers were stationed permanently on a hill south of Beirut to watch for shipping coming down the coast.[45] Off the coasts of Syria and Palestine the predominant wind pattern in summer was that of the daily cycle of land and sea breezes, the sea breezes being much stronger and extending up to twelve miles offshore.[46] With the current setting north at about two knots, these breezes offered the best conditions for ships returning from Egypt or the Holy Land to the West. The route via Palestine and Syria had been the most popular route to the West from Alexandria in the Roman period,[47] and it was still so in the thirteenth century.[48] Open-sea crossings from Alexandria or Acre to Cyprus or Rhodes against the *meltemi* could be very uncertain. In 1243 Frederick II's *bailli* in the Holy Land, Richard Filangieri, was blown off course while attempting to sail from Tyre to Apulia via the south coast of Cyprus and was wrecked off the coast of

[43] Balard, 'Escales génoises', p. 249 and diagram.
[44] *Weather in the Mediterranean*, vol. 1, p. 77.
[45] L. de Mas Latrie, ed., *Chronique d'Ernoul et de Bernard le Trésorier* (Paris, 1871), pp. 365–6. See also *L'estoire de Eracles Empereur et la conqueste de la terre d'Outremer*, in *R.H.C. Occ.*, vol. 2 (Paris, 1859), XXVI.8 (p. 226).
[46] Goldsmith & Sofer, 'Wave climatology', p. 8; *Weather in the Mediterranean*, vol. 1, pp. 93–5.
[47] Casson, *Ships and seamanship*, pp. 297–9; Semple, *Geography of the Mediterranean*, p. 599.   [48] Lane, *Venice*, p. 39, map 4 and p. 72.

Egypt.[49] In 1395 Ogier VIII d'Anglure was blown off course from Alexandria to Rhodes towards Cyprus when the *meltemi* strengthened and veered to the west.[50] Additionally, ships making this crossing had to be extremely watchful for the dangers of the Egyptian *khamsin*, which on occasions can blow right across the Mediterranean on to the coast of Cyprus. Louis IX was almost wrecked on the south coast of Cyprus in 1254 by the *khamsin*.[51] Not surprisingly, when the Florentines established a route for their great galleys to Alexandria and Beirut in the fifteenth century, the galleys went to Alexandria first and only then to Beirut before returning home.[52] From Acre the route to Cyprus recommended by the Marciana portolan lay along the coast to Tripoli or even Latakia and then west to make landfall at Cape Andreas.[53] In 1232 King Henry I of Cyprus crossed from Acre to Cyprus with the royal fleet via Tyre, Sidon, and Cape Greco south of Famagusta.[54] If a ship did cross to the south coast of Cyprus, it could then expect a difficult haul against the *meltemi* to either Rhodes or Crete. A better choice of route was to continue north from Tripoli towards Antioch and to turn west with the current along the Cilician and Lycian coasts to Rhodes. Here the land and sea breezes would continue to be of assistance. The main dangers lay in the Bay of Attalya from the strong squalls which can descend suddenly off the Taurus mountains. In the Middle Ages this stretch of sea had a notorious reputation, on which many writers commented.[55] In 1384 three Italian pilgrims, Frescobaldi, Gucci, and Sigoli, were caught in the Bay of Attalya by a northerly storm in April and blown right across the Mediterranean on to the Egyptian coast, where they were very nearly wrecked.[56] But in spite of the dangers of the Bay of Attalya, this route along the southern coast of Asia Minor remained a very popular alternative to the open-sea crossing south of Cyprus.

[49] Philip de Novare, *Wars of Frederick II*, p. 180.
[50] Bonnardot & Longnon, *Saint voyage*, pp. 79–81.
[51] Joinville, *Life of St. Louis*, pp. 182–7.
[52] Mallet, *Florentine galleys*, p. 65 and map 2.
[53] Portolan fragment from the Marciana Library, Venice, in Kretschmer, *Italienischen Portolane*, p. 235.
[54] Philip de Novare, *Wars of Frederick II*, pp. 145–6.
[55] Fulcher of Chartres, *Historia Hierosolymitana*, III.59 (pp. 811–12); Bellorini & Hoade, *Holy places*, pp. 89, 148–9, 185; Ludolph von Suchem, *Description of the Holy Land*, p. 13; Nicolaus de Marthono 'Nicolai de Marthono, notarii, liber peregrinationis ad Loca Sancta', ed. L. Legrand in *Revue de l'Orient latin*, 3 (1895), 566–669, here p. 638; Roger of Hoveden, *Chronica*, pp. 158–9.
[56] Bellorini & Hoade, *Holy places*, pp. 89, 148–9, 185.

Any glance at one of the late medieval portolans with their listings of the numerous small ports along this coast will confirm this.[57] As in the western Mediterranean, the routes through the Aegean to Constantinople were more varied than elsewhere because of the large number of Byzantine ports and, from 1204, Latin colonies scattered around the sea. The many passages through the various island groups also diffused the routes. However, in general terms there were three: one up the east coast of the Balkans, another along the west coast of Asia Minor, and a third through the Cyclades and across to Chios. All three came together from Lesbos north to Tenedos and the approaches to the Dardanelles. The western route involved voyages into the teeth of the *meltemi* at least as far as Kafirevs Straight between Andros and Negropont (Evvoia). Michael Choniates on Keos in the twelfth century complained bitterly about the north wind, which kept him isolated on his island.[58] After the seizure of Negropont by Venice, Venetian ships normally made their way north through the Gulf of Petalioi to Negropont city (Chalkis) and the Gulf of Evvoia, exiting into the Aegean through Trikeri Strait. In certain periods the way north may have been blocked by the bridge to the mainland at Negropont,[59] but in others this seems to have been down. Either that or it was somehow possible to go through the bridge. Certainly the *Compasso de Navegare* envisaged it as being possible to go past Negropont to the north in the second half of the thirteenth century.[60] The central route through the Cyclades was really an almost infinitely diverse series of routes amongst the various islands. Ships might pick their way through any one of the numerous channels according to weather conditions and their starting position. Both the *Compasso de Navegare* and Gratiosus Benincasa devoted large sections to the Cyclades, the *Scala de Romania*, the *Compasso* mentioning several small lighthouses on some of the islands.[61] The eastern route up the coast of Asia Minor was a dangerous one off a rocky lee shore strewn

[57] See Motzo, *Compasso di Navegare*, pp. 58–60; *Portolan Parma-Magliabecchi* and *Portolan Rizo* in Kretschmer, *Italienischen Portolane*, pp. 329–32, 523–30.

[58] Michael Choniates, Μιχ Ακομινάτου Σωζόμενα, ed. S. Lampros (Athens, 1879–80), vol. 2, p. 144 cited in E. Malamut, 'Les îles de la mer Egée de la fin du XIᵉ siècle à 1204', *Byzantion*, 52 (1982), 310–50; here p. 316.

[59] A. D. Andrews, *The Turkish threat to Venice 1453–1463*, Ph.D. thesis, University of Pennsylvania, 1962, p. 204; Nicolaus de Marthono, 'Liber peregrinationis', pp. 654–5.   [60] Motzo, *Compasso di Navegare*, pp. 41–3.

[61] Ibid., pp. 48–56, 123–6; *Portolan des Gratiosus Benincasa*, in Kretschmer, *Italienischen Portolane*, pp. 382–6.

with islands, reefs, and shoals. As Ruy Gonzalez de Clavijo commented: 'the voyage from Rhodes to Chios is dangerous, as the land of Turkey is very close on the right hand; and there are many islands, both inhabited and desert, on the other side; so that it is dangerous to sail over this route, at night, or in bad weather'.[62] These dangers were offset, to some extent, by the fact that the current set generally northwards and could be quite strong through some of the channels and also by the fact that close in to land the *meltemi* was reduced by convection and easterly and westerly land and sea breezes might be helpful.[63] Even so, de Clavijo took 55 days for his voyage from Rhodes to Constantinople and was constantly held in port by contrary winds.[64] In the twelfth century Nicholas Muzalon had reached Cyprus from Constantinople in only ten days.[65] Differences of this order of magnitude between times for voyages north and south along this coast were the norm throughout the period. As we saw above, a Genoese ship made Chios from Pera in three days in 1453, but took 20 days in the other direction.

All three Aegean routes came together between Lesbos and Tenedos for the approach to the Dardanelles. To the difficulties of the adverse current in these straits, which could reach up to six or seven knots, were added the constant north-east prevailing winds. Ships had to wait around in the approaches for the wind to shift to the south or west in order for them to mount the straits against the current. For that reason Tenedos was an extremely important haven. De Clavijo's ship remained there for 14 days waiting for the wind to shift.[66] At times the waters around Tenedos must have been crowded with shipping waiting for a favourable opportunity to enter the Dardanelles. No wonder that when John V Cantacuzenus ceded Tenedos to Venice in 1376, Genoa went to war with her rival for possession of the island.[67] The adverse currents and winds in the Dardanelles meant that mounting them could be a slow and tedious business. Conse-

---

[62] De Clavijo, *Embassy*, p. 19.
[63] *Weather in the Mediterranean*, vol. 1, p. 79 and vol. 2, p. 64.
[64] De Clavijo, *Embassy*, p. 19–28.
[65] A. Kazhdan & G. Constable, *People and power in Byzantium: an introduction to modern Byzantine studies* (Washington, 1982), p. 42.
[66] De Clavijo *Embassy*, pp. 25–7.
[67] F. Thiriet, 'Venise et l'occupation de Ténédos au XIVᵉ siècle', *Mélanges d'archéologie et d'histoire publiés par l'Ecole française de Rome*, 65 (1953), 219–45; D. M. Vaughan, *Europe and the Turk: a pattern of alliances 1350–1700* (Liverpool, 1954), p. 32.

quently, the port of Gallipoli on the northern side, which had the best water supplies in the straits, assumed a critical importance.[68] These major Mediterranean sea lanes or trunk routes both crossed each other in certain sectors and also passed through certain narrowly confined stretches of sea in others. During peak periods of the year for navigation, particularly in spring and again in autumn, these sectors must have been crowded with shipping. Such sectors included the Ligurian Sea between Genoa, Elba, Corsica, and Hyères; the waters around the Balearics and south-west to the coast of Spain at Cape de Gata; the south-west tip of Sardinia around the islands of S. Pietro and S. Antioco; the Lipari islands and approaches to the Straits of Messina from the north; the Straits of Otranto and west coast of the Peloponnesus south to Modon; the southern coast of Asia Minor from Rhodes to Alanya; the quadrilateral bounded by Famagusta, Tripoli, Beirut, and Limassol; and the approaches to the Dardanelles north of Lesbos. Not surprisingly, it was precisely these areas which were the favourite hunting grounds of pirates and corsairs of all persuasions throughout the period.[69]

With the exception of the waters around Cape de Gata, and to a lesser extent of those around the Balearics and along the southern coast of Asia Minor, all of these focal sectors of the trunk routes were on the one hand within easy striking distance of the northern coasts of the sea and on the other hand at a considerable distance from its southern and eastern coasts. Christian corsairs and war fleets had no logistical difficulties operating in these sectors. Their Muslim counterparts, however, had very great ones. From Alexandria to the waters off Tripoli and Famagusta via the coast is a round trip of about 700 miles. To Rhodes and Crete it is about 600 miles as the crow flies; somewhere between 1000 and 1500 miles if coastal routes are taken. From Tunis to the Straits of Otranto and return is about 1100 miles; to the Ligurian Sea about 1500 miles. Algiers to the Gulf of the Lion and return is about 1000 miles. If the galleys could not be watered en route, the major part of their cruising range, that is the 1100 miles calculated in chapter 2, would be expended simply reaching their hunting grounds and returning home. Until the Turks seized naval bases on the Mediterranean shores of Asia Minor in the thirteenth century, the ability of Muslim powers to maintain a maritime presence along the trunk routes and to threaten Christian shipping seriously was very

---

[68] Vaughan, *Europe and the Turk*, p. 46 n. *. [69] See below, pp. 156–8.

limited unless they could secure possession of advance bases along those routes. Moreover, without them, Muslim maritime traffic attempting to use the trunk routes could not be protected from Christian war fleets and corsairs operating out of nearby bases along the northern coasts. Only when Muslim war fleets and corsairs could operate along the trunk routes in these focal sectors for long periods of time could they make the routes unsafe for their Christian counterparts and Christian maritime traffic and thereby enable Muslim shipping to use the routes with a degree of assurance. At other times the latter was compelled either to use the navigationally more dangerous, and therefore economically less efficient, southern coastal routes or else to take its chances with Christian corsairs along the trunk routes.

The importance of control of advanced supply bases close in to proposed areas of operation is evinced by the reverse situation to that which we have considered here: the difficulties faced by Christian fleets operating off the southern shores of the sea. From the eleventh to the fourteenth centuries Christian fleets operating off the Maghreb habitually staged at advanced bases such as Sicily, Pantelleria, Favignana, the Balearics, Malta, Cagliari in Sardinia, and other islands whenever they could. When they could not, their operation was limited to cruising raids. The Genoese and Pisans in particular, lacking advanced staging bases, found it impossible to mount more than cruising raids in the twelfth and thirteenth centuries. The Normans of Sicily, on the other hand, were able to sustain a naval presence along the coasts of the Maghreb from their bases on the south coast of Sicily and at Malta, Pantelleria, and Djerba. An Aragonese presence could only be maintained after the acquisition of the Balearics (1230), Sicily (1282), and Djerba (1284). The loss of Sicily (1295–1409) and the Balearics (1276–1343) by the Aragonese crown presented great difficulties to Catalan shipping. The Aragonese conquest of Sardinia (1323–4) is to be explained at least partially by their need to compensate for the loss of Sicily and the Balearics.[70] In the eastern Mediterranean, Byzantine attacks on the coasts of Egypt, Syria, and Palestine were invariably staged from Cyprus.[71]

[70] Yarrison, *Force as an instrument of policy*, pp. 30, 32–3, 53, 56, 59, 60–2, 95–9, 99 and maps 3C and 3D, 101–2, 105–6 and table 3, 158–9, 210.
[71] R. J. H. Jenkins, 'Cyprus between Byzantium and Islam, A.D. 688–965', in G. E. Mylonas & D. Raymond, eds., *Studies presented to David Moore Robinson*

Control of the islands and mainland bases which dominated the trunk routes, and in particular the crucial sectors of them to which notice has been drawn, became the major focus of attention in the wider struggle for maritime supremacy. Islam posed its most serious threat to Christian maritime traffic precisely in that period from the late eighth century to the early eleventh when it held the chain of islands from Cyprus in the east to the Balearics in the west and when it secured a toehold on the mainlands of southern France and Italy. Throughout the entire Middle Ages and into the sixteenth century naval expeditions were usually launched either to gain control of, or to defend possession of, these islands and mainland bases. Engagements between naval forces usually occurred either when fleets moved forward to establish or defend advance bases and encountered enemy defence forces, or else when fleets attempted to recover possession of advance bases or to sweep enemy corsairs from the sea lanes and encountered enemy fleets defending them.

The nexus between geography and technology, which had been instrumental in establishing the predominance of the trunk routes in the Mediterranean, influenced profoundly the course of maritime struggles. The foci of those struggles and the patterns into which their conduct fell had their origins in the peculiar characteristics of seafaring as they had developed as a product of man's attempts to achieve his objectives as best he could in the face of the obstacles of nature with the limited technology at his disposal.

(Saint Louis, 1953), vol. II, 1006–14, here pp. 1012–13; C. P. Kyrris, 'The nature of the Arab–Byzantine relations in Cyprus from the middle of the 7th to the middle of the 10th century A.D.', *Graeco-Arabica*, 3 (1984), 149–75, here p. 171.

4. The ninth and tenth centuries: Islam, Byzantium, and the West

When he was still as yet only governor of Syria, the first of the Umayyad caliphs, Mu'āwiyyah, launched the initial Muslim challenge to Byzantine maritime domination of the Mediterranean with a raid on Cyprus in AD 649, just seventeen years after the death of Muhammad.[1] Soon afterwards, in 655, the Muslims won their first great naval victory over the Byzantines off Phoenix, near Chelidonia in Lycia.[2] From then on Islam was to challenge Christendom at sea in the Mediterranean for a thousand years. In the early Middle Ages, *pace* the great naval assaults on Constantinople itself in 673–9 and 717–18, the most serious threat from Islam developed in the ninth and tenth centuries. During that period Muslims were able in some cases to capture and hold, and in other cases to compromise seriously Christian authority over, all of the islands and some of the important mainland regions and bases along the trunk routes of the sea. Cyprus saw a shared condominium of power between the Abbasid Caliphate and Byzantium (figure 26).[3] Muslim fleets, *ghazi* squadrons, and corsair ships operated from Umayyad Spain, Aghlabid Tunisia, the Balearics, Sicily, Bari, Taranto, Monte Garigliano, Fraxinetum, Crete, Tarsus and Tripoli in Syria, and to some degree from Corsica, Sardinia, Rhodes, and Cyprus. Their operations took the form of corsair cruises by single ships or small flotillas, raids on coasts and islands for booty and slaves by *ghazi* squadrons pursuing the *ghazw* of *jihād*, and full-scale invasions by large fleets. Such operations posed extremely serious threats to Frankish, Italian, and Byzantine shipping in the Gulf of the Lion and the Tyrrhenian, Ionian, Adriatic, and Aegean seas. Moreover, they were able to detract greatly from the quality of Christian society and government in southern France, southern Italy, and the Aegean coasts and islands. In the West the

---

[1] Stratos, 'Naval engagement at Phoenix', p. 231.   [2] Ibid., *passim*.
[3] Christides, *Conquest of Crete*, pp. 168–72; Jenkins, 'Cyprus between Byzantium and Islam', *passim*; Kyrris, 'Arab–Byzantine relations in Cyprus', *passim*.

dimensions of this threat were reflected strongly in the preoccupation with the Muslim of the various *Chanson de geste* cycles. It was of this period that Ibn Khaldūn wrote later, with great exaggeration, that: 'the Muslims gained control over the whole Mediterranean. Their power and domination over it was vast. The Christian nations could do nothing against the Muslim fleets, anywhere in the Mediterranean. All the time the Muslims rode its waves for conquest.'[4]

Commencing with raids from the Balearics and Umayyad Spain, Muslim corsairs succeeded in establishing a virtual Muslim province in parts of southern France in the ninth and tenth centuries.[5] From their fortress base at Candia in Crete a band of 10 000 Spanish Muslims, originally exiled from Spain by the Umayyads after an abortive revolt in Cordova and later expelled from Egypt after a long sojourn in Alexandria, whence they sailed to Crete, exercised a tyranny over shipping in the southern Aegean between *c.* 824 and 961. Some of the nearby islands, such as Naxos, Paros, Cythera, and Aegina were occupied at various times and it is even possible that Athens may have been occupied for a while.[6] Significantly, the ninth-century *Rhodian Sea Law* discussed more than once the problems which might arise when a ship was captured by pirates.[7] From Syria *ghazi* fleets from Tarsus and Tripoli made numerous raids into the Aegean between 842 and 963, marshalling their fleets in Cyprus.[8]

[4] Ibn Khaldūn, *The Muqqadimah; an introduction to history*, trans. F. Rosenthal (Princeton, 1958), vol. 2, p. 41. See also H. Ahrweiler, 'Course et piraterie dans la Méditerranée orientale aux IVème-XVème siècles (empire byzantin)', in *Course et piraterie*, vol. 1, 7–29, here p. 15; F. Gabrielli, 'Greeks and Arabs in the central Mediterranean area', *D.O.P.*, 18 (1964), 57–65, here pp. 60–1: Gateau, 'Voyage d'Ibn Jubayr', pp. 290–1; Lev, 'The Fātimid navy', p. 221.

[5] P. Senac, *Musulmans et Sarrasins dans le sud de la Gaule du VIIIe au XIe siècle* (Paris, 1980). Cf. Colom, 'Navegaciones mediterraneas', pp. 19–23; Ch.-E. Dufourcq, *La vie quotidienne dans les ports méditerranéens au moyen-âge (Provence–Languedoc–Catalogne)* (Paris, 1975), pp. 23–5.

[6] H. Ahrweiler, 'Les ports byzantins (VIIe–IXe siècles)', in *La navigazione mediterranea nell'alto medioevo*, vol. 1, 259–83, here pp. 270, 274–7; E. W. Brooks, 'The Arab conquest of Crete', *English Historical Review*, 28 (1913), 431–43; Christides, 'Raids of the Moslems of Crete', pp. 79–82, 86–9, 91–9; Christides, *Conquest of Crete*, pp. 81–96, 126–8, 157–68; Gabrielli, 'Greeks and Arabs', *passim*; Lev, 'The Fātimid navy', p. 223; G. C. Miles, 'Byzantium and the Arabs: relations in Crete and the Aegean area', *D.O.P.*, 18 (1964), 1–32; K. M. Setton, 'On the raids of the Moslems in the Aegean in the ninth and tenth centuries and their alleged occupation of Athens', *American journal of archaeology*, 58 (1954), 311–19.

[7] W. Ashburner, ed. *ΝΟΜΟΣ ΡΟΔΙΩΝ ΝΑΥΤΙΚΟΣ: The Rhodian sea-law* (Oxford, 1909), pp. 83, 95.

[8] Christides, *Conquest of Crete*, pp. 39, 159–61; Jenkins, 'Cyprus between Byzantium and Islam', pp. 1012–13.

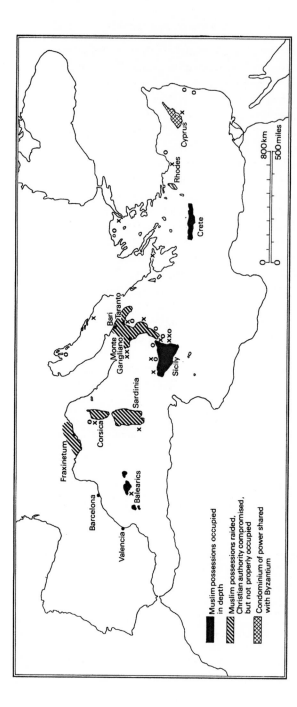

Muslim possessions

Balearics	902–1229	Malta	869–1091
Barcelona	711–802	Monte Garigliano	882/3–915
Bari	840–71	Rhodes	654–?
Corsica	c. 900–1015	Sardinia	c. 900–1015
Crete	c. 824–961	Sicily	827–c. 1070
Cyprus	649–965	Taranto	840–880
Fraxinetum	c. 888–975	Valencia	c. 711–1238

Major naval engagements   x – Christian victories   o – Muslim victories

Apulia	858 (o)	Crotone	840 (o)	Milazzo	880 (x), 888 (o)
Attalya	790 (o)	Cyprus	963 (x)	Naples	842 (x), 879 (x)
Beirut	975 (o)	Dubrovnik	867 (x)	Palermo	1063 (x)
Cape Stilo	880 (x)	Lemnos	923 (x)	Quarnero	841 (o)
Cefalu	859 (o)	Lycia	1035 (x)	Sardinia	1015 (x)
Corinth	879 (x)	Majorca	813 (x)	Syracuse	827 (x), 868 (x), 878 (o)
Corsica	806 (o), 807 (x)	Messina	965 (o), 1005–6 (x)	Taranto	867 (x)
				Thasos	829 (o)
				Tyre	998 (o)

Figure 26 Muslim possessions along the trunk routes and major naval engagements, *c.* AD 800–1000

From Aghlabid, and later Fatimid, Sicily, from the Maghreb, and from Spain, Muslim fleets and corsairs raided the Adriatic and Tyrrhenian repeatedly in the ninth century, occupying Monte Garigliano from 822–3 to 915, Bari from 840 to 871, Taranto from 840 to 880, raiding Rome in 846 and 876, and continuing to terrorize the Adriatic and Tyrrhenian coasts of Italy through into the eleventh century.[9] It is important to remember that the operations of the Muslim corsairs in this period amounted to more than just piracy. The corsairs were *ghazis*. Their *ghazw* was a form of *jihād*, perhaps the pre-eminent form, designed and intended to advance the frontiers of the Muslim world, the *dar al-Islam*, into the world of war, the *dar al-ḥarb*. Their operations were officially sanctioned and were as conscious and identifiable an attempt to acquire control over space, both land and sea, as the more familiar and recognizable invasions by armies and fleets.

The period marks the high point of the offensive at sea of various Muslim powers, such as the Abbasid Caliphate, the Umayyads of Cordova, the Aghlabids of Tunisia and Sicily, the Fatimids of North Africa and Sicily, and various corsair emirs of the Balearics, Crete, and other islands; for example, the notorious Mujahīd al-Muwaffak of Denia and the Balearics (1009–44)[10] In this period the areas of operations of Muslim fleets and corsairs were within easy striking distance from their advance bases on the various islands and on the northern mainland. The Gulf of the Lion was only 250 miles north of the Balearics. Fraxinetum dominated the Ligurian Sea. The Tyrrhenian was sandwiched between Sicily and Sardinia. A 250-mile cruise from Bari or Taranto covered the entire Balkan coast from

9 A. Ahmad, *A history of Islamic Sicily* (Edinburgh, 1975), pp. 17–21, 28–9, 33–6; Christides, *Conquest of Crete*, pp. 158–9; H. C. Krueger, 'The Italian cities and the Arabs before 1095', in M. W. Baldwin, ed., *The first hundred years* (vol. 1 of K. M. Setton, ed., *A history of the Crusades*) (Philadelphia, 1955), pp. 40–53; Lev, 'The Fātimid navy', pp. 231–2; G. Musca, *L'emirato di Bari 847–871* (Bari, 1978): U. Rizzitano, 'Gli Arabi in Italia', in *L'Occidente e l'Islam nell'alto medioevo* (Settimane di studio del Centro italiano di studi sull'alto medioevo, XII) (Spoleto, 1965), 93–114; M. Talbi, *L'émirat Aghlabide 184–296/800–909: histoire politique* (Paris, 1966), pp. 389–536; Yarrison, *Force as an instrument of policy*, pp. 39–40, 229–30.
10 On the character of the corsair establishments see Lewis, *Naval power*, pp. 153–5. On Muslim naval activity see W. B. Kubiak, 'The Byzantine attack on Damietta in 853 and the Egyptian navy in the 9th century', *Byzantion*, 40 (1970), 45–66; Lev, 'The Fātimid navy', pp. 223–44; G. Levi della Vida, 'A papyrus reference to the Damietta raid of 853 A.D.', *Byzantion*, 17 (1944–5), 212–21.

Zara on the Quarnero in the north to Zante in the south. From Candia 250 miles would bring a ship to Negropont, Chios or Rhodes. From Muslim ports in northern Syria or from neutral Cyprus the entire southern coastline of Byzantine Asia Minor was easily accessible. When Ibn Khaldūn referred to Muslim control of the seas in this period, what he really meant, whether he realized it or not, was that Muslim territorial gains along the trunk routes had given Muslim shipping a freedom to move virtually wherever it liked in the Mediterranean and had denied that same freedom to Christian shipping. Although no one should suppose that the likes of Mujahīd al-Muwaffak were above preying on the ships of their co-religionists, since in the eleventh century Muslim pirates from the Libyan coast were the scourge of Egyptian maritime traffic to the Maghreb,[11] and although neither should it be supposed that Christian corsairs had been cleared from the seas or that Christian maritime traffic had ceased, since very clearly it had not,[12] nevertheless, a relative security for Muslim shipping was created by their territorial acquisitions and by the activities of their war fleets and corsairs. Muslim sea power, in the loosest sense of that phrase, contributed greatly in this period towards making it a prosperous one for the commercial economies of various Muslim states and towards promoting Muslim maritime traffic throughout the Mediterranean.[13]

In the long series of Muslim naval engagements in this period with fleets of the Carolingians, the Italian seaports, and the Byzantine empire, a clear pattern emerges. Without exception, all major engagements were fought somewhere along the trunk routes (figure 26). In terms of overall strategy, the struggle was waged for control of

[11] Goitein, *Mediterranean society*, pp. 327–8. Cf. C. Pellat, 'Ḳurṣān: I. The Western Mediterranean and the Atlantic', in *The encyclopaedia of Islam*, new edn, vol. 5, ed. C. E. Bosworth et al. (Leiden, 1980–3), pp. 503–5.

[12] See, for example, Cahen, 'Commercial relations', *passim*; A. Grabois, 'Navigation méditerranéenne au VIIIème siècle selon quelques sources hagiographiques', in *L'histoire à Nice: Actes du Colloque international de 1980* (Nice, 1983), 7–13; Talbi, *L'émirat Aghlabide*, pp. 530–6; Yarrison, *Force as an instrument of policy*, p. 39.

[13] Christides, *Conquest of Crete*, pp. 38, 48–9, 116–21; Lewis, *Naval power*, pp. 163–70. See also Ahrweiler, 'Course et piraterie', p. 15; Cahen, 'Commercial relations', p. 6; Gabrielli 'Greeks and Arabs', pp. 59–62; Lev, 'The Fāṭimid navy', pp. 223–4; A. R. Lewis, 'Mediterranean maritime commerce: A.D. 300–1100, shipping and trade', in *La navigazione mediterranea nell'alto medioevo*, vol. 2, 480–501, here pp. 497–8; Miles, 'Byzantium and the Arabs', pp. 14–20. On the prosperity of Mediterranean Islam in general in this period see M. Lombard, *The golden age of Islam* (Amsterdam, 1975), pp. 135–44, 148, 164–5, 175–6, 180–1, 194–6, 209–11, 225–8, 231–3.

the islands and mainland bases which dominated those trunk routes. Many modern historians have, of course, pointed to the crucial significance of the acquisition of the islands by Islam in the ninth and tenth centuries and of their loss in the tenth to the thirteenth.[14] But even at the time their crucial significance was appreciated. Al-Muqqadasi was fully aware of the covering effects provided by possession of the islands when he wrote that:

And in this sea there are three flourishing and well populated islands. One is Sicily ... then there is Crete ... and then Cyprus ... And this sea has two channels, which are well known, and on its coast are many towns and important fortresses and excellent *ribats*. A part of it is on the frontier of Rum towards the frontier of Spain. The people who are in control of this sea are the Rum and they very much impose their fear on the sea. The population of Sicily and Spain are the people most experienced in the sea and its frontiers and channels because they travel on it a great deal and make expeditions against their neighbours. And in this sea are their routes to Syria and Egypt.[15]

Al-Muqqadasi was writing at the end of the tenth century, at a time when Crete and Cyprus had already been lost to the Byzantines. The Balearics were still in Muslim hands, as was Sicily. The strategic situation along the trunk routes was in a state of flux with the Byzantines in the ascendant in the east and the Muslims not yet under serious threat from the Italians, Normans, and Spanish Christians in the west. Spanish and Sicilian Muslim shipping could still follow the trunk routes to Syria and Egypt because the Balearics, Sardinia, and Sicily were still in Muslim hands. It is doubtful whether the newly re-established Byzantine presence in Crete and Cyprus was capable of excluding Muslim shipping from the routes south of those islands, although it probably could from those north of them. When Sardinia

---

[14] Cahen, 'Commercial relations', p. 6; Christides, 'Raids of the Moslems of Crete', p. 76; Gateau, 'Voyage d'Ibn Jubayr', p. 291; Jenkins, 'Cyprus between Byzantium and Islam', p. 1011–13; S. (Y.) Labib, 'The era of Suleyman the Magnificent: crisis of orientation', *International journal of Middle East studies*, 10 (1979), 435–51, here p. 447; Lewis, 'Mediterranean maritime commerce', pp. 494, 499; C. Vanacker, 'Géographie économique de l'Afrique du Nord selon les auteurs arabes, du IXe siècle au milieu du XIIe siècle', *Annales: E.S.C.*, 28 (1973), 659–80, here pp. 659, 662; Yarrison, *Force as an instrument of policy, passim,* esp. pp. 53–6; E. Zechlin, *Maritime Weltgeschichte; Altertum und Mittelalter* (Hamburg, 1947), p. 219.
[15] Al-Muqqadasi, *Descriptio imperii Moslemici,* ed. M. J. de Goeje, 2nd edn (Leiden, 1906), p. 15. I am indebted to E. Ashtor for the translation.

was lost to the Pisans in the first half of the eleventh century and Sicily to the Normans in the second half, the situation was changed totally and Muslim shipping from then on would be confined largely to the southern coastal routes.

From the end of the tenth century the Muslim powers gradually began to lose their hold along the trunk routes to a resurgent Christendom. Bari and Taranto were recovered by the Byzantines as early as 880. Crete fell to them in 961 and Cyprus in 965. The corsairs' nest at Fraxinetum was exterminated by Provençal knights in 975. Mujahīd al-Muwaffak's control of Corsica and Sardinia was broken by the Pisans and Genoese from 1015 onwards. When the main strengths of Muslim power in Sicily were eroded by the Normans after about 1070 and Malta was taken by them in 1091, all that was left of the once impressive chain of Muslim possessions along the trunk routes were the Balearics and the Andalusian ports in the west. These were to resist successfully until they finally crumbled to the Aragonese *reconquista* in the 1230s. The reconquest of Valencia and the Balearics finally gave the Christian maritime powers all the advantages as far as the logistics of maritime competition and warfare in the western Mediterranean were concerned.[16]

Why were the Christian powers so successful in recovering these Muslim possessions in the north of the sea? Traditional historical explanations have recourse to cultural factors such as the 'dynamism' of Byzantium in the second half of the tenth century and of the Christian West in the eleventh and twelfth centuries as well as to the progressive loss of fighting spirit and economic aggression of Muslim societies such as the *taifa* emirates of Spain and the Aghlabid, and later Kalbite, emirate of Sicily in the eleventh century. In Lewis's view, Ibn Hauqal's disparaging comments about the corsairs of early Muslim Palermo reflect a softening in his own time (*c.* 972–3) of the nature of Muslim societies established and grown prosperous along the trunk routes.[17] Such factors may not be discounted, since it is quite clear that societies do evolve in the ways to which such explanations have recourse. In particular the continuing influence of Christian maritime traffic to Muslim Sicily and other such societies

[16] Colom, 'Navegaciones mediterraneas', *passim*, esp. p. 61; Dufourcq, *Vie quotidienne dans les ports*, p. 24.
[17] Ibn Hauqal, *Configuration de la terre (Kitab surat al-ard)*, trans. J. H. Kramer & G. Wiet (Paris, 1964), vol. I, p. 120. See also Lewis, *Naval power*, pp. 154–5, 204; Talbi, *L'émirat Aghlabide*, pp. 490, 529–36.

very probably contributed much towards persuading them that their best interests lay elsewhere than in war, the *razzia* of *jihād*, and piracy and privateering.[18] We shall see the same phenomenon occur later, in the *ghazi* emirates. Nevertheless there may also have been other factors which were equally important. Although possession of the islands and mainland bases provided havens for Muslim fleets and corsairs harrying the waters of the trunk routes and provided a measure of security for Muslim shipping plying those routes, it could never provide anything like complete protection or blanket coverage. Operating from their own island and mainland bases in the Aegean, Adriatic, and Tyrrhenian Seas, Christian fleets and corsairs were always within easy striking distance of the trunk routes and of the Muslim colonies planted along them. Ibn Hauqal complained about the ease with which the Byzantines could attack even the coasts of Syria and Egypt as early as AD 972.[19] Muslim acquisition of possessions along the trunk routes had moved the maritime frontiers of Islam beyond easily defensible geographical limits.

The logistical situation of the Muslim possessions along the trunk routes in the ninth and tenth centuries was in startling contrast to that of the Christian Crusader states in Syria and Palestine in the twelfth and thirteenth centuries. Whereas, as we shall see in the next chapter, the vital sea lanes to the latter were relatively immune to Muslim naval attack, those leading to the former from the Muslim southern mainland and connecting them together were constantly exposed to easy attack from the northern mainland whenever the various Christian societies found the resources and will to challenge for control of them. In the passage cited above, al-Muqqadasi made this perfectly clear. Reinforcement of the islands from the Muslim south and east was much more difficult than attacking them from the north because of the much greater distances involved and because of prevailing weathern patterns. Muslim powers to the south might mean well and even offer diplomatic assistance to their coreligionists along the trunk routes, but translating that sympathy into real military support was a different matter, as the Cretan Muslims found out when they tried to enlist the aid of the Fatimid al-Mu'izz against

[18] Cf. Talbi, *L'émirat Aghlabide*, pp. 534–5.
[19] Ibn Hauqal, *Configuration de la terre*, vol. 1, p. 199. See also Kubiak, 'Byzantine attack on Damietta', *passim*; Lev, 'The Fātimid navy', pp. 224, 239; Lewis, *Naval power*, p. 203.

the Byzantines.[20] Even in the fifteenth and sixteenth centuries distant islands were extremely difficult to reinforce effectively against conquest attempts from their proximity. The Venetian losses of their islands and the Hospitaller loss of Rhodes to the Ottomans demonstrated this very clearly.[21]

To hold its possessions along the trunk routes Islam needed to settle and colonise them in depth. But settlement of large numbers of peasants, artisans, and merchants was severely restricted by the fact that the sea lanes on which they depended for their lifeblood could never be completely secured. With the exception of fertile Sicily, which could be reached quickly and easily from Tunisia and could be, and was, reinforced relatively easily and frequently,[22] and to a lesser degree of Crete and perhaps of the Balearics also, Muslim settlement along the trunk routes was largely confined to corsair freebooters and those who serviced them.[23] In the case of Crete it has been argued strongly that the Muslim settlement on the island was not a corsairs' nest.[24] However, even if that is correct, Muslim settlement in Crete was largely confined to the capital, Candia, and does not appear to have been very extensive. Even after almost 140 years of Muslim occupation, when Nicephorus Phocas attacked in 960–1 the Cretan fleet could not engage his, nor the Cretan army oppose him in open battle. The Cretan Muslims withdrew behind the walls of Candia as soon as the Byzantines landed, and the struggle was eventually won by starving them into surrender.[25] In the long term such societies could not sustain successful opposition to the pressure for Christian reoccupation. In the second half of the tenth century a resurgent Byzantium pushed Islam back off the trunk routes in the east by reoccupying Cyprus, Rhodes, and Crete. In the eleventh century the same result was produced in the west by the aggressive drive of the Italian cities and Norman adventurers.

---

20 F. Dachraoui, 'La Crète dans le conflit entre Byzance et al-Muʿizz', *Cahiers de Tunisie*, 7 (1959), 307–18; Lev, 'The Fāṭimid navy', p. 236. However, on other factors related to the Fatimid and Egyptian failure to support the Muslims of Crete see Christides, 'Raids of the Moslems of Crete', pp. 92, 102–6; *Conquest of Crete*, p. 116.   21 Cf. Guilmartin, *Gunpowder and galleys*, p. 103.
22 Ahmad, *Islamic Sicily*, pp. 12–53.
23 Colom, 'Navegaciones mediterraneas', pp. 19–23, esp. p. 19; Lewis, *Naval power*, pp. 104, 108, 140–54; Talbi, *L'émirat Aghlabide*, pp. 490, 519.
24 Christides, 'Raids of the Moslems of Crete', pp. 78, 99; Christides, *Conquest of Crete*, pp. 38, 121–2 *et passim*; Miles, 'Byzantium and the Arabs', pp. 14–17. See also, in the case of southern France, Senac, *Musulmans et Sarrasins*.
25 Christides, *Conquest of Crete*, pp. 172–91.

Christian reconquest of the Muslim possessions along the trunk routes in the tenth and eleventh centuries laid the foundations for later Western domination of those routes, with all that that implied. The reconquest thus appears as one of the most fundamentally important historical processes in Mediterranean history. There is more than an element of accuracy in the conception that prior to the Christian reconquest of the trunk routes the Mediterranean had been divided into two hostile zones, the *dar al-Islam* and the *dar al-ḥarb*, with the navigationally natural major sea lanes marking the maritime frontiers. Islam was astride that frontier, but only insecurely. Ibn Khaldūn's claim that the entire sea was incorporated into the *dar-al-Islam* was fundamentally false. The reconquest transformed the frontier back into the axis of navigation which it was by nature and permitted the seamen of Christendom, of Western Christendom as it happened, to unify the maritime economy of the Mediterranean world.[26] Henceforth, until the rise of the Ottoman Turks, the only waters of the Mediterranean which could properly be said to lie within the *dar al-Islam* were those within the horizon of the Muslim-held southern and eastern coasts. The consequences of this change were revolutionary. They had an immediate and direct bearing on the outcome of both the Crusades and the rise of Western maritime traffic in the immediately succeeding period. Had mastery of the trunk routes for Christendom not been secured in the tenth and eleventh centuries, the Crusader states in Palestine and Syria could not have survived in the twelfth, even if the overland First Crusade had succeeded in establishing them. Neither could the maritime republics of the West have carried their maritime traffic to the Muslim and Byzantine worlds as they did, thus securing a predominance in trans-Mediterranean traffic for themselves.

[26] H. Ahrweiler, 'Les liaisons maritimes et continentales dans le monde byzantin', in Ragosta, *Navigazioni mediterranee*, 247–63; here p. 247.

5. The twelfth and thirteenth centuries: the Crusader states

The most striking expression of the surge of military and economic aggression of the Christian West in the late eleventh and early twelfth centuries was the establishment by the armies of the First Crusade of the Kingdom of Jerusalem, the Principality of Antioch, and the two counties of Edessa and Tripoli. These Crusader states on the mainland of Syria and Palestine were not all to be finally exterminated until 1291, almost two hundred years later. Their survival during the twelfth and thirteenth centuries was very largely a product of the fact that their essential resources of manpower and financial revenues could be replenished constantly through their maritime connections to the Christian West. From very soon after the capture of Jerusalem in 1099 the majority of the pilgrim traffic, which brought both unarmed pilgrims to worship at the holy places and also armed pilgrims, Crusaders, to participate in military campaigns, came by sea. It is true that the major Crusading armies came overland for the First Crusade, the Crusade of 1101, and the Second Crusade, and that the German armies did so also for the Third Crusade. However, the constant trickle of Crusaders arriving in small groups or as individuals to spend a time campaigning against the infidel almost invariably came by sea. Pilgrims of both kinds provided forces for war, settlers to secure the land, and liquid capital to establish a Frankish social and economic infrastructure. Their continual influx was absolutely essential for the continued survival of the Crusader states. So also was the maritime commerce between the ports of those states and the Christian West. This commerce provided perhaps the major source of fiscal revenues to the various lords of the Crusader states.[1] As such,

---

[1] C. Cahen, 'Orient latin et commerce du Levant', *Bulletin de la Faculté des lettres de Strasbourg*, 29 (1951), 328–46; J. Prawer, 'The Italians in the Latin Kingdom', in his *Crusader institutions* (Oxford, 1980), 217–49; J. Riley-Smith, 'Government in Latin Syria and the commercial privileges of foreign merchants', in D. Baker, ed., *Relations between East and West in the Middle Ages* (Edinburgh, 1973), 109–32.

the security of the sea lanes back to the West and to the Byzantine empire was of vital importance to the Crusader states in their struggle to maintain and expand their position. Now, seemingly, these extended sea lanes over 1000 miles in length were extremely vulnerable to Muslim naval attack. Yet there is comparatively little record of attempts made against them throughout the twelfth and thirteenth centuries. The history of the maritime security of the Crusader states in these two centuries in fact provides a classic illustration of the ways in which geographical factors and contemporary naval technology formed a nexus which favoured one of the two belligerents in the struggle at sea. It contributed very greatly to the security of the maritime supply lines to the Crusader states and constantly frustrated Muslim attempts to threaten Christian shipping on the sea lanes.

In 1099, when the armies of the First Crusade successfully stormed Jerusalem, the only Muslim power capable of disputing the waters of the Levant with ships from the Christian West or Byzantium was Fatimid Egypt. During the actual course of the Crusade in Syria and Palestine (1097–9), and in the years immediately succeeding, control of Levantine waters south of Cyprus lay with the Fatimids and in the north, between Cyprus and the mainland, with the Byzantines, except for those occasions on which a Crusading fleet from the West made an appearance.[2] In the northern Aegean two Turkish emirs had broken through temporarily to the coast in the 1090s to challenge the Byzantine navy, but had been defeated. Abu'l-Qasim, appointed governor of Nicaea by Suleiman ibn Qutalmish, attempted to make himself independent between 1086 and 1092. He tried to build a fleet at Kios at the head of the Gemlik Gulf on the Sea of Marmara, but before it could be launched it was destroyed by the Byzantine admiral Manuel Boutoumites.[3] Tzachas, the emir of Smyrna, mounted a much more formidable threat to Byzantine mastery of the Aegean. He won one battle at sea against Niketas Castamonites off Chios, but was eventually destroyed in 1092 by Constantine Dalassenus between Mitilini and Smyrna.[4] The successful campaigns of Alexius I Comnenus in Asia Minor in the wake of the Crusaders' passage hemmed the Seljuq sultanate of Iconium in the hinterland of

---

[2] Cf. J. Richard, 'La Méditerranée et ses relations avec son arrière-pays oriental (XIᶜ–XVᶜ siècles)', in Ragosta, *Navigazioni mediterranee*, 265–99; here p. 271.
[3] Anna Comnena, *Alexiad*, pp. 202–3.   [4] Ibid., pp. 233–6, 269–72.

Anatolia. It remained barred from the sea by the Byzantines and the Armenians of Cilicia until the thirteenth century.

At the time of the First Crusade the Fatimid navy numbered about 70 warships. Its headquarters were at Alexandria, but it also had other bases in Egypt at Damietta and Tinnis and in Palestine at Ascalon, Acre, and Tyre.[5] During the siege of Jerusalem units of the fleet operated from Ascalon, blockading the small Genoese squadron in Jaffa and forcing the dismantling of the Genoese ships. After the fall of Jerusalem the Egyptian fleet withdrew to Egypt.[6] During the next 25 years units of this fleet continued to contest the waters off the coasts of Syria and Palestine with various fleets from the West which arrived to participate in Crusading campaigns. Because the seaports such as Ascalon, Arsuf, Acre, Tyre, Sidon, Beirut, and Tripoli initially remained in Fatimid hands, Egyptian squadrons were able to use them as advance bases and to move easily from one port to another as the need arose. Because its fleet had the logistical resources which galleys needed, the Fatimid government was able to move squadrons around very effectively. It had units stationed in the various seaports all of the time whereas the Crusaders depended for their naval strength on transient fleets from the West which usually arrived unexpectedly to participate in a single season's campaigning and then returned home. Ships from Beirut and Tripoli acting in conjunction with land forces under the Seljuq Duqaq of Damascus ambushed and almost defeated Count Baldwin of Edessa at the Dog river in 1100 when he was marching south to assume the crown of Jerusalem.[7] A series of Egyptian land expeditions against the Kingdom of Jerusalem from 1099 through to 1105 were supplied by, and coordinated with, accompanying fleet movements. Squadrons either sent up from Egypt or moved from one of the Fatimid ports to another prevented the capture of some of them when they were besieged by the Crusaders at various times; Arsuf in 1100, Acre in 1103, and both Sidon and Tripoli in 1108.[8] Moreover, Muslim corsairs operating out of the Fatimid

[5] Ehrenkreutz, 'Place of Saladin', p. 102; Lev, 'The Fātimid navy', pp. 243–4.
[6] S. M. Foster, *Some aspects of maritime activity and the use of sea power in relation to the Crusading states, 1096–1169*, D. Phil. thesis, Oxford University, 1978, p. 5; Runciman, *Crusades*, vol. 1, p. 282.
[7] Fulcher of Chartres, *A history of the expedition to Jerusalem, 1095–1127*, trans. F. R. Ryan (New York, 1973), II.2–3 (pp. 138–41).
[8] M. Mollat, 'Problèmes navals de l'histoire des croisades', *Cahiers de civilization médiévale*, 10 (1967), 345–59, here p. 347; Runciman, *Crusades*, vol. 1, pp. 295–7, 309 and vol. 2, pp. 64, 78, 80, 87, 89.

ports were able to harass Christian pilgrim and commercial shipping moving along the coast to and from Jaffa.[9]

In the gradual process of reduction of the Fatimid seaports, the assistance of fleets of Crusaders from the Italian cities of Pisa, Genoa, and Venice, and of other Western Crusader fleets such as that of Sigurd I of Norway, was absolutely essential. Without the Christian fleets to cut off their maritime supply lines, the seaports could be reinforced with manpower and resupplied with provisions from the sea. At first the struggle at sea between the Fatimids and the various Western maritime powers was fairly evenly poised. The Egyptians won a major encounter with a composite Italian fleet off Sidon in 1108 but were twice defeated two years later, by the Genoese and Pisans off Beirut and by the Venetians off Sidon.[10] In spite of a determined and sustained resistance by the Fatimids, the Crusaders gradually took the seaports one after another and by 1110 all of them had been lost except for Ascalon in the far south and Tyre. With their string of advance bases lost, the Fatimid squadrons increasingly suffered from a lack of manoeuvrability and lost the initiative. The Muslim corsairs also disappeared.

In 1123, when the Crusaders were tightening the ring around Tyre, a Venetian Crusader fleet dealt the Fatimid fleet a final blow by virtually destroying its last major squadron in a pitched battle off Ascalon.[11] In the following year the only response that the Caliph in Cairo could make to desperate appeals for assistance from the besieged city of Tyre was that he could no longer do anything. Deprived of its maritime support, Tyre capitulated to a combined assault by the forces of the Kingdom of Jerusalem and the Venetians.[12] Just what the loss of this last effective advance base on the Syro-Palestinian coast meant was vividly demonstrated two years later. The Fatimids built a new fleet of about 20 galleys and sent it north on a cruise to harass the shipping lanes and plunder the coasts of the Crusader states. Fulcher of Chartres reported that:

> They explored and stealthily examined the coast as far as the city of Beirut, hunting and searching from port to port to see if they could

---

[9] Fulcher of Chartres, *History*, II.6.5 (p. 149), II.44.5 (p. 200); Runciman, *Crusades*, vol. 2, p. 87; Saewulf, *An account of the pilgrimage of Saewulf to Jerusalem and the Holy Land in the years 1102 and 1103 from our Lord's incarnation*, trans. the bishop of Clifton, in *P.P.T.S.L.*, vol. 4 (London, 1896), 1–55, here p. 28.

[10] Runciman, *Crusades*, vol. 2, pp. 91–2.

[11] Fulcher of Chartres, *History*, III.20 (pp. 243–5); Runciman, *Crusades*, vol. 2, p. 167.

[12] Runciman, *Crusades*, vol. 2, pp. 167–70.

find any advantage for themselves which would be a disadvantage for the Christians. But since they were then suffering greatly from lack of fresh water they were obliged to make a landing in order to fill their buckets from the streams and springs and thus assuage their thirst. However, the citizens of the aforementioned city took this ill and boldly came out against them at once . . . Our knights with their lances and our bowmen with their arrows drove them into the sea and in this way unexpectedly routed them. They promptly hoisted sail and directed their course toward Tripoli, then Cyprus.[13]

It is clear what happened. The fleet had been deprived of watering facilities beyond Ascalon and was probably too large to use those there. Fulcher of Chartres numbered the fleet at 75 ships, although a figure of about 20 is probably nearer the truth.[14] Ascalon did not have a harbour at all. William of Tyre referred to the 'harbourless shores of Ascalon'.[15] Moreover, the town had no river or stream, and was dependent upon wells for its water supply. In all probability the size of the fleet had precluded watering at Ascalon. The Egyptian commander attempted to operate beyond his safe radius of action, trusting in his numbers to enable him to water the fleet by force of arms. He failed.[16] Significantly, it was around Beirut that he ran out of water. Did his supplies actually run dry, or was it rather that he no longer had sufficient water for the return voyage? As we shall see, the area around Beirut marked just about the limit of the radius of action of galleys operating from bases in Egypt. When Ascalon fell to Baldwin III of Jerusalem in 1153, to the accompaniment of much wailing throughout the Muslim world, the Egyptian fleet had no watering facilities beyond Tinnis and al-Faramā on Lake Manzalah in the Nile delta. But even these bases do not seem to have been much used, and throughout the twelfth and thirteenth centuries the Egyptian fleets continued to operate from their traditional home bases at Alexandria and Damietta. In the twelfth century, before its conquest by Richard Coeur de Lion, Byzantine authority in Cyprus was weak, and no doubt single corsair galleys or small squadrons might hope to water at deserted or isolated coves and streams on Cyprus. This was probably

---

[13] Fulcher of Chartres, *History*, III.56 (p. 296). Cf. William of Tyre, *A history of deeds done beyond the sea*, trans. E. A. Babcock & A. C. Krey (New York, 1941), XIII.20 (vol. 2, p. 32).   [14] Fulcher of Chartres, *History*, III.56 (p. 296).
[15] William of Tyre, *History*, XII.25 (vol. 1, p. 553).
[16] Cf. Foster, *Aspects of maritime activity*, pp. 15, 210.

what the Egyptian commander hoped to do in 1126 when he set sail for Cyprus after the disaster at Beirut. But if such a recourse might suffice for a few ships, it would not for major fleets and squadrons except in a dire emergency. They were normally limited to the radius of action which water supplies taken on board in Egypt would allow.

Leaving the West at the opening of the sailing season in late March or early April, or alternatively in late July or early August in order to reach the Holy Land and return home before winter, and following the trunk routes, merchant shipping from the Christian West would agglomerate off the approaches to the Holy Land in late April or early May and again in late September or early October. These were the two passages, *transiti*, to which William of Tyre referred.[17] The remarkable bunching of sailings from the West for the Holy Land in early spring in particular was caused as much by navigational concerns as by economic concerns to reach markets and supplies before the competition. The ships arrived in large numbers over short periods of time. Saewulf counted 30 large ships in Jaffa harbour in mid October 1102.[18] Around 1172 Theoderich counted 80 ships in port at Acre at Easter.[19] Because the arrival and departure of the ships were so bunched together chronologically, and because mostly the vessels would have come in to make landfall around Tripoli or Beirut, they ought to have been particularly susceptible to interception by Muslim raiders. Muslim corsairs or Fatimid raiding squadrons operating in the waters between Cyprus, Beirut, and Tripoli should have had easy pickings. However, this was not the case, and there are several reasons which explain why.

Egyptian galleys operating out of Alexandria, making a watering stop at Damietta if desired, could choose from two routes to the main hunting grounds between Cyprus and the coast (figure 27). They could take a direct route across the open sea on a north-east heading. Such a choice of route, however, exposed them to the dangers of being swamped if caught far from land in bad weather. It also meant that they could expect to have the *meltemi* blowing consistently into their bows from about 45–60° on the port bow if it backed to the north. This was too adverse a direction for them to maintain a course without time-consuming tacking. If it swung to the west, of course, they would

[17] See above, 3–4.   [18] Saewulf, *Pilgrimage*, pp. 7–8.
[19] Theoderich, *Description of the holy places*, trans. A. Stewart, in *P.P.T.S.L.*, vol. 5 (London, 1896), 1–86; here pp. 59–60.

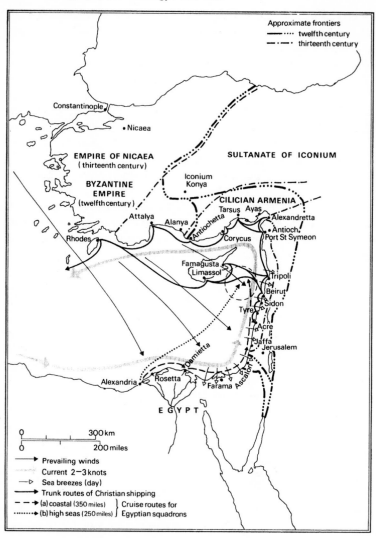

Figure 27 The maritime security of the Crusader states

be all right. A coastal route, on the other hand, would give them the consistent assistance of the two- to three-knot current and of the reliable daily cycle of land and sea breezes. This was, in fact, by far the better choice of route. The Egyptian navy had always used coastal routes in the Fatimid period.[20] If the *meltemi* was steady from the north-west, the galleys ought to be able to use their sails, reaching with the wind on the port beam, until they reached Ascalon. After that they would have to rely on the land and sea breezes or use their oars for the final 200 or so miles. A cruise of approximately 350 miles was necessary merely to reach the hunting grounds. If they returned by the same route, the round trip was about 700 miles. If they took the more dangerous direct route home, then it was about 600 miles. At an average continuous speed of two knots, approximately eleven to thirteen days would be spent merely getting to the strike zone and returning home, of which seven or eight would probably be spent on the outward voyage and four or five on the return voyage because of the pattern of the prevailing winds. A squadron could spend no more than seven to nine days on station before being forced to return for water. Even that assumes that a commander would be prepared to take the risk of calculating the duration of the return voyage sufficiently finely to reach home just as the last of the water was consumed. How many commanders would be prepared to take that risk? How many crews would accept it even if the commander wished to? Egyptian crews in this period were not slaves but free men, even if their social status was poor.[21] Surely there would always be some allowance made for emergencies; perhaps two or three days' supply. This means that the actual time which could be spent in the strike zone was probably less than a week. If Egyptian galleys of this period were using amphorae to carry their water, as is most probable, and if the efficiency of amphorae as water containers was about 30% less than that of barrels, then the amount of time which could be spent on station would have been pared to almost nothing. The function of Egyptian raiders would have been reduced to merely cruising to the waters off Tripoli and then returning home immediately, hoping to pick up prizes en route rather than lying in wait for them where they could be most easily intercepted.

[20] Lev, 'The Fātimid navy', p. 251.
[21] Ayalon, 'Mamluks and naval power', pp. 2–7; Ehrenkreutz, 'Place of Saladin', pp. 105, 111; Fahmy, *Muslim naval organization*, pp. 98–106; Levi della Vida, 'Papyrus reference to the Damietta raid', p. 218.

Whatever the difficulties and variables involved in these calculations, and I accept that they are theoretical calculations only, their general thrust is to confirm the historical observation that the logistical ability of the Egypian fleet to threaten seriously the strategic security of the Crusader states by striking at their maritime supply lines was extremely limited.[22] Because of the agglomerated nature of the arrival and departure of Western shipping in and from the Holy Land, had Egyptian squadrons been able to stay on station in the waters between Cyprus and Tripoli for even a month or so, they would have been able to deal crippling blows to the economies and manpower of the Crusader states. But because of the logistical limitations of the war galley, they could not do so. Their function became limited to one of sending out small raiding flotillas which might hope to water at a deserted beach on Cyprus or which, failing that, would have to return home almost immediately. Raiding flotillas are precisely what we find mentioned in the sources.[23] Although they often proved to be a nuisance, they could not affect fundamentally the lifeblood of the Crusader states.

Other factors added their influence to that of the range of galleys to exacerbate the problems facing the Egyptians. Because the objectives of corsairs or raiding flotillas were to capture their prey rather than to sink it, they had to intercept well out to sea, where the sailing ships could not simply run for the protection of the Crusader coasts. South of Beirut shipping hugged the coast and, unless the wind was easterly, which is extremely uncommon during the day in summer, ships could easily be beached to escape capture. War galleys no longer had rams below water, and therefore could not hole ships below the water line and sink them easily. Their beaks could hole a ship above the water line, but any attempt to sink a ship in this way would be a long drawn-out process. The galleys of Richard Coeur de Lion had to go to remarkable lengths to sink the large Muslim ship sent by Saladin from Beirut to the relief of Acre in 1191. Richard's men could not board the ship from their galleys because of its high freeboard and missile firepower. The only way it could be stopped was to send a diver overboard to lash its steering oars in such a position as to cause it to sail around in circles. Then repeated ramming with the galleys' beaks was necessary to sink it, that is if the Latin sources are correct and it

[22] Ehrenkreutz, 'Place of Saladin', pp. 102, 108.
[23] See also Foster, *Aspects of maritime activity*, pp. 311–313.

was in fact sunk by enemy action. The Muslim sources say that the captain sank it himself when he saw that capture was inevitable.[24] Large sailing ships, riding high out of the water and of a tonnage perhaps up to ten times that of attacking galleys, could not easily be stopped if they were sailing before a steady and favourable wind. Indeed the inability of galleys to stop and capture large round ships under sail was a commonplace. Muslim galleys from Tyre and Sidon were unable to stop Saewulf's ship on his return from the Holy Land in 1103.[25] In 1264 the Genoese admiral Simone Grillo had to abandon his futile attempts to capture a large Venetian round ship, the *Roccafortis*, even though his squadron managed to capture all the other smaller Venetian ships in its convoy.[26] Fourteenth- and fifteenth-century Venetian pilgrim cogs habitually managed to repel Turkish corsairs, and the Genoese had similar experiences.[27] In the fifteenth century Venice ordered the construction of large sailing ships specifically to combat the threat of corsair galleys.[28] In 1453, during the siege of Constantinople, four large Christian sailing ships, three Genoese and one Byzantine, successfully held off a reported 150 Ottoman galleys in the Bosphorus and sank many of them.[29] The figure of 150 is not to be taken literally, but the sailing ships were certainly outnumbered by many times.

Galleys had to intercept well out to sea and then had difficulty stopping and boarding their prey, unless, of course, the sea was a flat calm. Moreover, it was extremely dangerous for Egyptian galleys to remain out at sea patrolling to intercept incoming ships because they had no friendly coast to run for should the weather turn bad. If it did, a whole squadron could be sunk. Furthermore, given the small size of galleys and their lack of height above water, they had a limited range

---

[24] Ehrenkreutz, 'Place of Saladin', p. 115. The sources are Abū Shāma, *Le livre des deux jardins: histoire des deux règnes, celui de Nour ed-Dīn et celui de Salāh ed-Dīn*, in *R.H.C.Or.*, vols. 4–5 (Paris, 1898, 1906), here vol. 5, pp. 11–12; Ambroise, *L'estoire*, p. 359; Behā ed-Dīn, *Anecdotes et beaux traits de la vie du sultan Youssof (Salāh ed-Dīn)*, in *R.H.C. Or.*, vol. 3 (Paris, 1884), pp. 220–1; 'Imad ad-Dīn, *Al-Fath al-Qussī fī'l-Fath al-Qudsī*, ed. C. Landberg (Leiden, 1888), p. 337.

[25] Saewulf, *Pilgrimage*, pp. 27–8.   [26] Lane, *Venetian ships*, pp. 4–5.

[27] Heers, *Gênes*, pp. 278–9, 451; Hyde, 'Navigation', p. 530.

[28] Hocquet, *Le sel: Voiliers*, pp. 547–50.

[29] Makarios Melissenos, *The chronicle of the siege of Constantinople, April 2 to May 29, 1453*, in George Sphrantzes, *The fall of the Byzantine empire: a chronicle by George Sphrantzes, 1401–1477*, trans. M. Philippides (Amherst, 1980), pp. 106–8; A. Pertusi, *Testi inediti e poco noti sulla caduta di Constantinopoli*, ed. A. Carile (Bologna, 1983), p. 69.

of visibility. Consequently they had difficulty setting up any sort of effective 'blockade' at all.[30] After all, even the small quadrilateral of sea between Cyprus, Tripoli, and Beirut was still about 4000 square miles. In the reverse situation in the fourteenth century, Marino Sanudo Torsello admitted the inability of his proposed Crusader squadron to cover the wide reaches of the sea and to prevent completely Muslim and Christian shipping reaching Egypt.[31] With luck Egyptian raiding squadrons might intercept one or two isolated incoming ships, but that would be just a pin prick to the logistical security of the Crusader states, not a body blow. Outgoing ships could simply stay in port and wait for the Egyptians to go home.

The inability of Egyptian squadrons to operate effectively in the maritime approaches to the Holy Land helps greatly to explain a number of apparently puzzling historical phenomena: the paucity of reports of raids on shipping until the era of Saladin, the dearth of major fleet actions between the Egyptian navy and the various fleets which appeared in Levantine waters from time to time, and the failure of the lords of the Crusader states to acquire their own ships to protect their coasts and sea lanes.

It was not that they lacked the resources to do so. Baldwin III of Jerusalem compiled a fleet of 20 ships for the assault on Ascalon in 1153.[32] Reynald of Chatillon and Thoros of Armenia raided Cyprus in 1156 with a fleet which they had put together.[33] Raymond III of Tripoli fitted out twelve galleys in 1160 to convey his sister Melissande to Constantinople and, when the negotiations for her marriage to Manuel I collapsed, he used them to raid Cyprus.[34] Amalric I employed ships on the Nile to cut off support to Alexandria from upper Egypt during his campaign of 1167.[35] In 1182 Acre and Tyre supplied a fleet of 33 galleys with which Baldwin IV of Jerusalem broke a naval blockade of Beirut by galleys of Saladin's Egyptian fleet.[36] The Templars and Hospitallers and some of the great vassals of the Crusader states certainly owned and operated ships at various times during the twelfth century. Reynald of Chatillon, Prince of Oultrejourdain, built a small fleet in 1183 which he transported

---

[30] See the comments of Lane on the ineffectiveness of 'blockading' in the Middle Ages in his *Venice*, pp. 67–8.   [31] Marino Sanudo, *Liber secretorum*, I.4.2 (p. 28).
[32] Foster, *Aspects of maritime activity*, p. 333; Runciman, *Crusades*, vol. 2, pp. 338–9.
[33] Runciman, *Crusades*, vol. 2, pp. 347–8.
[34] Ibid., vol. 2, p. 360.   [35] Ibid., vol. 2, p. 375.
[36] Ehrenkreutz, 'Place of Saladin', p. 109; Runciman, *Crusades*, vol. 2, pp. 432–3.

overland and launched in the Gulf of Aqaba to raid the Red Sea.[37] Usāmah ibn Munqidh recorded that some corsairs operated out of Crusader ports against Muslim shipping. Probably they were resident Italians.[38] In fact the lords of the Crusader states were quite wealthy enough to have acquired and maintained ships had they perceived a need to do so. Even in the thirteenth century the revenues of the single city of Acre were about the same as those of the Kingdom of England.[39] The argument that the Crusader states, like the Muslim world, were starved of shipbuilding materials, particularly timber, and could not build their own ships is meaningless.[40] The ships could simply have been bought from the West if necessary. In any case, the Crusader states had access to the Lebanon in the County of Tripoli, which still had plentiful timber supplies in the twelfth century, and to the forests of the Taurus mountains through their Armenian and Byzantine allies. Cyprus also had forests on its mountains which could have been tapped if necessary. Neither is the argument that the rulers of the Crusader states were inhibited by their cultural conservatism as feudal knights from developing a maritime infrastructure, both commercial and military, any more meaningful.[41] These were highly pragmatic men. The occasional forays which they did make at sea were not eccentricities, as has been suggested, but rather show very clearly that where a need or benefit was perceived they were more than capable of developing a maritime capability, and often a successful one. Cultural conservatism is a notoriously unreliable argument for historical causation.

As long as the Crusader states remained on the defensive, merely holding on to the territories which they already held, they really had no need for any permanent naval force. Since the Crusaders held the entire coastline of Palestine and Syria, Egyptian squadrons could do no more than disrupt the sea lanes temporarily during the short

[37] J. Delaville le Roulx, ed., *Cartulaire général de l'ordre des Hospitaliers de St. Jean de Jérusalem (1100–1310)* (Paris, 1894–1906), vol. 1, nos. 159, 181, 207; Mollat, 'Problèmes navals', p. 349; J. Richard, *Le Comté de Tripoli sous la dynastie toulousaine (1102–1187)* (Paris, 1945), p. 54. [38] Usāmah, *Memoirs*, p. 110.

[39] In the 1240s Richard of Cornwall was informed by the military orders that the revenues of Acre were around 50 000 pounds of silver a year. This was roughly equivalent to the income of Henry III of England at the time. See Riley-Smith, 'Government in Latin Syria', p. 109 and n. 5.

[40] Mollat, 'Problèmes navals', pp. 348–9.

[41] A. Ben-Ami, *Social change in a hostile environment: the Crusaders' Kingdom of Jerusalem* (Princeton, 1969), pp. 60–4.

periods for which they could maintain themselves off the Crusader coasts. The only times when lack of a Crusader maritime presence really made itself felt was when the Kingdom of Jerusalem went on the offensive to the south, against Ascalon in 1153 and Egypt in the 1160s, and then again after Hattin during the struggle with Saladin when the strategic situation reverted to what it had been before 1124. For these few occasions it made better sense to use fleets scrambled together hastily or to use fleets provided by their Italian or Byzantine allies. In 1153 a scratch feet assembled in the ports of the Crusader states was used against Ascalon. In the 1160s, particularly in 1169, it was the Byzantine fleet which cooperated in the Crusader attack on Egypt. After 1187 the Italians and other Western powers provided the necessary naval assistance. In fact the only powers which did maintain anything like a professional, permanent war fleet in the twelfth century were Fatimid Egypt, the Byzantine empire, and the Kingdom of Sicily. Even Venice, Genoa, and Pisa at this time still assembled war fleets from their commercial shipping when the need arose. This was normal practice for all other maritime powers also and it is not surprising, therefore, given the highly spasmodic nature of their needs for maritime strength, that the Crusader states did so also.

One accepts, of course, that a factor contributing to the lack of Egyptian naval activity from the mid 1120s onwards was that the Fatimid government itself went into a period of decline and inactivity from that time. But its fleet by no means disintegrated. Even in the 1150s it could still count 70 or more warships. And, like the lords of the Crusader states, when the need was felt and the possibility of successful use of the fleet was perceived, the Fatimids were more than capable of throwing it into action. Between 1150 and 1155, as a result of the increasing pressure mounted by the Kingdom of Jerusalem on Ascalon, the Fatimids made proposals to Nūr-ad-Dīn in Damascus for a joint naval and land campaign, and they themselves sent out no less than four raiding fleets to the coast of the Kingdom.[42] Seventy Fatimid ships relieved Ascalon in June 1153 and enabled the city to hold out for another two months even though they could not prevent its ultimate fall. The Egyptian fleet was, then, still capable of offensive

---

[42] M. W. Baldwin, 'The Latin states under Baldwin III and Amalric I, 1143–1174', in Baldwin, ed., *The first hundred years*, 528–61, here pp. 537–9; Ehrenkreutz, 'Place of Saladin', p. 102; H. A. R. Gibb, 'The career of Nūr-ad-Dīn', in Baldwin, *The first hundred years*, 513–27, here p. 518; Mollat, 'Problèmes navals', p. 348; Runciman, *Crusades*, vol. 2, p. 338.

operations in the 1150s and its failure to operate against the maritime supply lines of the Crusader states during the period from 1126 to 1150 and then again after 1155 is to be attributed to the nature of the objectives for which it might have been used, to the limitations of its radius of action, and to the inadequate offensive capabilities of galleys against large sailing ships. The flurry of activity between 1150 and 1155 was all associated with concern for Ascalon.

That these parameters are accurate may be demonstrated by analysis of the last great attempt made by an Egyptian sultan in the Middle Ages to contest the waters of the Mediterranean with ships of the Christian West: that of Saladin from 1179 to 1191. In 1168 a large part of the Egyptian fleet had been destroyed accidentally by fire in its base at Cairo during the Egyptian campaign of Amalric I of Jerusalem.[43] In the following year, deprived of any real war fleet, the only response that Saladin had been able to make to the expected arrival of a huge Byzantine armada had been to send a small squadron of six galleys north to Cyprus to watch out for it.[44] From 1168 Egypt seems to have had no major naval force, and consequently its ports of Damietta, Tinnis, and Alexandria had been vulnerable to attacks by Byzantine and Sicilian fleets.[45] But in 1177 Saladin ordered the building of a new fleet and by spring 1179 he had 60 galleys and 20 oared transports (*ṭarīda*) in Alexandria harbour.[46] From then until his defeat before the walls of Acre in 1191, Saladin attempted to use this Egyptian fleet to threaten the maritime security of the Crusader states at the same time as he mounted increasing pressure on them by land. Notwithstanding the fleets built and used by some later Mamluk sultans of Egypt, Saladin was the only Egyptian sultan of the post-Fatimid period to demonstrate any sustained commitment to challenging the dominance of the Christians at sea. His failure is therefore all the more instructive.

From 1179 to 1182 Saladin merely tested the muscle and sinews of his fleet. Clearly he attempted to whip it into fighting condition gradually by sending detachments out on raiding cruises. And these raiding squadrons had some success; capturing one or two isolated Christian merchant ships, landing on the Syrian coast, and even

---

[43] Ehrenkreutz, 'Place of Saladin', p. 103; M. C. Lyons & D. E. P. Jackson, *Saladin: the politics of the holy war* (Cambridge, 1982), p. 22.

[44] Ehrenkreutz, 'Place of Saladin', pp. 103, 105–6.

[45] Ibid., pp. 103–5; Runciman, *Crusades*, vol. 2, pp. 385–8, 403, 414–15.

[46] Ehrenkreutz, 'Place of Saladin', pp. 105–6.

raiding Acre harbour.[47] Then in 1182 Saladin launched his most ambitious strike: a combined land and sea assault on Beirut. Saladin's choice of target was surely no accident. As we saw above, Beirut commanded the approaches of the major trunk routes to landfall in the Crusader states. Had Saladin succeeded in taking the city, he would both have cut the Crusader states in two by land and also have acquired an advanced naval base from which squadrons of his Egyptian fleet could really have created havoc in the maritime approaches to the Holy Land. Just how serious such a threat from regular squadrons of the Ayyubid fleet would have been was to be shown in the next decade when, after Saladin's death, an independent corsair emir by the name of Usāmah operated corsair galleys from Beirut with very dire consequences for Christian shipping on its way to Tyre and Acre. According to *L'estoire de Eracles Empereur*, Usāmah's galleys had captured 14 000 Christians, whom he sold into slavery, by the time that his depredations provoked a Crusader reconquest of Beirut in 1197.[48] However, Saladin's attack on Beirut in 1182 failed because the Egyptian squadron of some 30 galleys could not consolidate a beach head before the town and then was driven back to Egypt by a Crusader fleet of 33 galleys which had been hastily scratched together in Acre and Tyre.[49] The defeat of this Egyptian squadron, which had been preparing for just such a test as this for three years, by the makeshift Crusader fleet does not speak wonders for the morale and abilities of Saladin's crews. From then until the fall of the Kingdom of Jerusalem at Hattin in July 1187 the successes of the Egyptian fleet were limited to the occasional capture of isolated merchant ships.[50] Just how limited the strike capacity of the Egyptian fleet still was in this period is illustrated by one of its cruises in 1183, a cruise hailed by 'Imad ad-Dīn as one of its great victories. Under the command of Abu Bakr, the fleet captured a large Christian merchant ship carrying merchants and 375 knights to the beleaguered Kingdom of Jerusalem. The important point to note is that the fleet left Egypt on 21 May and returned with its prize a bare nine days later.[51]

[47] Ibid., pp. 106–8.
[48] *L'estoire de Eracles*, XXVI.8 (p. 226). Cf. XXIV.3 (p. 109) and XXVII.6 (p. 224). See also de Mas Latrie, *Chronique d'Ernoul*, pp. 311–17; Ibn al-Athir, *Extrait de la chronique intitulée Kamel-altevarykh par Ibn-Alatyr*, in *R.H.C. Or.*, vols. 1–2 (Paris, 1872–7), here vol. 2, pp. 85–6.
[49] Ehrenkreutz, 'Place of Saladin', pp. 108–9; Runciman, *Crusades*, vol. 2, pp. 432–3.
[50] Ehrenkreutz, 'Place of Saladin', pp. 109–10.
[51] Abū Shāma, *Livre des deux jardins*, vol. 4, pp. 239–40.

Obviously Abu Bakr had taken his prize en route immediately upon reaching the shipping lanes and had run for home straight away. The incident illustrates to what extent the operations of the Egyptian fleet were characterized as short raiding cruises in this period.

On Saturday 4 July 1187, at the Horns of Hattin, Saladin all but destroyed the field army of the Kingdom of Jerusalem and within a few months Frankish rule in the Holy Land had been reduced to the immediate environs of a few coastal cities: Antioch, Tyre, Tripoli, and Tortosa. Yet within a decade Frankish control had been re-established over the entire coastline with the exception of the two Syrian ports of Latakia and Jabala, which had been virtually demolished and made inoperable. The immediate survival and subsequent remarkable re-establishment of the Crusader states after Hattin was a direct result of Christian ability to move freely on the seas, to supply men and equipment by sea, and of the failure of Saladin's challenge to Christian sea power.

His naval attacks on Acre in 1179 and Beirut in 1182 had already shown that Saladin was aware of the strategic advantages that possession of a Palestinian or Syrian port would give him in the struggle at sea in particular and the overall struggle for the Holy Land in general. When Acre, the greatest seaport on the whole coast, the 'Constantinople of the Franks',[52] fell into his hands on 10 July 1187, the entire strategic situation in Levantine waters was fundamentally altered. Saladin clearly perceived what possession of the great seaport might mean to him. He was advised by his emirs at the time to destroy Acre so that if it was ever retaken by the Franks it could not be used by them as a supply base from which to re-establish their presence in the Holy Land.[53] However, conscious of the influence that an Egyptian squadron stationed at Acre might have on the strategic situation, Saladin declined their advice. In fact he ordered the defences of the city to be strengthened and then brought up ten galleys from Egypt to station in the port.[54] One might wonder why he did not bring the entire Egyptian fleet up to Acre. Apart from the obvious consideration that he did not wish to leave Egypt unprotected from the sea, another possibility is that after the failure of the fleet during the attack on Beirut in 1182 he reposed little confidence in its fighting qualities

---

[52] Ibid., p. 210. From a letter written on Saladin's behalf by his secretary, the qadi al-Fāḍil, to the vizier of the Abbasid caliph in Bagdhad.

[53] 'Imad ad-Dīn, *Al-Fatḥ*, p. 118, cited in Ehrenkreutz, 'Place of Saladin', p. 112.

[54] Ehrenkreutz, 'Place of Saladin', p. 110.

and was unwilling to place it in a position where it might become committed to a major fleet action. 'Imad ad-Dīn commented very unfavourably on the fighting qualities of the Egyptian crews after the defeat of a squadron from Acre off Tyre at the end of 1187.[55] Saladin may also have been influenced by the general reluctance of all rulers to commit fleets in open battle. In galley warfare decisive victories were extremely difficult to obtain, and the consequences in terms of losses of large quantities of skilled manpower in the eventuality of defeat were very serious. Ships were comparatively easy to replace. Skilled crews were not. The theme appears in the Byzantine military manuals of the middle Byzantine period and then recurs constantly until the end of galley warfare in the Mediterranean.[56] Since galley warfare was essentially amphibious warfare and fleets were normally used in conjunction with land forces to achieve terrestrial objectives, fleets clashed in pitched battle only in exceptional circumstances. Most commanders normally tried to avoid pitched battles at sea. But the real explanation for Saladin's decision was probably that there was no need to commit the entire fleet to Acre in 1187 in any case. There were no significant Christian naval forces in Levantine waters as yet and a small squadron could operate just as effectively as a large fleet for the tasks Saladin had in mind: commerce raiding and harassment of supply lines.

That Saladin was unwilling to let the Egyptian fleet challenge major Christian naval forces in open battle was then shown clearly during his campaign in northern Syria from July to September 1188. In response to appeals for aid from the Holy Land, William II of Sicily sent his famed admiral Margaritus of Brindisi with 50 galleys to the Levant in the spring of 1188.[57] Saladin was unwilling to commit the Egyptian fleet to battle with the combat-hardened Sicilians and allowed Margaritus to move along the Palestinian and Syrian coasts unmolested. Sicilian assistance probably saved both Tripoli and Tyre, certainly reinforced Antioch, and generally enabled the Franks to maintain themselves through the critical year of 1188 and the winter of 1188–9 before any other Crusader forces reached the East.[58]

[55] 'Imad ad-Dīn, *Al-Fatḥ*, p. 81, quoted in Ehrenkreutz, 'Place of Saladin', p. 111. See also p. 109.
[56] Christides, *Conquest of Crete*, p. 60; R. H. Dolley, 'Naval tactics in the heydey of the Byzantine thalassocracy', *Atti del VIII Congresso internazionale di studi bizantini* (Rome, 1953), vol. 1, pp. 324–9; Ehrenkreutz, 'Place of Saladin', p. 109 n. 103; Guilmartin, *Gunpowder and galleys*, pp. 21, 74–5.
[57] Ehrenkreutz, 'Place of Saladin', p. 112; Runciman, *Crusades*, vol. 3, pp. 18–19.
[58] Runciman, *Crusades*, vol. 3, pp. 4, 18–19.

Guy of Lusignan, king of Jerusalem, in an act of high gallantry which many have seen as mere foolhardiness, pitched camp before Acre on 28 August 1189. He commenced a 'siege' of the city, accompanied by a naval 'blockade' of it by a Pisan fleet of 52 ships which had reached Tyre in April. With his forces outnumbered by at least two to one by the garrison of the city, Guy's position was initially extremely precarious.[59] However, during the autumn of 1189 massive reinforcements from the West poured on to the beaches around Acre. Fleets arrived from England, Denmark, Flanders, Frisia, Germany, Italy in general, and Genoa and Venice in particular. Although their numbers cannot be estimated with any accuracy, there is no doubt that by New Year 1190 hundreds of Christian ships of all types were either beached or anchored around the city. Even at the time of Saladin's own arrival on the scene in early September 1189, 'Imad ad-Dīn said that the Christian ships had transformed the beaches into a forest of masts.[60] As the Crusader ring closed around Acre and Saladin found himself increasingly unable to supply and reinforce the city by land, he was forced to resort to supplying it by sea.[61] On Christmas Day 1189 his Armenian admiral Husam ad-Dīn Lū' Lū' fought his way into the port with 50 galleys of the Egyptian fleet.[62] A second large relief fleet, probably comprised of virtually every ship left in Egypt, also managed to fight its way through in July 1190.[63] The commitment of the crews to the defence of Acre meant that the ships could not be extricated. Saladin was caught in a tactically impossible situation. With their crews immobilized in Acre manning the walls, the Egyptian ships were powerless. Although he made two attempts to do so, Saladin could not even use them effectively to attack the Christian ships around Acre.[64] From that point on, Saladin's ability to supply and reinforce the garrison of Acre became very limited. Throughout the summer of 1190 and the winter of 1190–1 he still managed to slip occasional ships through the Christian blockade, but these were only small merchant ships and it became increasingly difficult as time wore on.[65] When the galleys of Richard Coeur de Lion quite by chance intercepted and sank the large relief ship from Beirut as they arrived off the coast on 7 June 1191, Saladin's

[59] Ibid., pp. 19–23.
[60] Cited from Behā ed-Dīn by Abū Shāma, *Livre des deux jardins*, vol. 4, p. 413.
[61] Ehrenkreutz, 'Place of Saladin', pp. 112–15.
[62] Ibid., p. 113; Runciman, *Crusades*, vol. 3, p. 27.
[63] Runciman, *Crusades*, vol. 3, p. 28.
[64] Ehrenkreutz, 'Place of Saladin', pp. 113–14. [65] Ibid., pp. 113–15.

last die was cast. The garrison of Acre was doomed and its surrender followed a month later, on 14 July. The entire Egyptian fleet with all its crews fell into the hands of the Crusaders and Saladin's attempted challenge to Christian dominance at sea was at an end.

In fact the sultan had realized the consequences of having the Egyptian fleet bottled up in Acre well before the loss of the city. Whereas in 1187 he had ordered the defences of Acre to be strengthened, in the winter of 1190–1 he ordered Sidon and Jebail to be destroyed and Jaffa, Arsuf, and Caesarea mined so that they could be demolished at short notice if necessary.[66] The final demolition of Ascalon was one of the terms of the truce eventually drawn up between Saladin and Richard.[67] He was already preparing for the consequences of losing the battle of the seaways. When Acre capitulated and the entire Egyptian fleet in the harbour was captured, the survival and recovery of the Crusader states was virtually assured. The capture of the fleet was as important as the capture of Acre itself; as was shown by the Crusaders' insistence that the surrender of the garrison would be accepted only if the fleet was not destroyed.[68]

Saladin died in 1193 and within a short time the Ayyubid sultanate fragmented into a coterie of rival states. In these circumstances the fact that Jebail, Sidon, Beirut, Jabala, and Latakia were still in Muslim hands counted for little as far as the strategic situation at sea was concerned. As we saw, the emir Usāmah, Saladin's governor of Beirut, made himself independent, and his piratical activities became a severe nuisance. But his forces were inadequate to really upset the strategic balance of power and none of the Ayyubid rulers could put any significant fleet to sea. By 1197 Jebail, Sidon, and Beirut had been recovered by the Franks and Jabala and Latakia could not provide the quality of facilities necessary if Muslim squadrons and corsairs were to use them on a large scale as bases for effective operations against Christian shipping. The strategic situation at sea reverted to that which had prevailed throughout the twelfth century until Saladin's attempted build-up of the Egyptian navy.

Over the course of the thirteenth century, the history of the

---

[66] 'Imad ad-Dīn, cited by Abū Shāma, *Livre des deux jardins*, vol. 4, p. 462. According to Al-Maqrizi, the ports were in fact actually destroyed. Al-Maqrizi, *Histoire d'Egypte de Makrizi*, trans. E. Blochet in *Revue de l'Orient latin*, 8 (1900–1), 165–212, 501–53; 9 (1902), 6–163, 465–530; 10 (1903–4), 248–371; 11 (1905–8), 192–239; here 9 (1902), p. 51.

[67] Ehrenkreutz, 'Place of Saladin', pp. 115–16; Runciman, *Crusades*, vol. 3, pp. 72–3.

[68] Behā ed-Dīn, *The life of Saladin*, trans. C. W. Wilson (London, 1897), p. 266.

Crusader states in Syria and Palestine is remarkable for the mounting pressure placed upon them by land by the Egyptian Ayyubid and Mamluk sultans, while at the same time there was a virtual absence of pressure applied to their coasts and vital sea lanes. Under Saladin's Ayyubid successors (1193–1252) and then the Mamluks (1250–91), the Egyptian fleet never posed a serious threat to the maritime life lines of the Crusader states. In fact there were only two major naval expeditions sent out from Egypt during this period: one to Ascalon in 1247 and the other to Cyprus in 1270.[69] Both ended in dismal failure. During the course of the gradual Mamluk reduction of the Crusader states on the mainland, the Egyptian fleet was never used in conjunction with land forces against the port cities. Rather it was overwhelming superiority on land which produced the eventual Muslim successes. Indeed, in most cases many of the defenders were evacuated by sea as the Muslims poured over the land walls.[70] Nor did squadrons of the Egyptian fleet operating as commerce raiders pose any threat to Christian maritime traffic in Levantine waters. In the thirteenth century command of the Levantine seas clearly lay with the Italians.

Two arguments have been advanced to explain the lack of Egyptian maritime initiative in the thirteenth century, both of which are perfectly acceptable and may be verified by reference to historical fact. On the one hand, the later Ayyubids profited economically from Christian commerce with Egypt in the first half of the thirteenth century and did not pursue a particularly aggressive stance towards the Crusader states.[71] As had the Aghlabid and Kalbite emirs of Sicily before them, and as did the Turkish *ghazi* emirs and the Ottoman sultans after them, they derived substantial benefits from Christian maritime traffic to their domains. They turned the maritime commerce of the Christian West with the Levant into an asset for themselves and had little interest in disrupting it. On the other hand, the Mamluks came from a background of Turkish nomadism, and were trained as cavalry in Egypt. They did not esteem naval warfare highly and may even have had a profound dislike for the sea.[72] Yet

---

[69] Ayalon, 'Mamluks and naval power', p. 5; Runciman, *Crusades*, vol. 3, p. 227.

[70] Runciman, *Crusades*, vol. 3, pp. 318, 406–7, 418–23.

[71] H. A. R. Gibb, 'The Aiyūbids', in Wolff & Hazard, *The later Crusades*, pp. 693–714. See also C. Cahen, *Orient et Occident au temps des Croisades* (Paris, 1983), pp. 182–3.

[72] Ayalon, 'Mamluks and naval power', *passim*; Levi della Vida, 'Papyrus reference to the Damietta raid', p. 218.

tastes and dislikes very often have root causes in circumstances which are much more concrete than mere cultural heritage. Attributing failure to change to cultural conservatism is always a hazardous business. Guilmartin has shown just how false it is in the case of the survival of the galley for naval warfare in the Mediterranean.[73] Very often a recourse to cultural heritage and conservatism as an explanation for historical causation is due to nothing more than an inability to see that the particular failure to change in question had good reasons lying behind it. No one likes very much that at which he cannot succeed. Expressed dislike for something may be no more than a self-delusory justification for inability to succeed. There was nothing in the Arab or Turkish mentality in general to justify recourse to it as an explanation of this Mamluk attitude. After all, Saladin's own Kurdish heritage hardly gave him any more empathy for the sea and naval warfare than an Arab or a Turk would have had. Yet he showed a willingness to utilize sea power when he perceived a use for it. Other Turks and Arabs, as much desert dwellers and cavalrymen as the Mamluks, had already taken to the sea with aplomb and were to continue to do so: under the Umayyads in the seventh and eighth centuries, the Abbasid governors of North Africa in the eighth century, the Cretan Arabs in the ninth and tenth centuries, the Fatimids in the tenth and eleventh centuries, various Western Muslim regimes throughout the entire early Middle Ages, particularly the Aghlabids of Tunisia and the Umayyads of Spain in the ninth century, and the *ghazi* emirs of Asia Minor in the fourteenth century.[74] Other Arabs, of course, had a long and distinguished tradition of seafaring in the Indian Ocean. Was there not more to this Egyptian dislike for the sea and naval warfare in the thirteenth century than mere cultural conservatism?

One of the major reasons for the lack of Egyptian naval operations in the thirteenth century may have been that the logistical lessons of the twelfth century and of Saladin's failure had been well and truly learnt. Why, when the Ayyubids and Mamluks eventually did gain control of the Syro-Palestinian seaports, did they follow Saladin's second pattern of dealing with them rather than his first? Rather than

[73] Guilmartin, *Gunpowder and galleys*, pp. 36–7.
[74] Although it is hardly a profound analysis of the subject, see A. Ali, 'The Arabs as seafarers', *Islamic culture*, 54 (1980), 211–22. See also Christides, 'Raids of the Moslems of Crete', pp. 89–90; Christides, 'Naval guides', pp. 86–7; Kubiak, 'Byzantine attack on Damietta', *passim*; Lev, 'The Fātimid navy', *passim*.

refortifying them and using them as bases for their own ships, they destroyed them.[75] The Palestinian coast was deliberately turned into a wasteland of ruined fortresses and demolished harbour works, upon which pilgrims commented consistently throughout the rest of the Middle Ages. The more northerly coast of Syria, where the Mamluks had less to fear from any attempted Christian seaborne expedition to recover the Holy Land, seems to have been much less affected than the coast from Tyre south. And, although the Palestinian ports were destroyed as centres of naval operations, they were far from destroyed as commercial centres. Throughout the fourteenth and fifteenth centuries they were visited regularly by Western merchant and pilgrim shipping.[76] The military capabilities of the Palestinian ports were destroyed in the initial conquest by the Mamluks but, after the danger of their reoccupation by the Crusaders had passed, the purely commercial facilities of the ports were reactivated by the Egyptian governments. The destruction was carried out not simply because the Egyptian rulers disliked the sea. They may have done so, but they were still sufficiently pragmatic to have developed naval forces and a supporting maritime infrastructure if they thought that they could achieve something by it and the risks were not too great. On occasions, when the possibility of successful use of sea power was perceived, the Mamluks of Egypt did operate naval forces at various times during the late Middle Ages.[77] But Saladin had learnt his lesson, and in general so had they. By the late thirteenth century it had become virtually impossible for Egypt to build up and maintain on a permanent basis a fleet which could match the numbers and experience of those of the Italians, the Catalans, the Kingdom of Cyprus, and later of the Hospitallers of Rhodes. The combined weight of Christian sea power had become too great for the Mamluks to

---

[75] Ayalon, 'Mamluks and naval power', pp. 8–9; D. Ayalon, 'Egypt as a dominant factor in Syria and Palestine during the Islamic period', in *Egypt and Palestine: a millennium of association (868–1948)* (Jerusalem, 1984), 17–47, here p. 36; Runciman, *Crusades*, vol. 3, pp. 407, 421–3.

[76] E. Ashtor, *Levant trade in the later Middle Ages* (Princeton, 1983), *passim* under the various ports; Richard 'La Méditerranée', p. 292.

[77] For example, in 1366–8, 1384, 1424–6, 1433–4, 1439–40, 1442, 1444, 1459, 1460 and 1464. See Andrews, *Turkish threat to Venice*, p. 378; Ashtor, *Levant trade*, pp. 92–6, 99–102, 129, 295, 302, 309, 452, 480; H. Luke, 'The Kingdom of Cyprus, 1369–1489', in H. W. Hazard, ed., *The fourteenth and fifteenth centuries* (vol. 3 of K. M. Setton, ed., *A history of the Crusades*) (Madison, 1975), 361–95, here p. 372; Richard, 'La Méditerranée', p. 295; E. Rossi, 'The Hospitallers at Rhodes, 1421–1523', in Hazard, *The fourteenth and fifteenth centuries*, 314–39, here pp. 319–20.

defend the Palestinian coast by naval forces.[78] Destruction of the military capabilities of the ports then became the only logical means of defence. Above all the sultans feared seaborne reoccupation of the port cities and re-establishment of the logistical situation of the twelfth and early thirteenth centuries. In the event they successfully prevented a recurrence of the situation which had occurred after the Third Crusade when the Crusader states had been reconstructed from the basis of the port cities. The advice which Saladin's emirs had offered him at Acre was now taken, with successful results; but for sound military reasons rather than for dislike of the sea.

[78] See also Richard, 'La Méditerranée, pp. 283–4.

6. Maritime traffic: The 'guerre de course'

At the same time as the fleets of Pisa, Genoa, Venice, and other maritime powers of the Christian West were confronting the navies of the Fatimids and Ayyubids in the waters of the Levant, a far wider confrontation at sea was beginning all over the Mediterranean; a confrontation whose outcome was to have infinitely greater importance in the long term than the wars of the Crusades. In the eleventh century there commenced a decisive movement by the merchant marine of the Christian West to establish its dominance over those of Byzantium and Islam in Mediterranean maritime shipping and commerce. In fact, of course, and particularly because of the key role played by the *guerre de course* in both, the essentially naval and strategic struggle between the three civilizations on the one hand and the competition in maritime traffic on the other were integrally connected and part and parcel of the same historical phenomenon.

Because of its complex and multiplex nature, the parameters and evolution of this competition in maritime traffic between the merchant marines of the three civilizations are even now obscure, despite an enormous historical scholarship devoted to the subject over the past century. The rich European archives have been ransacked to document what was beyond a shadow of doubt an enormous growth of shipping and maritime commerce in Western seaports such as Genoa, Pisa, Venice, Marseilles, Barcelona, Montpellier, and Dubrovnik. But hardly even the barest outlines of how what is commonly accepted to have been a marked decline in Byzantine maritime traffic actually occurred are known because of the extreme paucity of surviving Byzantine sources. The same is true of the Muslim world. Historians are generally agreed that from the eleventh to the fifteenth centuries Muslim shipping lost completely, or almost completely, whatever share of trans-Mediterranean maritime commerce it had had prior to then. But how this actually happened, seen from the Muslim point of view, is unclear. Surviving Muslim sources are known to be much better than Byzantine ones, but difficulties of language and of access to them have meant that historical research in European languages has been based largely on chronicles and a few administrative texts. At the *IVème Colloque international d'histoire maritime* at Paris in 1959, the sources for the maritime traffic of the Christian West in the late Middle Ages were explored at length.[1] At the same meeting the meagre survivals from the late Byzantine empire were presented also.[2] Admittedly the meeting was devoted to Europe, but the absence of an Islamicist to present a survey of the holdings in Muslim archives and of the Arabic and Turkish literature was sorely felt.[3] Other scholars have also lamented the inaccessibility of Muslim, particularly Ottoman, sources,[4] although the wealth of what may one day be made available from Muslim sources has been indicated by B. Lewis.[5]

The European archives certainly reveal a very great increase in voyages made by ships of the Christian West to the Byzantine and Muslim worlds and from place to place within those worlds during the period from the twelfth to the fifteenth centuries. However, they reveal absolutely nothing about any contemporary survival or disappearance of Byzantine and Muslim maritime traffic. Naturally enough, European sources were written by Europeans and were concerned with European ships, merchants, and seamen. This was the case even on those rare occasions where they were written abroad, within the Muslim or Byzantine worlds. The occasional references to Muslim or Byzantine shipping which they do preserve are entirely incidental since almost invariably they refer to instances in which Muslim or Byzantine shipowners or merchants were involved in business dealings with their counterparts from the Christian West. Very rarely indeed do they reveal anything about Muslim or

---

[1] M. Mollat, ed., *Les sources de l'histoire maritime en Europe du moyen-âge au XVIIIe siècle* (IVème Colloque international d'histoire maritime, Paris, 1959) (Paris, 1962). See esp. R. H. Bautier, 'Les sources de l'histoire du commerce international en Méditerranée (XIIe–XVe siècle)', ibid., 137–79.

[2] H. Antoniadis-Bibicou, 'Sources byzantines pour servir à l'histoire maritime', ibid., 121–36.

[3] See the comments of Bautier et al., ibid., 177–9.

[4] Braudel, *Mediterranean*, p. 13; A. C. Hess, 'The evolution of the Ottoman seaborne empire in the age of the oceanic discoveries', *American Historical Review*, 75 (1970), 1892–1919, here pp. 1892–5.

[5] B. Lewis, 'Sources for the economic history of the Middle East', in M. A. Cook, ed., *Studies in the economic history of the Middle East from the rise of Islam to the present day* (London, 1970), 78–92, esp. pp. 82–4.

Byzantine maritime traffic when there was no involvement with that of the Christian West. In fact, the European archives may be positively misleading, since they may give the impression that the shipping of the Christian West displaced its Muslim and Byzantine competitors when there is no way of really knowing whether that was the case or not. At present no quantitative assessment of a decline or survival of either Muslim or Byzantine maritime traffic can be made. Since that is so, the evidence of the European archives must be treated with great caution.

European scholars have claimed that from the eleventh century onwards an evolutionary, some would say revolutionary, process saw trans-Mediterranean maritime traffic fall almost entirely into the hands of the seaports of the Christian West. But should the question be put in these terms at all? One of the essential problems which still remains to be clarified, remarkably enough, is the true degree to which the ships and merchants of Byzantium and Islam actually voyaged to the Christian West in the period prior to the supposed Western drive to eliminate competition in trans-Mediterranean traffic; that is, in the ninth to the first half of the eleventh centuries. What evidence there is, and admittedly the Byzantine and Muslim sources are exiguous, suggests that in fact they rarely did so. Alternatively stated, the evidence, including European evidence, would suggest that the only Western ports frequented by Byzantines and Muslims in any numbers in this period were those in the far south of the Christian West in close proximity to Muslim and Byzantine territories in southern Italy, Sicily, the Balearics, and Spain. Such Western ports included those in Catalonia and ports such as Amalfi in southern Italy. This being the case, there is little point in the claim that shipping of the Christian West gradually eliminated its Byzantine and Muslim competition from trans-Mediterranean traffic from the eleventh century onwards.

What trans-Mediterranean traffic was in the hands of Muslims in the preceding period primarily connected Egypt and the Levant with Muslim North Africa, Sicily, and Andalusia, and to some extent with Byzantium, rather than with the Christian West. Indeed the commercial orientation of Mediterranean Muslim societies in the period was towards the east and south; towards Persia, the Indian Ocean, and the Sahara, rather than across the sea to the Christian West.[6] Aghlabid and Kalbite Sicily had commercial contacts with the mainland of

[6] Yarrison, *Force as an instrument of policy*, p. 39.

southern Italy, as would be expected,[7] but for Muslim societies on the southern and eastern shores of the Mediterranean the West had few commodities which could induce Muslim shipowners to sail to its ports. Moreover, some Muslim scholars of the Mālikī school held that travel to the *dār al-ḥarb*, the land of war, for purposes of trade was illicit.[8] The Mālikī school was particularly influential in the Maghreb and it is possible, though one would not wish to make too much of the point, that its influence may have dissuaded some Maghrebis from sailing to the Christian West. An absence of Muslim maritime traffic to the West is suggested by the dearth of commercial contacts between Egyptian Jewish merchants of the Cairo Geniza community and the West.[9] Social, intellectual, and travel contacts existed between these Jews and their co-religionists in the West, but not commercial contacts. But admittedly, whether the commerce of the Egyptian Jewish community was representative of that of the Mediterranean Muslim world in general is debatable. The famous text of Ibn Khordadbeh referring to the Rhadanite Jewish merchants travelling to and fro between Carolingian Europe, the Middle East, and China, appears to qualify the testimony of the Geniza records, at least for an earlier period.[10] On the other hand, Ibn Khordadbeh's is a unique text unsupported by any other evidence relating to these Rhadanite merchants. Whatever the true interpretation of the evidence of the Cairo Geniza and Ibn Khordadbeh should be, it is clear that in the period prior to the Crusades shipowners from the Muslim world did not sail their vessels to the ports of the Christian West in Catalonia, the Languedoc, Provence, Liguria and Tuscany, and the northern Adriatic in any great numbers or with any great frequency.[11]

Byzantine maritime traffic to the West, except certainly to the Byzantine province of South Italy, was also probably minimal in this period, and may have been so since the seventh century.[12]

---

[7] Talbi, *L'émirat Aghlabide*, pp. 529–36.

[8] Yarrison, *Force as an instrument of policy*, pp. 267–82.

[9] A. O. Citarella, 'A puzzling question concerning the relations between the Jewish communities of Christian Europe and those represented in the Geniza documents', *Journal of the American Oriental Society*, 111 (1971), 390–7; S. D. Goitein, 'Mediterranean trade in the eleventh century: some facts and problems', in Cook, *Studies*, 51–62, here p. 55; Idem, *Mediterranean society*, pp. 211, 214.

[10] R. S. Lopez and I. W. Raymond, *Medieval trade in the Mediterranean world* (New York, n.d.), pp. 31–3.

[11] Cahen, 'Commercial relations', pp. 16, 22; Cahen, *Orient et Occident*, pp. 37–41.

[12] Ahrweiler, 'Ports byzantins', p. 276. However, see below, pp. 148–52.

As far as the shipping of the Christian West in this period is concerned, there is now little doubt that Ibn Khaldūn exaggerated wildly the degree of its disappearance in the ninth and tenth centuries. In spite of the Muslim acquisition of the islands along the trunk routes in this period, which turned those routes into the maritime frontier between Islam and Christendom, and which permitted Muslim shipping to use them in a way in which it was not able to in both the preceding and subsequent periods, Western shipping also managed to use them in this period and to proceed from them to the Muslim and Byzantine worlds. Recent research has pointed ever more convincingly to the conclusion that the later growth of the maritime traffic of the Christian West was not a sudden development from nothing at the time of the First Crusade but rather was founded securely on a continuous previous experience in the eleventh century and earlier.[13] Trans-Mediterranean maritime traffic between the Christian West and the Byzantine and Muslim worlds was very largely in the hands of the West as early as the tenth and eleventh centuries, although the total size of that traffic was certainly minuscule by comparison to what it later became. Western merchants and shipowners had far more incentive to sail their ships to Muslim and Byzantine ports than did their Muslim and Byzantine counterparts to do the reverse. The historical process of the growth of the maritime traffic of the West from the late eleventh century onwards should be seen in terms of a massive expansion of a traffic which had existed previously, but only on a small scale, rather than in terms of displacement of Muslim and Byzantine competition.

Some scholars have gone further and extended the analysis from trans-Mediterranean traffic to regional traffic. They have claimed that particularly from the thirteenth century onwards, merchants and ships from Genoa and Venice especially, but also from Catalonia and other areas, displaced their Byzantine and Muslim counterparts within the internal maritime traffic of their own regions. Ashtor has argued repeatedly that Italian, Ragusan, and Catalan shipping

[13] Cahen, 'Commercial relations', *passim*; Cahen, *Orient et Occident*, pp. 37–41; C. Cahen, 'Quelques mots sur le déclin commercial du monde musulman à la fin du moyen-âge', in Cook, *Studies*, 31–6, here p. 32; Grabois, 'Navigation méditerranéenne', pp. 10–11. See also G. Airaldi, 'Groping in the dark: the emergence of Genoa in the early Middle Ages', in *Miscellanea di studi storici, II* (Genoa, 1983), 7–17; B. Z. Kedar, 'Mercanti genovesi in Alessandria d'Egitto negli anni sessanta del secolo XI', ibid., 19–30; Talbi, *L'émirat Aghlabide*, pp. 531–6; Yarrison, *Force as an instrument of policy*, p. 39.

virtually eliminated Muslim competition in the waters of the Levant from the fourteenth century onwards, and has attributed the causes of this historical phenomenon to a general technological decline in the Muslim Near East accompanied by a rapid acquisition of technological superiority by the Christian West.[14] Yarrison has seen Maghrebin shipping largely eliminated by European competition from the twelfth century and Fisher has claimed that in the sixteenth century the maritime commerce of the Maghreb was almost entirely in the hands of the Christian West.[15] Earle would have it that a brief attempt in the early sixteenth century, following the Ottoman expansion, to extend Ottoman maritime traffic across the Mediterranean was short lived and that by the seventeenth century practically all trade between the Muslim world and the Christian West was carried in Christian ships.[16] Even Cahen, an Islamicist, accepts that from the period of the Crusades the ships and seamen of the Christian West 'acquièrent la maîtrise et presque l'esclusivité du commerce méditerranéen'. In Egypt, the twelfth century was a period of transition towards this state of affairs, he declares.[17]

Although such claims certainly embody a great deal of truth, historians ought to be wary of their parameters, their extent, and their implications. They are made primarily on the basis of European evidence and, as suggested above, that may be misleading. What is needed is an examination by historians consciously investigating the evidence for survival of shipping and maritime traffic in Egypt, the Byzantine empire, Turkey, and the Maghreb from the twelfth to the sixteenth centuries. Malowist, for example, has insisted that even

[14] E. Ashtor, 'Aspetti della espansione italiana nel basso medioevo', *Rivista storica italiana*, 90 (1978), 5–29; E. Ashtor, 'Le Proche-Orient au bas moyen-âge: une région sousdévelopée, une économie en déclin', in A. Guarducci, ed., *Sviluppo e sottosviluppo in Europa e fuori d'Europa dal secolo XIII alla rivoluzione industriale* (Prato, 1983), 375–433; E. Ashtor, 'The economic decline of the Middle East during the later Middle Ages – an outline', *Asian and African studies*, 15 (1981), 253–86; E. Ashtor, 'L'artigleria veneziana e il commercio di Levante', in *Armi e cultura nel Bresciano 1420–1870* (Brescia, 1981), 141–54; E. Ashtor, 'L'ascendant technologique de l'Occident médiéval', *Revue Suisse d'histoire*, 33 (1983), 385–413. But see also his latest work, *Levant trade*, pp. 213–14, 333–6, 383, 395, 452–3 *et passim*. In this work Ashtor is more guarded and, although he reiterates his theme forcefully, he also draws attention to surviving Muslim maritime traffic.
[15] G. Fisher, *Barbary legend: war, trade and piracy in North Africa 1415–1830* (Oxford, 1957), p. 20; Yarrison, *Force as an instrument of policy*, p. 234.
[16] Earle, *Corsairs*, pp. 8–9.
[17] Cahen, 'Douanes et commerce', pp. 218–23; Cahen, *Orient et Occident*, pp. 137–8. See also Labib, 'Era of Suleyman the Magnificent', p. 447.

though the Christian West penetrated the carrying trade between the Maghreb and Egypt, it nevertheless captured only a part of that traffic.[18] Labib also has documented a significant survival of Egyptian maritime commerce in the late Middle Ages.[19] For the Ottoman sultanate, Inalcik has provided a refreshing alternative point of view.[20] For late Byzantine maritime traffic and that of Greek subjects of the Ottomans, Laiou-Thomadakis, Oikonomides, Luttrell and others have recently begun to explore the evidence for its survival.[21] Even if it was true that the shipping of the Christian West acquired a dominance in trans-Mediterranean traffic, there is still a need to distinguish between this, what Heers has called the 'grand trafic maritime', and the enormous volume of traffic carried in small boats by *cabotage*, coastal tramping.[22] Braudel has drawn attention in no uncertain manner to the importance of small boats and *cabotage* through into the fifteenth and sixteenth centuries.[23]

The West penetrated the regional maritime traffic and *cabotage* of the Muslim world to some degree. That much is clear. An impressive array of evidence has been amassed for large numbers of Muslims from the Maghreb and Andalusia travelling between the Maghreb, Egypt, and the Levant on Western ships.[24] In the second half of the fifteenth century, Venice even went so far as to operate, although only intermittently, a regular state galley service between Tunis, Tripoli

[18] M. Malowist, 'Les fondements de l'expansion Européene en Afrique au XVᵉ siècle: Europe, Maghreb, et Soudan occidental', *Acta Poloniae historica*, 18 (1968), 155–79, here p. 156.

[19] S. Y. Labib, *Handelsgeschichte Ägyptens im Spätmittelalter (1171–1517)* (Wiesbaden, 1965).

[20] H. Inalcik, *The Ottoman empire: the classical age 1300–1600* (London, 1973), pp. 121–39.

[21] Laiou-Thomadakis, 'Byzantine economy'; A. Luttrell, 'Late-medieval galley oarsmen', in Ragosta, *Le genti del mare mediterraneo*, vol. 1, 87–101, here pp. 100–1; Oikonomides, *Hommes d'affaires*.

[22] J. Heers, 'Types de navires et specialisation des trafics en Méditerranée à la fin du moyen-âge', in Mollat, *Le navire et l'économie maritime*, 107–17.

[23] Braudel, *Mediterranean*, pp. 103–8, 295–312.

[24] Ashtor, 'Ascendant technologique', pp. 404–7; Ashtor, 'Economic decline', pp. 282–3; Ashtor, 'Proche-Orient', pp. 423–6; Ashtor, *Levant trade*, pp. 213–14, 333–6, 395, 452–3, 481 *et passim*; Carrère, *Barcelone*, p. 236; Earle, *Corsairs*, p. 9; Heers, *Gênes*, p. 476; J. Heers, 'Le royaume de Grenade et la politique marchande de Gênes en Occident (XVᵉ siècle)', *Le moyen-âge*, 63 (4ᵉ série, 12) (1957), 87–121, here pp. 90, 100, 104–7, *et passim*. See also the interesting accounts of voyages by Muslims from Tunis on Genoese and Venetian galleys *c.* 1463–70 in R. Brunschwig, ed., *Deux récits de voyages en Afrique du Nord au XVᵉ siècle: 'Abdalbasiṭ b. Halil et Adorne* (Paris, 1936).

(Libya), Alexandria, and Beirut: the *galee de trafego*.[25] Florence and Genoa also operated galleys to Egypt and the Maghreb. In the early fourteenth century the ships of a remarkable Genoese merchant and slave trader, Segurano Salvaygo, plied between the Black Sea and Egypt flying the flag of the Mamluk sultans.[26] In a famous passage of his *Muqqadimah*, Ibn Khaldūn lamented the decline of Muslim naval strength and maritime traffic at the end of the fourteenth century:

Then, the naval strength of the Muslims declined once more, because of the weakness of the ruling dynasty. Maritime habits were forgotten under the impact of the strong Bedouin attitude prevailing in the Maghrib, and as a result of the discontinuance of Spanish habits. The Christians resumed their former, famous maritime training, and (renewed) their constant activity in (the Mediterranean) and their experience with conditions there. (They again showed) their former superiority over others on the high seas of (the Mediterranean) and in (Mediterranean) shipping. The Muslims came to be strangers to the Mediterranean. The only exceptions are a few inhabitants of the coastal regions, who are active on (the sea). They ought to have many assistants and supporters, or they ought to have support from the dynasties to enable them to recruit help and to work towards the goal of (increased seafaring activities).[27]

Ibn Khaldūn's analysis was extravagant. He was identifying and placing the decline of Maghrebin and Egyptian maritime traffic within a context of Western expansion. In fact, a plethora of evidence reveals the continuation of a Muslim merchant marine. Labib has shown that, although there was certainly a decline in Egyptian maritime commerce in the later Middle Ages and the role of Egyptian shipping in trans-Mediterranean traffic gradually weakened, nevertheless, significant numbers of Muslim ships continued to ply the waters between Egypt, the Maghreb, Syria, and Asia Minor. Muslim maritime traffic between the Maghreb and Egypt continued through-

---

[25] Ashtor, *Levant trade*, p. 461; Heers, 'Royaume de Grenade', pp. 104–7; Lane, *Venice*, pp. 339, 349–50 and map 9 (p. 341); A. Tenenti & C. Viventi, 'Le film d'un grand système de navigation: les galères marchandes vénitiennes, XIVᵉ–XVIᵉ siècles', *Annales: E.S.C.*, 16 (1961), 83–6.

[26] B. Z. Kedar, 'Segurano-Sakrān Salvaygo: un mercante genovese al servizio dei sultani mamalucchi, *c.* 1303–1322', in *Fatti ed idee di storia economica: studi dedicati a Franco Borlandi* (Bologna, 1977), 75–91.

[27] Ibn Khaldūn, *Muqaddimah*, vol. 2, p. 46.

out the period.[28] In the thirteenth century, Muslim merchants from Egypt, Palestine, and Syria voyaged north and south along the coast to Cilician Armenia in spite of the Crusader presence. With the rise of the *ghazi* emirates on the south and west coasts of Asia Minor in the fourteenth century, and the Ottoman sultanate in the fifteenth and sixteenth centuries, this north–south traffic in the eastern Mediterra nean was extended into the Aegean.[29] Seen from the opposite point of view, the situation was very different from that depicted by Ibn Khaldūn. According to Marino Sanudo Torsello in the early fourteenth century, Cilicia was a major source of timber, pitch, and slaves for Egypt, and the *marina*, that is the merchant marine as well as the naval forces, of the Mamluk sultan was 'magna'.[30] The existence of a Turkish merchant marine in the fourteenth to sixteenth centuries plying the waters of the Black Sea, the Aegean, and the eastern Mediterranean south to Egypt is sufficiently well attested not to need documentation.

Alexandria harbour had two different basins: an old and a new harbour. At the end of the fourteenth century and in the early fifteenth, the old harbour was reserved for the exclusive use of Muslim shipping.[31] Moreover, what would have been the point of all those late medieval Crusade propaganda treatises which advocated a maritime blockade of Egypt had there not been an Egyptian merchant marine?[32] As Marino Sanudo Torsello said, one of the tasks of projected Crusader squadrons was to be to intercept Christian shipping carrying contraband war materials to Egypt, or even enriching the sultan's coffers through normal trade, but another was to be to seize all Muslim ships attempting to enter or leave the country: the galleys . . . are necessary . . . to carry the offensive to the infidels,

---

[28] Ashtor, *Levant trade, passim*; Labib, *Handelsgeschichte Ägyptens*, pp. 100–1, 337–440, and esp. p. 404.

[29] Ashtor, *Levant trade*, p. 311; L. de Mas Latrie, *Histoire de l'île de Chypre sous le règne des princes de la maison de Lusignan*, vol. 2 (Paris, 1852), pp. 74–9; Labib, *Handelsgeschichte Ägyptens*, pp. 110–11; Emmanuel Piloti, *Traité d'Emmanuel Piloti sur le passage en Terre Sainte (1420)*, ed. P. H. Dopp (Louvain, 1958), pp. 137–40; Richard, 'La Méditerranée', p. 296.

[30] Marino Sanudo, *Liber Secretorum*, I.4.2 (p. 28). See also I.4.1 (p. 27), I.4.4 (p. 29).

[31] Gilbert de Lannoy, *Oeuvres de Ghillebert de Lannoy: voyageur, diplomate et moraliste*, ed. C. Potvin (Louvain, 1878), pp. 101–10; Nicolaus de Marthono, *Liber peregrinationis*, p. 587.

[32] A. S. Atiya, *The Crusade in the later Middle Ages* (New York, 1965), pp. 58–61, 120–2, *et passim*; W. Heyd, *Histoire du commerce du Levant au moyen-âge*, trans. F. Raynaud (Leipzig, 1885–6), vol. 2, p. 28.

and especially against those who sail and cross the sea to parts subject to the sultan, both disobedient faithful [Catholics] and schismatics [Byzantines and members of other Eastern rites], although Saracens and other infidels also.[33]

If Maghrebin shipping had been virtually eliminated by competition from the Christian West, then how was it possible for Abū-l-Ḥasan 'Ali I, the Marinid sultan of Morocco, to send a fleet of 16 galleys to the Balearics in 1338?[34] Two years later, in 1340, Abū-l-Ḥasan also joined with Yusuf I, the Nasrid sultan of Granada, to convoy an army of 8000–10 000 men across the Straits of Gibraltar, to put together a war fleet of 60 galleys and a support fleet of some 190 other ships, and to win a decisive battle over the navy of Castile. During the period *c.* 1337–44, the general maritime strength of the Maghreb and Granada seems at least to have matched and perhaps to have surpassed that of Aragon and Castile.[35] Such naval forces and expertise could not have been deployed for war had there not been a strong background of maritime tradition and merchant shipping in North Africa and Granada at the time. Maghrebin and Andalusian rulers did not maintain permanent standing navies of more than a few ships. Like almost all other maritime powers of the Mediterranean in the Middle Ages, they assembled war fleets from the shipping of their subjects and by building limited numbers of war galleys whenever naval operations were planned. But in fact the Maghreb had known a continuous tradition of commercial seafaring.[36] Corsair and war fleets also had operated from the Maghreb in previous centuries. The Almoravids and Almohads in the eleventh to thirteenth centuries had both deployed naval forces at various times, although it is true that formal Maghrebin naval power had not been maintained continuously and had been distributed unevenly.[37]

Perhaps the best index of the continued existence of Muslim maritime traffic everywhere is the continuous seizure of Muslim ships by Western corsairs and pirates throughout the entire period.[38]

---

[33] Marino Sanudo, *Liber Secretorum*, 1.4.7 (p. 31).

[34] Colom, 'Navegaciones mediterraneas', p. 36.

[35] Robson, 'Catalan fleet', pp. 389, 392, 398–9, 403, 406–7.

[36] Yarrison, *Force as an instrument of policy*, pp. 248–9 and appendix B-12, -13, -27–8, -36, -39, -41, -51, -55–8.

[37] Ibid., pp. 12, 227–31, 234–5, 241–5 and appendix B-28, -39, -51, -62–3.

[38] Ashtor, *Levant trade, passim*; R. I. Burns, 'Piracy as an Islamic–Christian interface in the thirteenth century', *Viator*, 11 (1980), 165–78, here pp. 169–70; Carrère, *Barcelone*, pp. 246, 247, 250: Ch.-E. Dufourcq, *L'Espagne catalane et le Maghrib*

Thriving piracy and privateering always indicate a flourishing maritime traffic rather than its absence. In 1328 the Dominican friar Guillaume Adam complained bitterly that claims made by Muslims to the Genoese Officium Robarie, an office set up in 1296 to compensate victims of piracies committed by Genoese subjects, had stopped Genoese corsairs preying on Muslim shipping and was thus impeding the prosecution of the Holy War.[39]

In the political disorder following the capture of Constantinople by the Fourth Crusade in 1204, Venetian, and later Genoese, shipping had unique opportunities to penetrate the regional maritime traffic of the Byzantine areas in the Black Sea and the Aegean. As early as the second half of the thirteenth century, the Venetians had clearly captured a significant share of the *cabotage* of the Aegean.[40] Subsequently, they and the Genoese gained control of a large share of the trade in provisioning of the Byzantine capital.[41] The political weakness of the imperial government following the Palaeologan restoration of 1261 allowed them to do so. Throughout the fourteenth and fifteenth centuries, the participation of Genoese and Venetian shipping in the maritime traffic of Romania, and to a lesser degree that of other maritime cities of the Christian West also, is well attested and was undoubtedly very significant.[42] On the other hand, there is no doubt that maritime traffic was continued on a large scale by Byzantines and by Greeks in ex-Byzantine territories falling under Ottoman control. In the 1340s Alexius Apokaukos based his power

aux XIIIe et XIVe siècles (Paris, 1965), pp. 574, 594–5; M. T. Ferrer i Mallol, 'Els corsaris castellans i la campanya di Pero Niño al Mediterrani (1404)', *A.E.M.*, 5 (1968), 265–338, here pp. 299–300; J. Guiral, 'Course et piraterie à Valence de 1410 à 1430', *A.E.M.*, 10 (1980), 759–65, here pp. 761, 763; Heyd, *Histoire du commerce*, vol. 1, p. 415; Inalcik, *Ottoman empire*, p. 128; Malowist, 'Expansion Européene', p. 174; A. Tenenti, 'Venezia e la pirateria nel Levante 1300c.–1460c.' in A. Pertusi, ed., *Venezia e il Levante fino al secolo XV. Vol. 1: storia – diritto – economia* (Florence, 1973), 703–71, here pp. 717–21; Yarrison, *Force as an instrument of policy*, pp. 180–3, 184–90, 207–8 and appendix B – *passim*.

[39] L. de Mas Latrie, '*L'Officium Robarie* ou l'Office de la piraterie à Gênes au moyen-âge', *Bibliothèque de l'Ecole des Chartes*, 53 (1892), 262–72.

[40] G. Morgan, 'The Venetian claims commission of 1278', *Byzantinische Zeitschrift*, 69 (1976), 411–38, here table I, pp. 427–32.

[41] M. Balard, 'Gênes et la mer noire (XIIIe–XVe siècles)', *Revue historique*, 270 (1983), 31–54, here pp. 41–2; Heers, *Gênes*, pp. 362–72, 385–406; Heyd, *Histoire du commerce*, vol. 1, pp. 529–30; A. (E.) Laiou(-Thomadakis), 'The provisioning of Constantinople during the winter of 1306–1307', *Byzantion*, 37 (1967), 91–113, here pp. 92–7; Laiou-Thomadakis, 'Byzantine economy', pp. 184–9.

[42] See in particular Balard, *Romanie Génoise*; Thiriet, *Romanie Vénitienne*.

on Byzantine shipowners and merchants in his attempt to control the imperial throne.[43] When he had defeated Apokaukos, John VI Cantacuzenus reduced the *kommerkion* paid by Byzantine merchants on their goods from 10% to 2% and this resulted in a rapid expansion of the Byzantine merchant marine. According to John VI himself, 200 merchantmen (ὁλκάδες) were constructed in short order.[44] If John's own figure of 200 ships should be treated with some reservation, at least a significant expansion in the size of the Byzantine merchant marine is indicated.

Recent research has accumulated an impressive amount of evidence concerning Byzantine and Greek shipowners and maritime traffic in the fourteenth and fifteenth centuries in the Black Sea and the Aegean. Greek ships trading with the Genoese at Caffa are attested from 1290 through to 1386.[45] Byzantine ships frequented Venetian and Genoese colonies such as Caffa, Tana, Chilia, Chios, Modon, Coron, Negropont, and Crete.[46] In 1360–1, Byzantines owned 30% of the ships engaged in the grain trade from the Genoese colony of Chilia to Pera/Constantinople; and this is according to Genoese records from a Genoese port.[47] Some Byzantine seaports, such as Monemvasia and Thessalonica, clearly were thriving in this period.[48] And again, perhaps the best evidence for the continuation of a Byzantine merchant marine in the Aegean and Black Sea areas is the continuous evidence of Western corsairs preying on their shipping.[49]

Even for trans-Mediterranean traffic, the *grand trafic maritime*, in which the West undoubtedly achieved a predominance by the fourteenth and fifteenth centuries, there is a need for some caution.

---

[43] Laiou-Thomadakis, 'Byzantine economy', p. 193; Oikonomides, *Hommes d'affaires*, p. 47 n. 45.

[44] John VI Cantacuzenus, *Historiarum libri IV*, in J. P. Migne, ed., *Patrologiae cursus completus: series Graeca posterior*, vol. 154 (Paris, 1866), IV.12 (coll. 95–6). See also Laiou-Thomadakis, 'Byzantine economy', pp. 192–3; Oikonomides, *Hommes d'affaires*, p. 48.

[45] Balard, *Romanie Génoise*, pp. 337–8; Laiou-Thomadakis, 'Byzantine economy', pp. 190–2.

[46] Laiou-Thomadakis, 'Byzantine economy', pp. 187–202, 205–10; Oikonomides, *Hommes d'affaires*, pp. 74–84.   [47] Balard, 'Gênes et la mer noire', pp. 51–2.

[48] Laiou-Thomadakis, 'Byzantine economy', pp. 205–8; Oikonomides, *Hommes d'affaires*, pp. 87–8.

[49] Ahrweiler, 'Course et piraterie', pp. 20–2; Ahrweiler, *Byzance et la mer*, pp. 288–92; Balard, *Romanie Génoise*, pp. 587–98; Balard, 'Bataille du Bosphore', p. 441; P. Charanis, 'Piracy in the Aegean during the reign of Michael VIII Palaeologus', *Annuaire de l'Institut de philologie et d'histoire orientales et slaves*, 10 (1950), 127–36, here pp. 134–5; B. Krekic, *Dubrovnik (Raguse) et le Levant au moyen-âge* (Paris, 1961), p. 82.

The European evidence still inevitably casts a distorted shadow and the subject has never been studied with the deliberate intention of correcting the nature of the sources. Examination of evidence alternative to the European may yet modify significantly the parameters of the predominance of the Christian West, if not the fact of that predominance itself. Let us ask, for example, why Ibn Jubayr made all his voyages in 1183–5 on Genoese ships. Perhaps from Acre and Trapani he could not easily catch a Muslim ship, or at least a suitable Muslim ship. But would this have been the case from Ceuta? Was it true that as early as 1183 there were no Muslim ships in the Maghreb and Andalusia able to take pilgrims, travellers, and merchants from the Muslim West to the Levant? Was Muslim shipping already driven from the sea lanes? Obviously not, for Usāmah ibn Munqidh reported Muslim ships carrying pilgrims between the Maghreb and Egypt in the same period as though there was nothing unusual about it at all.[50] As we saw above, at least one of these Muslim ships was comparable in size to contemporary Western ships.[51] Around the year 1150, abbot Nikolás Bergsson reported Muslims in Pisa, and around 1165, Benjamin of Tudela reported them in Montpellier also.[52] Neither author said explicitly that these Muslims came to Pisa and Montpellier on their own ships, but both certainly gave the impression that this was the case. A wreck of what may have been a Maghrebin Muslim ship of the late twelfth century has recently been found at Marsala in Sicily.[53] In the early thirteenth century a Muslim merchant from Egypt, al-Fakīm of Alexandria, was to be found in Marseilles, and in the same period Jewish merchants from Muslim North Africa were to be found in Genoa. Whether any of them came on his own ship is unclear.[54] However, in 1266–8 a Muslim merchant ship, probably from Tunis, was certainly attacked and burnt in port at Trapani.[55] In the fourteenth and fifteenth centuries, Muslim and Jewish ships and merchants from the Maghreb were to be found in Majorca, Valencia, Barcelona, Sardinia, and

---

[50] Usāmah ibn Munqidh, *Memoirs*, pp. 110, 210.   [51] See above, pp. 44–5.

[52] Benjamin of Tudela, *The itinerary of Benjamin of Tudela*, trans. M. W. Adler (London, 1907), p. 3; M. Scovazzi, 'Il viaggio in Italia del monaco islandese Nikolás', *Nuova rivista storica*, 51 (1967), 358–62, here p. 360.

[53] Purpura, 'Un relitto di età Normanna a Marsala'.

[54] L. Blancard, ed., *Documents inédits sur le commerce de Marseille au moyen-âge* (Marseilles, 1884–5), vol. I, pp. 18–19; S. D. Goitein, ed., *Letters of medieval Jewish traders* (Princeton, 1973), pp. 56–62.

[55] Filangieri, *Registri*, vol. 14, ed. J. Mazzoleni (Naples, 1961), p. 81.

Sicily trafficking with their counterparts from the Christian West.[56] The Muslim world had not abandoned trans-Mediterranean commerce entirely. In the fifteenth century we find Turks from Bursa in port at Chios with three ships and talking of going on to Alexandria with Granadan and Maghrebin merchants on board. So also we find a Maghrebin shipmaster visiting Chios and Ottoman territories with his ship and carrying Moorish merchants on board.[57] Throughout the period from the twelfth to the fifteenth centuries, before the emergence of an Ottoman merchant marine, Muslim ships and merchants continued to participate in trans-Mediterranean traffic to some degree at least. If their share of that traffic was certainly overshadowed by the massive contemporaneous increase of the maritime traffic of the Christian West, nevertheless their ships, merchants, and seamen did not disappear from the sea lanes entirely. The reasons why Ibn Jubayr travelled on a Genoese ship from Ceuta to Alexandria did not lie in a simple lack of ships. They were far more complex than that.

Trans-Mediterranean traffic on the part of the Byzantines is usually considered to have been discontinued even earlier than that of the Muslims. For example, Ahrweiler has posited the discontinuance of Byzantine maritime traffic with Italy as early as the seventh to ninth centuries.[58] But was this really the case, or is it more likely that the apparent disappearance of Byzantines from trans-Mediterranean traffic may be no more than a creation of the dearth of sources for Byzantine shipping in the subsequent period? In the ninth century the emperor Nicephorus I, in an effort to raise revenues, obligated provincial shipowners to buy lands belonging to the fisc in the maritime provinces and required shipowners in the capital to make a forced loan of twelve pounds of gold to the government. Obviously such shipowners were engaged in more than localized trade within the empire. Most probably the provincial shipowners in question were

---

[56] E. Ashtor, 'The Jews in the Mediterranean trade in the fifteenth century', in J. Schneider, ed., *Wirtschaftskräfte und Wirtschaftswege. I: Mittelmeer und Kontinent. Festschrift für Hermann Kellenbenz* (Nuremberg, 1978), 441–54, here pp. 441–2; Colom, 'Navegaciones mediterraneas', pp. 49, 51, 58; Delgado, 'Mediterráneo Nazarí', table I; Ch.-E. Dufourcq, 'Les relations de la Péninsule Ibérique et de l'Afrique du Nord au XIVe siècle', *A.E.M.*, 7 (1970–1), 39–66, here pp. 58–9; Ch.-E. Dufourcq, 'Chrétiens et musulmans durant les dernières siècles du moyen-âge', *A.E.M.*, 10 (1980), 207–26, here p. 222; Dufourcq, *Vie quotidienne dans les ports*, p. 130; Guiral, 'Course et piraterie à Valence', p. 760; Yarrison, *Force as an instrument of policy*, p. 263.

[57] Heers, *Gênes*, p. 399.

[58] Ahrweiler, 'Ports byzantins', p. 276; Ahrweiler, 'Liaisons maritimes', pp. 254, 260.

primarily those of Lycia and Cilicia who were growing fat on trade with the Muslim Levant to their south.[59] Both Muslim and Byzantine sources of the tenth century refer to Byzantine spies operating in Muslim ports under the guise of merchants.[60] How would it have been possible for them to have passed themselves off successfully in this way if Byzantine merchants did not habitually frequent the ports in question? And if they did, how did they get there? Are we to assume that they never used their own ships but rather travelled on Muslim ones? The actions of Nicephorus I would not suggest so.

As far as southern Italy itself is concerned, Guillou's studies of the Byzantine province there in the tenth and eleventh centuries have shown a prosperous commercial economy exporting commodities such as corn, oil, and mulberry leaves to Constantinople and a society which was in constant contact with the capital of its empire.[61] Is it possible that all maritime traffic between Byzantine South Italy and Constantinople was in the hands of ships from the Italian province? Surely Byzantines from Constantinople and the Aegean world were also involved, and is it not likely, although admittedly I know of no positive evidence to support the case, that Byzantine traffic with its province of South Italy spilt over into non-Byzantine areas in the Adriatic and Tyrrhenian Seas? Ahrweiler herself has pointed to a period of prosperity experienced by certain ports and islands such as Patras, Naupactus, Cephalonia, Corfu, and Durazzo on the west coast of the Balkans during the ninth and tenth centuries when the Muslims of Crete made the sea route around the Peloponnesus unsafe.[62] The west coast of the Balkans became the jumping-off point for traffic with Byzantine South Italy, and there can be little doubt that some of that traffic was carried in ships from the ports and islands in question.

In the twelfth century it is absolutely clear that Byzantine ships and merchants frequented Levantine waters south as far as Egypt. The Cairo Geniza materials recorded both Byzantine ships and merchants in Egypt in the eleventh and twelfth centuries.[63] At the time of the

[59] H. (Antoniadis-) Bibicou, 'Problèmes de la marine byzantine', *Annales: E.S.C.*, 13 (1958), 327–38; here p. 333.
[60] Christides, *Conquest of Crete*, p. 57; Christides, 'Naval guides', p. 91.
[61] A. Guillou, 'Production and profits in the Byzantine province of Italy (tenth to eleventh centuries): an expanding society', *D.O.P.*, 28 (1974), 89–109.
[62] Ahrweiler, 'Liaisons maritimes', p. 255.
[63] Goitein, *Mediterranean society*, vol. 1, pp. 45, 328; S. D. Goitein, 'Mediterranean trade preceding the Crusades: some facts and problems', *Diogenes*, 59 (1967), 47–62, here p. 51.

First Crusade Raymond of Aguilers reported Greek ships bringing supplies to the armies at Antioch and referred to the role of English and Genoese Crusader fleets making the seas south from Cyprus safe for Greek shipping.[64] During the Second Crusade the remnants of the French army were shipped from Attalya to Antioch by Greek ships, which beyond doubt belonged to local Byzantine seamen from Cilicia and Lycia.[65] After the capture of Acre by Saladin's armies in 1187 Ibn al-Athir referred to the city as a port frequented by Frankish and Greek merchants.[66] Also in the twelfth century, Benjamin of Tudela reported Greek merchants present in the western Mediterranean at Tarragona and Beziers.[67] The record of Byzantine ships and merchants going south to Egypt was in fact continuous throughout the thirteenth, fourteenth, and fifteenth centuries also. [68] How was it possible in the twelfth century for Alexius I and Manuel I Comnenus to rebuild the Byzantine navy to a strength which made Byzantium one of the most formidable maritime powers in the Mediterranean if they did not have a lively tradition of commercial seafaring and shipbuilding on which to draw?[69] On the elementary basis of a regional *cabotage* in the Aegean and Black Seas? That seems hardly likely. Throughout history states which have developed a major military maritime capability have always done so on the foundation of a strong commercial maritime tradition of their subjects. Although I do not have either the opportunity or the inclination to enter here into a debate still currently raging, it is true that many Byzantinists now see the Comneni century as a period in which the Byzantine economy flourished.[70] That would have been impossible without a Byzantine merchant marine in contact with other parts of the Mediterranean world. In discussing the attack by Manuel I on Corfu in 1149 John Kinnamos said that the emperor assembled a fleet of

[64] Raymond d'Aguilers, *Historia Francorum qui ceperunt Iherusalem*, trans. J. H. & L. L. Hill (Philadelphia, 1968), pp. 88, 113.
[65] Odo of Deuil, *De profectione Ludovici VII in Orientem*, trans. V. G. Berry (New York, 1947), pp. 129–43.
[66] Ibn al-Athir, *Kamel-altevarykh*, vol. 1, p. 689.
[67] Benjamin of Tudela, *Itinerary*, pp. 2, 3.
[68] Laiou-Thomadakis, 'Byzantine economy', pp. 193, 206; Oikonomides, *Hommes d'affaires*, p. 89.
[69] Ahrweiler, *Byzance et la mer*, pp. 175–279; M. Sesan, 'La flotte byzantine à l'époque des Comnènes et des Anges (1081–1204)', *Byzantinoslavica*, 21 (1960), 48–53.
[70] See, for example, M. F. Hendy, 'Byzantium, 1081–1204: an economic reappraisal', *Transactions of the Royal Historical Society*, 20 (1970), 31–52; J. Herrin, 'The collapse of the Byzantine empire in the twelfth century: a study of a medieval economy', *Birmingham historical journal*, 12 (1970), 188–203.

over 500 triremes and 1000 horse transports and supply ships.[71] Even allowing for the Byzantine chronicler's exaggeration of the numbers, there is no doubt that the fleet was very large and, more importantly, that the support and supply fleet numbered some hundreds of ships. These latter must have been gathered from the merchant marine of the empire.

In the fourteenth and fifteenth centuries, Byzantine shipmasters, some of them, for example a certain Manuel Cabasilas, acting as agents for the Byzantine emperor himself, took considerable quantities of grain to Genoa on Byzantine ships.[72] Indeed, in the fifteenth century Byzantine merchants may even have had a *logia* at Genoa.[73] Treaties between Venice and Genoa on the one hand and the Byzantine empire on the other certainly envisaged that Byzantine merchants and ships could visit those cities.[74] And if in practice severe difficulties were put in the way of their doing so, and the emperor had cause to complain about the treatment they sometimes received, that merely shows that they did attempt to sail their ships to Genoa, Venice, and the colonial ports of those two powers.[75] In the fifteenth century, Greek or Byzantine ships were to be found at both Venice and Dubrovnik.[76] Moreover, it is clear that not only did Greek or Byzantine ships operate to and fro between their home ports in Byzantine or Ottoman territories and the south and west of the Mediterranean, but they also participated in the carrying trade all around the sea. Their ships moved between the ports of foreign powers, picking up passengers and cargoes as the opportunity arose, just as did the ships of the Christian West. In March 1345 a certain unidentified English pilgrim took a Greek ship from Coron to Rhodes,[77] and in 1395 Ogier VIII d'Anglure travelled from Rhodes to Venice on a Greek ship.[78] More significantly still, in the fifteenth century a Byzantine shipmaster called Manuel Zaliotus, from Constantinople, traded in grain between Sicily and Dubrovnik.[79] The evidence for a continuing Greek or Byzantine participation in trans-

---

[71] John Kinnamos, *Deeds of John and Manuel Comnenus*, trans. C. M. Brand (New York, 1976), III.2 (p. 76).

[72] Balard, *Romanie Génoise*, p. 337; Laiou-Thomadakis, 'Byzantine economy', pp. 217–21. See also Melissenos, *Chronicle of the siege of Constantinople*, p. 106.

[73] L. T. Belgrano, 'Seconda serie di documenti riguardanti la colonia di Pera', *Atti della Società ligure di storia patria*, 13 (1884), 932–1003; here p. 975.

[74] Oikonomides, *Hommes d'affaires*, p. 83.   [75] Ibid., pp. 83–5.

[76] Laiou-Thomadakis, 'Byzantine economy', p. 210; Oikonomides, *Hommes d'affaires*, p. 84.   [77] E. Hoade, ed., *Western pilgrims* (Jerusalem, 1952), p. 56.

[78] Bonnardot & Longnon, *Saint voyage*, pp. 95–9.

[79] Laiou-Thomadakis, 'Byzantine economy', p. 210.

Mediterranean traffic remains to be collected systematically but it is quite clear that, like those of the Muslims, their ships were far from driven from the sea lanes in the fourteenth and fifteenth centuries. Both Greeks and Muslims continued to operate in maritime traffic throughout the entire Middle Ages and into the sixteenth century. If the ships and merchants of the Christian West did displace their Greek and Muslim counterparts from the sea lanes over the course of the twelfth to sixteenth centuries, or if alternatively they developed and expanded their own trans-Mediterranean traffic, from which the latter were largely excluded, then the degree of that displacement or exclusion certainly cannot be quantified. All that is possible is to build up impressionistic pictures based on examples. But in history such pictures are as often misleading as they are revealing, and in this case they may be particularly so since the nature of the evidence is so extremely one-sided: West European in origin. That being said, there is still no doubt whatsoever that the period witnessed an enormous expansion of the maritime traffic of the Christian West. In the case of the Byzantine–Greek world, by the fifteenth century the ships and merchants of Genoa, Venice, Barcelona, and to a lesser degree a few other maritime cities of the West, not only controlled the lion's share of its maritime traffic with the West but also had a considerable share of its internal *cabotage*. In the case of the Muslim world also, the Christian West controlled the vast bulk of its trans-Mediterranean traffic with both the West and the Byzantine–Greek world and had penetrated its internal *cabotage* to some degree at least. From the twelfth century onwards the Christian West gradually asserted its predominance in the great trans-Mediterranean traffic between the West and the Muslim and Greek worlds.

The root causes of the commercial and maritime thrust of the Christian West which produced what Lopez and others have called the 'Commercial Revolution of the Middle Ages', and what Halphen long ago characterized as the 'conquête de la Méditerranée', have stimulated much speculation. In general, historians have turned to cultural factors for an explanation of the success of the West: an innovativeness in, and receptivity towards, technology; the aggressive dynamic of Crusader Europe; the galvanizing effects of religious faith; the unique position of the urban bourgeoisie in medieval Europe; and the development of a bourgeois, if not 'capitalist' ethic.[80]

---

[80] See, for example, L. Halphen, 'La conquête de la Méditerranée par les Européens au XIe et au XIIe siècles', in *Mélanges d'histoire offerts à Henri Pirenne* (Brussels,

In other words, historians have looked to the *mentalité* of the medieval Christian West for their causation. Such cultural factors of *mentalité* are intrinsically unsatisfying as causal explanations because they are totally relative, if for no other reason. Their validity exists only by comparison to the *mentalité* of others. They should be assessed critically by comparison to the Greek and Muslim worlds rather than treated in isolation, as has too often been the case. Nevertheless, although, as I argued previously in another context, cultural factors are notoriously unreliable as a source of historical causation, they do form part of any essay in causation and may not be discounted completely. But to them should be added, in this context, the consequences of the nexus between Mediterranean geography and maritime technology operating within the milieu of a perpetual *guerre de course* embracing the entire sea.

Outright illegal piracy on the one hand and legitimized corsair activity under the licence of political authorities, privateering or *guerre de course*, on the other were endemic throughout the Mediterranean from the twelfth to the sixteenth centuries. No region or time period was free from them, and there was no maritime city, state, or people whose seamen did not participate in them.[81] Pirate and corsair crews were cosmopolitan. Captains of all races roved the seas in the

1926), vol. 1, 175–80; H. C. Krueger, 'Economic aspects of expanding Europe', in M. Clagett, ed., *Twelfth-century Europe and the foundations of modern society* (Madison, 1961), 59–76; R. S. Lopez, *The Commercial Revolution of the Middle Ages, 950–1350* (Englewood Cliffs, 1971), pp. 97–102; Santamaría Arandez, 'Reconquista', pp. 50–5; L. White jr, 'The Crusades and the technological thrust of the West', in V. J. Parry & M. E. Yapp, eds., *War, technology and society in the Middle East* (London, 1975), 97–112.

[81] On piracy and privateering in general see P. Adam, 'Esquisse d'une typologie de la course et de la piraterie', in *Course et piraterie* vol. 2, 917–55; Ahrweiler, *Byzance et la mer*, pp. 288–92; Ahrweiler, 'Course et piraterie'; Balard, *Romanie Génoise*, pp. 587–98; Braudel, *Mediterranean*, pp. 865–91 *et passim*; Burns, 'Piracy'; Charanis, 'Piracy in the Aegean'; Dufourcq, *L'Espagne catalane*, pp. 82–4, 428–40, 496–8, 573–6 *et passim*; M.-L. Favreau, 'Die italienische Levante-Piraterie und die Sicherheit der Seewege nach Syrien im 12. und 13. Jahrhundert', *Vierteljahrschrift für Wirtschafts- und Sozialgeschichte*, 65 (1978), 463–510; Ferrer i Mallol, 'Corsaris castellans'; Guilmartin, *Gunpowder and galleys, passim*; Heers, *Gênes*, pp. 300–7; M. Mollat, 'Essai d'orientation pour l'étude de la guerre de course et la piraterie (XIII⁵–XV⁵ siècles)', *A.E.M.*, 10 (1980), 743–9; Tenenti, 'Venezia e la pirateria'; A. Tenenti, 'I corsari in Mediterraneo all'inizio del Cinquecento', *Rivista storica italiana*, 72 (1960), 234–87; M. Fontenay & A. Tenenti, 'Course et piraterie méditerranéenes de la fin du moyen-âge au début du XIXème siècle', in *Course et piraterie*, vol. 1, 78–136; Yarrison, *Force as an instrument of policy, passim*.

On the organization of privateering see L. Balletto, 'Mercanti, corsari e pirati nei mari della Corsica (sec. XIII)', in *Miscellanea di storia italiana e mediterranea per Nino Lamboglia* (Genoa, 1978), 171–263; Unali, *Marinai*.

service of anyone who would pay or license them. Before the Fourth Crusade the Angeli emperors of Byzantium issued letters of marque to Western corsairs who entered their service, licensing them to operate as privateers against other Western corsairs infesting the Aegean.[82] Genoese, Pisans, Franks, and perhaps even Muslims were corsairs for Byzantium in the thirteenth century.[83] Greeks served the *ghazi* emirs of Aydin in the fourteenth.[84] The Barbary corsairs of the sixteenth century included renegade Christians among their numbers.[85] There was no sharp distinction between the peaceful merchantman and the pirate on the one hand and the man of war and the corsair on the other. Around 1195 a Genoese merchant by the name of Gafforio, who had been unjustly fined or despoiled by the Byzantine admiral Michael Stryphnus, turned pirate and inflicted great damage on Byzantine coasts and shipping in the Sea of Marmara and the upper Aegean.[86] Boccaccio related the story of the merchant Landolfo Rufolo of Ravello who, when his business affairs in Cyprus did not prosper, sold his great merchant ship and bought a small, fast ship with which to go privateering against the Turks. After a year of successful plundering, his ship was sheltering in a bay of one of the Greek islands when it was surprised, plundered, and sunk by two Genoese *cocche* returning from Constantinople.[87] Few merchantmen voyaged totally unarmed,[88] and, if the right prey was encountered, few were above seizing it. As opportunities presented themselves, and as circumstances dictated, war fleets casually snapped up ships of all persuasions. Piracy and privateering were business for investment, and in fact formed an integral part of the economic system.[89] They

---

[82] F. Miklosich & J. Müller, eds., *Acta et diplomata graeca medii aevi sacra et profana*, vol. 3 (Vienna, 1865), pp. 48–9; Niketas Choniates, *O city of Byzantium, annals of Niketas Choniates*, trans. H. J. Magoulias (Detroit, 1984), pp. 264–5; A. Sanguineti & G. Bertolotto, 'Nuova serie di documenti sulle relazioni di Genova coll'Impero bizantino', *Atti della Società ligure di storia patria*, 28 (1896–98), 337–573, here pp. 467–8.

[83] Ahrweiler, 'Course et piraterie', pp. 16–17; Morgan, 'Venetian claims commission', table I (pp. 427–32).

[84] Ahrweiler, *Byzance et la mer*, pp. 376–8; C. Foss, *Ephesus after antiquity: a late antique, Byzantine, and Turkish city* (Cambridge, 1979), p. 150; Oikonomides, *Hommes d'affaires*, pp. 86–7.

[85] Lane-Poole, *Barbary corsairs*, p. 200; Traselli, 'Naufragi', p. 507.

[86] Choniates, *O city of Byzantium*, pp. 264–5.

[87] Boccaccio, *Decameron*, II.4 (pp. 93–7). See also Dufourcq, *Vie quotidienne dans les ports*, p. 125; Unali, *Marinai*, pp. 17, 139.

[88] Heers, *Gênes*, pp. 300–2; Unali, *Marinai*, p. 19.

[89] Balletto, 'Mercanti, corsari e pirati', *passim*; Unali, *Marinai*, pp. 16–21 *et passim*.

were licensed, aided, and abetted by political authorities, who provided facilities and took a cut of the profits.[90] Skilful use of corsairs by political authorities could serve as an instrument of state policy, as it did for Aragon in the thirteenth and fourteenth centuries.[91] They were encouraged by the system of reprisals, under which political authorities granted to individuals the right to take recourse against the countrymen of someone who had injured them or caused them loss.[92] In fact, piracy and privateering were as omnipresent a hazard of seafaring as the weather. The statutes of Marseilles, Pisa, Dubrovnik, and Venice, and the laws of the Kingdom of Jerusalem all listed loss of cargo from piracy and privateering along with that from shipwreck as normal circumstances under which the *tractator* of a *commenda* contract was freed from all obligation to his *commendator* who had supplied him with the capital for his voyage.[93]

Religion provided only a degree of protection. Christian pirates and corsairs happily plundered the ships of their Christian political and economic competitors as well as those of Muslims. Whether Muslim corsairs attacked Muslim shipping on an equal scale is less clear. The evidence for that aspect of their activities is very exiguous, although in the eleventh and twelfth centuries pirates from Libya and Djerba certainly preyed on Muslim shipping following the routes along the southern coasts.[94] Outright criminal pirates might be a scourge to all, but they were in a minority. Most of the sea robbers who infested the sea lanes were corsairs, privateers, and their commissions make it clear that their primary targets were ships of other religions except for when conditions of intra-religious war or reprisals made the ships of specified co-religionists legitimate targets also.[95] One of the primary objectives of all corsairs was the capture of slaves. Since co-religionists could only rarely or with difficulty be sold as slaves, this also helped to promote the character of the *guerre de*

[90] Braudel, *Mediterranean*, pp. 867, 869; H. Bresc, 'Course et piraterie en Sicile (1250–1450)', *A.E.M.*, 10 (1980), 751–7, here pp. 754–6; Charanis, 'Piracy in the Aegean', pp. 129–30; Heers, *Gênes*, pp. 300–7; Mollat, 'Essai d'orientation', p. 744; Unali, *Marinai*, p. 123.

[91] Yarrison, *Force as an instrument of policy*, p. 114.

[92] Unali, *Marinai*, pp. 139–51.

[93] J. H. Pryor, 'Mediterranean commerce in the Middle Ages: a voyage under contract of commenda', *Viator*, 14 (1983), 133–94; here p. 147.

[94] Goitein, *Mediterranean society*, vol. 1, pp. 327–8; Pellat, 'Ḳurṣān: I', p. 503.

[95] Burns, 'Piracy', pp. 165, 168; Dufourcq, 'Chrétiens et musulmans', pp. 209–11; Dufourcq, *Vie quotidienne dans les ports*, p. 124; Unali, *Marinai*, p. 143.

course as primarily an inter-religious struggle.[96] As far as inter-religious conditions were concerned, the natural state of affairs at sea was one of war between Islam and Christianity. Peace treaties and truces were merely momentary aberrations from the norm. The larger framework of the *guerre de course* was an inter-religious one, although at certain times and in certain zones the intra-religious framework predominated; for example, in the Aegean and Levant during the twelfth and thirteenth centuries, where, because there were no significant numbers of Muslim or Byzantine corsairs, those from the Italian maritime cities had the seas virtually to themselves.[97] A similar situation may have prevailed in the western Mediterranean in the second half of the twelfth century.[98] Within the larger framework of the inter-religious *guerre de course*, there certainly existed an intra-religious free-for-all, and the boundaries between the two were by no means well defined, but over the centuries the larger framework predominated.

Pirates and corsairs were not unintelligent men. They had to be skilled and experienced in the ways of the sea and of the ships and men who sailed it if they were to be successful. They knew as well as anyone that they would be most likely to take prizes easily in those few focal sectors of the sea lanes where shipping agglomerated at particular times of the year for navigational and economic reasons. Whenever possible, they based themselves in close proximity to those sectors. When that was not possible, they cruised to them and lurked there in ambush for as long as their supplies would last.[99] Not surprisingly, the zones identified by the historical sources as being the favourite haunts of corsairs were precisely those same zones which were identified above as focal sectors of the sea lanes where the routes intersected each other or passed through narrowly confined seas.[100]

---

[96] Aymard, 'Chiourmes et galères', p. 60; Luttrell, 'Galley oarsmen', p. 88; Fontenay & Tenenti, 'Course et piraterie', pp. 117–19.

[97] Ahrweiler, 'Course et piraterie', pp. 16–17; C. M. Brand, *Byzantium confronts the West, 1180–1204* (Cambridge, Mass., 1968), pp. 42–3, 208–21; G. W. Day, *Genoese involvement with Byzantium 1155–1204: a diplomatic and prosopographical study*, Ph.D. thesis, University of Illinois, 1978, pp. 64–72; Favreau, 'Italienische Levante-Piraterie'; J. Fotheringham, 'Genoa and the Fourth Crusade', *English historical review*, 25 (1910), 26–57, here pp. 27–32.

[98] G. Pistarino, 'Genova e l'Islam nel Mediterraneo occidentale (secoli XII–XIII)', *A.E.M.*, 10 (1980), 189–205; here pp. 114, 201.

[99] Ahrweiler, 'Course et piraterie', pp. 12–13; Bresc, 'Course et piraterie en Sicile', p. 756; Guilmartin, *Gunpowder and galleys*, pp. 97–8; Fontenay & Tenenti, 'Course et piraterie', pp. 85–92.   [100] See above, p. 99.

In the twelfth century the port at the mouth of the river Finike at the western end of the Bay of Attalya became known as 'Portus Pisanorum' because it was used by Pisan corsairs.[101] It was ideally positioned to dominate the routes east from Rhodes to Cyprus and south to the Holy Land and Egypt. Rhodes and the waters around it were a favourite haunt of Christian corsairs, especially Catalans in the fourteenth and fifteenth centuries and Maltese in the sixteenth and seventeenth.[102] Cyprus and Rhodes provided refuges and bases for Catalan corsairs in the fifteenth century, and the expeditions of the Mamluk sultans Barsbay and Jaqmaq against the two islands were motivated by reprisal against the authorities who gave them shelter.[103] It was no accident that under the Gattilusi, Mitilini (Lesbos) became the centre of corsair activity for the northern Aegean and the approaches to the Dardanelles.[104] Sapienza island, off Modon at the south-west tip of the Peloponnesus, was a notorious resort for corsairs of all persuasions from the fourteenth to the seventeenth centuries.[105] After the fall of Modon to the Ottomans in 1499, it and other ports along the west coast of the Balkans and in the Ionian islands, such as Zonchio/Navarino, Durazzo, Avlona, Prevesa, Lepanto, and the island of Santa Maura (Levkas) became the main bases for Ottoman corsairs.[106] Catalan and Sicilian corsairs frequented the Straits of Otranto in the fourteenth century,[107] as did the Barbary corsairs in the seventeenth.[108] In the western Mediterranean, ports such as Hyères, La Ciotat, Fréjus, and Monaco were lairs from which corsairs preyed on shipping in the Ligurian sea.[109] The waters of the Balearics were haunted by Maghrebin corsairs from the fourteenth century through into the sixteenth.[110] The west coasts of Corsica and Sardinia, and particularly the island of S. Pietro at the south-west tip of Sardinia, were favourite stamping-grounds for both Christian corsairs and also the Barbary corsairs.[111] The latter were

---

[101] Roger of Hoveden, *Chronica*, p. 158.
[102] Ashtor, *Levant trade, passim*; Earle, *Corsairs*, p. 144; Fontenay & Tenenti, 'Course et piraterie', p. 91; Inalcik, *Ottoman empire*, p. 128; Nicolaus de Marthono, *Liber peregrinationis*, p. 639. [103] Richard, 'La Méditerranée', p. 296.
[104] Heers, *Gênes*, pp. 306, 387.
[105] Earle, *Corsairs*, p. 58; Niccolò da Poggibonsi, *A voyage beyond the seas (1346–1350)*, ed. & trans. T. Bellorini & E. Hoade (Jerusalem, 1945), pp. 129–30.
[106] See below, pp. 187, 196. [107] Hoade, *Western pilgrims*, p. 55.
[108] See below, p. 194. [109] Heers, *Gênes*, pp. 303–7.
[110] Colom, 'Navegaciones mediterraneas', pp. 59, 67, 70–3.
[111] Carrère, *Barcelone*, p. 253; Earle, *Corsairs*, p. 58; Ferrer i Mallol, 'Corsaris castellans', *passim*; Heers, *Gênes*, pp. 304–5.

also fond of lurking around Cape de Gata, from where they could cover the routes from the Balearics to the Straits of Gibraltar.[112] In the twelfth and thirteenth centuries, the crucial period in which the ships and seamen of the Christian West established their dominance in trans-Mediterranean traffic, Islam held no possessions along the trunk routes except for Granada, Valencia, and the Balearics in the far west and a strip of the south coast of Asia Minor in the east, from Attalya to Alanya. Valencia and the Balearics were lost in the 1230s and the strip from Attalya to Alanya was only acquired between 1207 and 1220. Political factors discussed below[113] meant that until the fourteenth century it remained largely ineffectual as a base for Muslim corsairs. During these centuries it was Christian rather than Muslim fleets and corsairs which were able to roam the waters of the trunk routes at will. The establishment of the Crusader states in Syria and Palestine in 1098–9, the conquest of Cyprus by Richard Coeur de Lion in 1191, and the extensive settlement of Venetians and later Genoese throughout the Aegean and the Black Sea after the Fourth Crusade in 1204 and the Palaeologan restoration of the Byzantine empire in 1261 gave the seamen of Italy in particular and the West in general innumerable bases from which to infest the focal sectors of the trunk routes east of the Ionian Sea. Disintegration of the imperial Byzantine fleet after the death of Michael VIII Palaeologus permitted Western corsairs to establish themselves on the Aegean islands and to roam virtually wherever they wished.[114] In the western Mediterranean, the development of Genoese, Marseillese, Pisan, and Barcelonese sea power, the existence of powerful Sicilian fleets under the Norman, Hohenstaufen, and Angevin kings, and the conquest of Valencia and the Balearics, the hinge of the western Mediterranean, gave command of all of the sea except the southern coasts to the Christian West.[115] Against the ability of Western ships to move freely along the trunk routes, Muslim fleets and corsairs, and for that matter Byzantine ones also, were in a hopelessly inferior logistical position. Limitations of the radius of action of their galleys meant that all the war fleets and corsairs of Islam could ever do was to make brief raiding forays on to the sea lanes of the trunk routes. They could never establish themselves in any numbers for extended periods

---

[112] Braudel, *Mediterranean*, pp. 880–1; Earle, *Corsairs*, p. 58; Fontenay & Tenenti, 'Course et piraterie', p. 86.   [113] See below, pp. 165–7.
[114] Ahrweiler, 'Course et piraterie', pp. 9–11.
[115] Yarrison, *Force as an instrument of policy*, passim.

of time across the routes in the crucial focal zones. Over the entire sea the logistical position of Muslim naval forces approximated that of Egypt vis-à-vis the Crusader states in the twelfth century. The Christian West, however, and particularly the Genoese, Venetians, and Barcelonese, could and did maintain a continuous naval presence along the trunk routes. The consequences were predictable. Trade follows the flag, or, put in a medieval context, trade flourished only where backed by sea power. Muslim ships, and to a considerable degree Byzantine ones also, could not use the trunk routes safely or easily. Ibn Jubayr travelled on Genoese ships not because there were no Muslim ships available but because it was safer and more convenient to travel on Christian ships, which both could use the navigationally safer, quicker, and more comfortable trunk routes and also were less vulnerable to corsair attack.[116] Muslim shipping attempting to operate along the trunk routes was exposed continuously to spoliation by a plethora of Western corsairs.

As we saw above, neither Muslim nor Greek shipping desisted entirely from trans-Mediterranean traffic along the trunk routes. And, just as was the case with treaties between Byzantium and the West, commercial treaties between the Western maritime powers and various Muslim states specifically permitted reciprocal commercial contacts.[117] If Muslim ships did not voyage to the ports of the Christian West on a scale equal to that of voyages of Western ships to the Muslim world, this was so, at least in part, because the waters of the trunk routes were extremely unsafe for them. The same was true for Byzantine shipping. It was the dangers of operating along the major sea lanes, rather than any simple lack of ships, which gave rise to practices whereby Muslims and Greeks travelled on Western ships, sent their cargoes on them, leased them, or actually bought and owned shares in them. However, even these recourses had their dangers. A Christian flag did not protect the person or merchandise of a Muslim if the ship were taken by Christian corsairs.[118] Moreover, ships'

[116] Cf. Gateau, 'Voyage d'Ibn Jubayr', pp. 290–2.
[117] Colom, 'Navegaciones mediterraneas', p. 46; L. de Mas Latrie, *Traités de paix et de commerce et documents divers concernant les relations des Chrétiens avec les Arabes de l'Afrique septentrionale au moyen-âge* (Paris, 1866), vol. 2, pp. 54, 64, 120, 124, 155, etc.
[118] Braudel, *Mediterranean*, pp. 867–8; Bresc, 'Course et piraterie en Sicile', p. 754; Colom, 'Navegaciones mediterraneas', pp. 53–4; Dufourcq, 'Chrétiens et musulmans', p. 215; Heers, 'Royaume de Grenade', pp. 90, 100; Unali, *Marinai*, p. 143.

masters were not above selling Muslim passengers into slavery.[119] Ships leased by Muslims or in which Muslims owned shares might still be plundered by Western corsairs even when sailing under a Western flag with which the corsair legally had no quarrel.[120] But even if not by any means completely effective, the use of practices such as these, as also the acquisition of citizenship of Western cities by Greeks,[121] reveals a systematic attempt by Muslims and Greeks to overcome the formidable obstacles which deterred them from operating their own ships along the trunk routes.

In 1450 the Mamluk sultan of Egypt commandeered a Ragusan ship in Alexandria harbour to convey an Egyptian envoy to Cyprus and to bring back grain from there and from Asia Minor.[122] This incident and others of a similar nature have been interpreted as evidence of a fundamental decline in the Egyptian merchant marine, of a simple lack of ships in Mamluk Egypt.[123] But in fact this is not at all what the incident reflected. A Mamluk sultan could always lay his hands on a ship if he wanted one. Rather it reflected the dangers which were to be faced by Egyptian ships in the waters around Cyprus and north to the Lycian coast. The sultan's motives were the same as those of Ibn Jubayr three centuries earlier. It was simply safer and more convenient to send the envoy on a Christian ship. When, fourteen years later, in 1464, an Egyptian envoy *was* sent to Cyprus on an Egyptian ship, he was captured by corsairs.[124] This is not to suggest that amongst all the known cases where Muslim rulers commandeered Western ships for their own purposes, there was never one where the motive was a temporary lack of Muslim ships, or at least of *suitable* Muslim ships. Specific types of ships were often needed for particular purposes and it may well have happened that occasionally a Muslim ruler did not have at his disposal the specific type of ship needed for the purpose he had in mind. To suggest otherwise would be to go too far and the circumstances of some cases suggest otherwise. After all, even in the Christian West, some rulers, such as Charles I of Anjou, king of Sicily, were forced on occasions to commandeer or

[119] Ashtor, *Levant trade*, pp. 223, 450; Braudel, *Mediterranean*, pp. 868–9; de Mas Latrie, *Traités de paix*, vol. 2, pp. 228–30; Piloti, *Traité*, pp. 229–30; Unali, *Marinai*, pp. 142–3.

[120] Dufourcq, 'Relations', p. 50; Unali, *Marinai*, p. 122.

[121] Laiou-Thomadakis, 'Byzantine economy', p. 212.

[122] Krekic, *Dubrovnik*, pp. 85–6.

[123] Ashtor, 'L'ascendant technologique', pp. 406–7; Ashtor, 'Economic decline', p. 283.   [124] Ashtor, *Levant trade*, p. 450.

negotiate a forced lease of particular types of ships temporarily unavailable to them in their own domains and needed for particular purposes. However, in the main, Muslim rulers did have available ships of their own subjects. When they used Western ships, they did so for more complex reasons. The practice in fact long predated any disappearance of Muslim shipping from Mediterranean traffic. In the middle of the eleventh century travellers from the Muslim West were already using Western ships to make the voyage to the Levant.[125] In 1192 Genoese corsairs seized a Venetian ship bound for Constantinople from Egypt carrying envoys from Saladin to the Byzantine emperor.[126] There is no question here that Saladin's envoys could have travelled on a Muslim ship had he wished them to do so. The sultan certainly had access to a ship for the purpose, even after the loss of his Egyptian fleet in Acre in 1191. Rather, Saladin chose to send his envoys on a Venetian ship because it was safer to do so given the infestation of the seas by Western corsairs, merchantmen, and war fleets. As it happened his precautions availed his envoys little. In the Muslim West similar sorts of situations occurred. In 1247 the emir of Tunis did send ambassadors to Genoa on a Muslim galley.[127] In the late thirteenth and early fourteenth centuries, when envoys from Maghrebin rulers to Aragon travelled to Barcelona on Catalan ships, they did so not because their masters could not lay their hands on a ship for the purpose but rather because their destination lay in waters in which no Muslim ship was safe.[128] When commercial treaties between Maghrebin rulers and Western powers gave those rulers the right to commandeer Western ships if necessary, they did so not because of any inadequacy in the Maghrebin merchant marine and lack of skill of Muslim seamen,[129] but because for certain purposes it was safer and easier for Muslims to travel on, and to ship cargoes on, Western ships.[130]

Obviously, no single factor explains the rise to predominance of the maritime traffic of the Christian West in the Middle Ages. I do not pretend that it does. It is interesting that Ibn Khaldūn explained it on the grounds of 'cultural' factors lying behind Muslim decline at sea: the influence of the desert Bedouin mentality and the political

[125] Cahen, *Orient et Occident*, p. 38.
[126] Charanis, 'Piracy in the Aegean', pp. 127–8.
[127] Pistarino, 'Genova e l'Islam', p. 204.
[128] Dufourcq, *L'Espagne catalane*, pp. 97, 145–6, 241–2, 444, 501–2.
[129] Ashtor, 'L'ascendant technologique', p. 406.
[130] De Mas Latrie, *Traités de paix*, vol. 2, pp. 52, 60–1, 117, 120, 125, 138–9, 254, 356.

weakness of Muslim powers.[131] Amongst modern historians, Ayalon would follow Ibn Khaldūn's first path, emphasizing the influence of the Turkish cavalry mentality in Mamluk Egypt.[132] Malowist and Santamaría Arández follow his second path, emphasizing the importance of political fragmentation and internal conflict within the Muslim world in general.[133] But since there is no doubt that internal fragmentation and conflict was much greater in the Christian West than in the Muslim world, it seems extremely hard to see how this can possibly be adduced as the cause of Muslim loss of maritime power. Ashtor wishes to explain it by the technological superiority of European industry and the shipping of the Christian West. The case for industry appears to be well proven, but, as we saw above,[134] that for shipping seems much less so. Certainly the case for a superiority in naval architecture and maritime technology by the Christian West over the Muslim world of such dimensions that it created cost efficiencies, navigational advantages, and freight securities of an order to lead to the demise of the Muslim merchant marine remains to be proven. But in any case the question of technological inferiority of the Muslim merchant marine is a false one. The processes by which the Christian West acquired its predominance in trans-Mediterranean traffic began in the twelfth century and were well advanced, if not complete, by the late fourteenth century, when the cog and great galley became common in merchant fleets of the West. Up to that time there is no question that both Greeks and Muslims had ships just as good as the light galleys and lateen-rigged round ships of the West. Yet they were unable to compete, if indeed they attempted to compete at all, with the ships and merchants of the West. The causes of the predominance of Western over Muslim shipping in trans-Mediterranean traffic lie not in technological superiority but elsewhere. Even ships every bit as good as those of the West would have made no difference whatsoever to the vulnerability of Muslim shipping to the cloud of Western corsairs, merchantmen, and war fleets along the trunk routes. Even if Muslims had begun, or did begin, to use cogs, carracks, and great galleys as soon as the Christian West, that would not have been altered. Muslim shipping and maritime traffic would have needed many other strengths to offset the advantages possessed

---

[131] See above, p. 142.
[132] Ayalon, 'Mamluks and naval warfare', pp. 5–6.
[133] Malowist, 'Expansion Européene', p. 155; Santamaría Arandez, 'Reconquista', pp. 50–5.   [134] See above, pp. 44–6, 67–9.

naturally by that of the Christian West if they were to match the growth of the latter in the high and later Middle Ages.

The degree of the West's advantage may be suggested by consideration of structural relativities and cost efficiencies in maritime traffic; although here, it must be admitted, we enter largely into the realm of hypothesis. Confined mainly to the southern routes along the African coasts of the sea from the twelfth century onwards, Muslim shipping between the Levant and the western Mediterranean must have suffered from severe structural inefficiencies by comparison to the merchant marines of the West. Was it the case that Ibn Jubayr was induced to travel on a Genoese ship from Ceuta to Alexandria in 1183 not only because the Genoese ship would be relatively immune from Christian corsairs along the trunk routes but also because it could be expected to make a faster passage than a Muslim ship forced to use the southern coastal routes and would have a greater expectation of reaching its destination safely since it would not have to brave the dangers of offshore navigational hazards for 2000 miles along a lee shore? For voyages from east to west the navigational advantages of the trunk routes over the southern coastal routes must have been even greater because of the adverse prevailing winds. These advantages must have created cost efficiencies for shipping able to use the trunk routes because of faster passage times and less frequent losses from shipwreck. However, without extensive series of data to make comparisons of passage times and to compare rates of loss of shipping by wreck, this cost efficiency/inefficiency cannot be quantified. Perhaps more extensive research in both Muslim and European archives may lead to such a quantification. The Datini archives suggest themselves as one source. However, at present it is not possible. Alternatively, if archival research ultimately fails to provide data to make such a quantification possible, then perhaps a theoretical quantification can be produced through mathematical model techniques. It ought to be possible to feed into hypothetical voyages known data about navigational hazards, prevailing winds, currents, and changing daily weather patterns derived from modern geographical, navigational, and meteorological sources and thus to arrive at some theoretical differential between the cost efficiencies of voyages along the southern coasts and those along the trunk routes. When Muslim merchants in the later Middle Ages travelled on Christian ships, bought shares in them, leased them, and shipped cargoes on them, did they do so solely to avoid the dangers of Western corsairs along the trunk routes, or was it that their motives were related also to costs and profits? Could they make more profit by doing so than by using Muslim shipping because of the cost efficiencies of the trunk routes?

7. The Turks

The Christian stranglehold on the waters of the trunk routes in the eastern Mediterranean was ended in the thirteenth century when the Seljuq sultan Kai-Khusrau I broke out of the confines of the Anatolian plateau through to the Bay of Attalya during the chaos which engulfed the Byzantine empire after the Fourth Crusade. He captured Attalya in 1207 and, following this Seljuq seizure of a Mediterranean coastline, the Turks quickly took to the sea. Indeed it is quite remarkable just how soon after their acquisition of a coastline the sources record Turkish ships and seamen. These Muslims were certainly not restrained by their non-maritime cultural heritage from appreciating the sea. Letters exchanged between Hugh I of Cyprus and Kai-Kā'ūs I in 1214–16 refer to Turkish merchants and ships in the Mediterranean and to ships of the sultan.[1] Clearly, Seljuq merchants and their ships began to ply the waters south to Cyprus, and perhaps to Egypt, in this period. Whether Turkish corsairs also began to operate in Levantine waters at the same time is not clear. Kai-Qubādh I pushed east along the coast to Alanya between 1220 and 1227,[2] and the superb naval arsenal which he built at Alanya was almost certainly intended for the maintenance of corsair flotillas or coastguard patrols.[3] The Persian chronicler Ibn Bībī referred to an emir of the coasts, *amīr-i sawāḥil*, who may possibly have commanded

---

[1] A. G. C. Savvides, *Byzantium in the Near East: its relations with the Seljuk Sultanate of Rum in Asia Minor the Armenians of Cilicia and the Mongols A.D. c. 1192–1237* (Thessalonica, 1981), pp. 140–5.

[2] C. Cahen, 'The Turks in Iran and Anatolia before the Mongol invasions', in Wolff & Hazard, *The later Crusades*, 661–92, here p. 682; C. Cahen, *Pre-Ottoman Turkey* (London, 1968), pp. 124–5; M. Th. Houtsma, 'Ueber eine Türkische Chronik zur Geschichte des Seljúqen Klein-Asiens', *Actes du Sixième Congrès international des Orientalistes tenu en 1883 à Leide*, part II (Leiden, 1884), 367–84, here pp. 381–3; Savvides, *Byzantium in the Near East*, pp. 87–8, 152–4.

[3] R. M. Riefstahl, *Turkish architecture in Southwestern Anatolia* (Cambridge, Mass., 1931), pp. 57–60 and plates 101, 106–9; S. Lloyd & D. Storm Rice, *Alanya ('Alā'iyya)* (London, 1958), pp. 16–18, fig. 5, and plates 1, 2, 5.

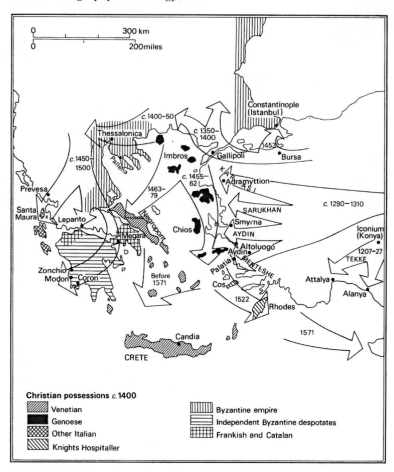

Major naval engagements
x – Christian victories
o – Muslim victories

Amorgos (1312)	x	Smyrna (1344)	x	Negropont (1470)	o
Chios (1319)	x	Imbros (1347)	x	Zonchio (1499)	o
Rhodes (1320)	x	Megara (1359)	x	Zonchio (1500)	o
Adramyttion (1334)	x	Attalya (1362)	x	Prevesa (1538)	o
Pallena (1344)	x	Gallipoli (1416)	x	Lepanto (1571)	x

Figure 28 The Turkish advance, *c.* 1200–1571

Seljuq ships in the Mediterranean around 1220–40,[4] and Alanya was within ideal striking range of the seas around Cyprus and Rhodes, through which the main Western shipping lanes to Egypt and the Holy Land ran. Perhaps fortunately for Christendom, the potential threat to the shipping of the West posed by this Turkish coastline was not fulfilled. In their last years the Seljuqs were fully occupied with affairs on their eastern borders and in the west seem to have been more interested in promoting the economic development of their domains by encouraging Western merchants and ships to visit their Mediterranean ports than in waging *jihād* against them at sea.[5] Then, in 1243, the Seljuq state was swept away by the Mongols, leaving a patchwork of *ghazi* emirates whose thirteenth-century history is shrouded in obscurity.[6] Not until late in the century were these *ghazi* emirs able to extend Turkish control of the coasts to the south-west and western coasts of Asia Minor. Only when they did so did Christian sources begin to show evidence of a Turkish corsair menace. By 1278 a Muslim pirate, one Saladinus, was operating from Ania, to the south of Ephesus, and by 1284 the raids of Turkish corsairs had extended to the Cyclades, the Sea of Marmara, and the Black Sea. In 1300 they were pillaging Chios.[7]

In the fourteenth century the operations of these Turkish corsairs were stepped up enormously. Perhaps as early as 1306–9 Marino Sanudo Torsello was already lamenting the depredations of the *ghazis* against the Kingdom of Armenia, Cyprus, and the Latins of the Aegean islands.[8] By *c.* 1330 Umur Pasha, who became emir of Aydin from 1334 to 1348, had made the fleet of Aydin, based at Smyrna and at Altoluogo, medieval Ephesus, the terror of the Aegean.[9] Ibn

[4] C. H. Imber, 'Ḳurṣān: II. In Turkish waters', in *The encyclopaedia of Islam*, new edn, vol. 5, ed. C. E. Bosworth et al. (Leiden, 1980–3), 505–7, here p. 505.

[5] Cf. M. E. Martin, 'The Venetian–Seljuk treaty of 1220', *English Historical Review*, 95 (1980), 321–30; Savvides, *Byzantium in the Near East*, p. 140.

[6] Cahen, *Pre-Ottoman Turkey*, pp. 125–32, 308–9; Cahen, *Orient et Occident*, p. 181; P. Lemerle, *L'émirat d'Aydin, Byzance, et l'Occident: recherches sur «La geste d'Umur Pacha»* (Paris, 1957), pp. 10–11; P. Wittek, *Das Fürstentum Mentesche: Studie zur Geschichte West-Kleinasiens im 13.-15. Jh.* (Istanbul, 1934), pp. 15–57. N. Roger, *En Asie Mineure: la Turquie du Ghazi* (Paris, 1930) was not available to me.   [7] Imber, 'Ḳurṣān: II', p. 505.

[8] Marino Sanudo, *Liber secretorum*, I.4.4 (p. 29), I.5.2 (p. 32).

[9] Foss, *Ephesus*, pp. 144–52; Heyd, *Histoire du commerce*, vol. 1, pp. 535–6; Imber, 'Ḳurṣān: II', pp. 505–6; Lemerle, *L'émirat d'Aydin*, pp. 50–64, 75, 84, 96, 127; Wittek, *Fürstentum Mentesche*, pp. 35–41; P. Wittek, *The rise of the Ottoman empire* (London, 1938), pp. 35–6.

Battuta and Nicephorus Gregoras testified to the raids of his galleys against shipping and islands, seizing booty and slaves and levying tribute.[10] At Palatia, medieval Miletus, to the south of Aydin, the fleet of the emirate of Menteshe was only comparatively less feared. Attalya was the seaport of the emirate of Tekke and Alanya was held by the Karamanids.[11] To the north, the emirate of Sarukhan held the coast of Phocaea and that of Karasi had a seaport at Adramyttion.[12] From this series of bases along the south and west coasts of Asia Minor the *ghazi* corsairs could strike easily at Byzantine and Western shipping along focal sectors of the trunk routes to Constantinople and the Black Sea and from Crete east to the Levant. Their final conquest of all the southern and western coasts of Asia Minor in the years *c.* 1290–1310 gave the Turks a strategic and logistical advantage such as Islam had not possessed in the eastern Mediterranean since the loss of Cyprus and Crete to the Byzantines in 961–5.

Assessment of the dimensions of the *ghazi* threat to Byzantine and Western maritime traffic in the fourteenth century is complicated by the fact that it was Christian as much as Muslim corsairs who turned the Aegean and eastern Mediterranean into a no-man's-land at this time.[13] Nevertheless, the *Dürstürnāme-i Enverī*, the *Song of Umur Pasha*, showed Umur attacking Western shipping around the Dardanelles in 1329, off Negropont in 1333, and in the Gulf of Volos in 1339 or 1340.[14] An array of evidence from Latin sources reported attacks on Western shipping by the Turks and in the 1340s the Great Council of Crete was lamenting the effects of the Turkish corsairs on

[10] Ibn Battuta, *The travels of Ibn Battuta, A.D. 1325–1354*, trans. H. A. R. Gibb (Hakluyt Soc. Works. Second series, 110, 117, 141) (Cambridge, 1958–71), vol. 2, pp. 445–6; Nicephorus Gregoras, *Byzantina historia*, ed. L. Schopenus & I. Bekker (Bonn, 1829–55), vol. 2, pp. 597–8.

[11] Cahen, *Pre-Ottoman Turkey*, pp. 299, 304; *Encyclopaedia of Islam*, ed. M. Th. Houtsma et al. (Leiden, 1913–31) under *Teke-Oghlu* and *Adalia*; Heyd, *Histoire du commerce*, vol. 1, pp. 534–5; Ibn Battuta, *Travels*, vol. 2, pp. 416–21; Wittek, *Fürstentum Mentesche*, pp. 15–57; Wittek, *Rise of the Ottoman empire*, pp. 34–5.

[12] Cahen, *Pre-Ottoman Turkey*, p. 309; Heyd, *Histoire du commerce*, vol. 1, p. 536; Lemerle, *L'émirat d'Aydin*, under *Qaresi, Saruhan, Yahşi*; Wittek, *Fürstentum Mentesche*, pp. 20–1.

[13] Ahrweiler, 'Course et piraterie', pp. 9–10, 20–2; Ashtor, *Levant trade*, p. 391; Balard, *Romanie Génoise*, pp. 587–98; Charanis, 'Piracy in the Aegean'; Favreau, 'Italienische Levante-Piraterie'; D. Jacoby, 'Les gens de mer dans la marine de guerre vénitienne de la Mer Egée aux XIV\^e et XV\^e siècles', in Ragosta, *Le genti del mare mediterraneo*, 169–201, here pp. 171–2; Tenenti, 'Venezia e la pirateria', pp. 747–66; Thiriet, *Romanie Vénitienne*, pp. 243–7.

[14] Lemerle, *L'émirat d'Aydin*, pp. 58–9, 84, 127.

business.[15] In 1339 Venice had to arm passengers to help the crews defend their ships and also to order ships' masters to resist rather than to surrender.[16] Genoa also insisted that her ships be armed and sail in convoy.[17] Both Genoa and Venice sent out armed escort galleys and established galley patrols and naval arsenals on their island possessions.[18] Departures were often delayed when corsairs were reported in the offing and the use of maritime insurance increased, with rates multiplying.[19] When describing the littoral of the southern coast of Asia Minor, Marino Sanudo Torsello was very conscious of the degree of security from Turkish corsairs offered by the various ports along the coast.[20] Genoa, Venice, and also their island possessions acting independently hastened to conclude treaties with Aydin and Menteshe and to establish consulates in Altoluogo and Palatia in attempts to protect their maritime traffic.[21]

The threat to Western shipping was certainly a real one, but in the fourteenth century the Christian powers of Genoa, Venice, the Hospitallers of Rhodes, and various Crusading Holy Leagues were able to contain it. Until their final absorption by the Ottomans, the *ghazi* emirates did not win a single major fleet engagement against the forces of the Christian West. Divided amongst themselves and engaged in a ruthless struggle for supremacy, none of them could muster sufficient strength at sea to succeed in open battle. As was seen above,[22] in the main their ships were smaller galleys, *kalite*, *qayīq*, and *iğribār*, rather than full-sized *kadīrge*, and these lighter galleys could

---

[15] Foss, *Ephesus*, p. 155; Heyd, *Histoire du commerce*, vol. 1, pp. 538, 545–6; A. Luttrell, 'The Hospitallers at Rhodes, 1306–1421', in Hazard, *The fourteenth and fifteenth centuries*, 278–313, here p. 287; A. Luttrell, 'Venice and the Knights Hospitallers of Rhodes in the fourteenth century', *Papers of the British School at Rome*, 26 (1958), 195–212, here p. 205; Tenenti, 'Venezia e la pirateria', pp. 721–3; Thiriet, *Romanie Vénitienne*, pp. 244–7; Thiriet 'Itineraires', p. 598.

[16] Tenenti, 'Venezia e la pirateria', pp. 757–8; Thiriet, *Romanie Vénitienne*, p. 244.

[17] Balard, *Romanie Génoise*, p. 596.

[18] Balard, *Romanie Génoise*, p. 597; Jacoby, 'Gens de mer', pp. 172–3, 189, 193 *et passim*; Tenenti, 'Venezia e la pirateria', pp. 747–66; Thiriet, *Romanie Vénitienne*, pp. 247–51.   [19] Balard, *Romanie Génoise*, p. 596.

[20] Marino Sanudo, *Liber Secretorum*, II.4.26 (pp. 88–90).

[21] Foss, *Ephesus*, pp. 151–5; Lemerle, *L'émirat d'Aydin*, pp. 229–35; Luttrell, 'Venice and the Knights Hospitallers', p. 206; Thiriet, *Romanie Vénitienne*, p. 246; Wittek, *Fürstentum Mentesche*, pp. 71–2; E. A. Zachariadou, 'Sept traités inédits entre Venise et les émirats d'Aydin et de Menteşe (1331–1407)', in *Studi Ottomani e pre-Ottomani* (Naples, 1976), pp. 229–40; E. A. Zachariadou, 'Prix et marchés des céréales en Romanie (1343–1405)', *Nuova rivista storica*, 61 (1977), 291–306, here pp. 294–7.   [22] See above, pp. 67–8.

not stand in formal battle against the heavier, well-armed *galee sottili* of the Christian West. In a later period, Ottoman fleets continued to include large numbers of *kalite* and were still inferior to *galee sottili* in open battle.[23] It also seems probable, if unprovable, that *ghazi* fleets always lacked the experience and discipline necessary to overcome the fierce determination and long training of the Hospitallers and Venetians in particular. Thus the Hospitallers won victories over Menteshe off Amorgos in 1312, off Rhodes in 1320, and over Aydin off Chios in 1319. In 1334 Umur Pasha was defeated and the fleet of Sarukhan was annihilated off Adramyttion. A Holy League fleet won a victory off Pallena and burnt the fleet of Aydin at Smyrna in 1344. Christian victories continued off Imbros in 1347 and Megara in 1359. The Hospitallers scored a final success over a squadron from Alanya in 1362.[24] Unable to defeat the battle fleets of the Christian West, the *ghazi* emirs were confined to Asia Minor and unable to occupy permanently any of the islands, which were the key to control of the shipping lanes. From bases in the islands on the other hand, Christian corsairs such as the Gattilusi of Mitilini could operate easily against any Muslim shipping; and also against Greek and Western shipping for that matter. The maritime powers could throw up screens of convoy escorts and galley patrols to ensure the safety of their own shipping along the sea lanes. In the south, the Hospitallers of Rhodes, the Venetians of Crete, and the royal galleys of the Kingdom of Cyprus succeeded to a large degree in protecting Western shipping along the sea lanes to Egypt and the Levant from the threat of Turkish corsairs. They were less successful in protecting it from the depredations of Western corsairs, particularly the Catalans. The potential offered to Islam by the superb geographical location of the *ghazi* emirates was never realized in the fourteenth century, and the struggle between the two faiths at sea in the Aegean became balanced and very confused.

In fact there is nothing to suggest that any of the *ghazi* emirs was ever concerned to develop maritime commerce on the part of his own

---

[23] Guilmartin, *Gunpowder and galleys*, p. 47.
[24] Foss, *Ephesus*, p. 145; Heyd, *Histoire du commerce*, vol. 1, pp. 538–9; G. Hill, *A history of Cyprus. Vols. 2 & 3: The Frankish period 1192–1571* (Cambridge, 1948), pp. 298, 320–3; Lemerle, *L'émirat d'Aydin*, pp. 96–9, 187–9, 202 and n. 2; Luttrell, 'Hospitallers at Rhodes', pp. 287–9, 293–7; Luttrell, 'Venice and the Knights Hospitallers', pp. 206 and n. 115; A. Luttrell, 'Gregory XI and the Turks: 1370–1378', *Orientalia Christiana periodica*, 46 (1980), 391–417, here p. 398; Wittek, *Fürstentum Mentesche*, pp. 55, 65.

subjects. Consequently they had no need to secure the sea lanes for Muslim shipping. From the earliest days of Islam, *ghazis* had had as their objectives winning glory in battle, enriching themselves with slaves and booty, and aggrandizing their states in any way possible. For the emirs of the fourteenth century, the use of sea power was but a means to those ends. Commerce raiding was only one such means, and not necessarily the best one. Indeed the *ghazi* fleets were used as much or more for ravaging Byzantine and Western possessions for slaves and booty and for extracting tribute. As early as 1318 corsairs from Anatolia raided Santorini.[25] Umur Pasha raided Chios in 1330, Gallipoli in 1332, Negropont, Boudonitsa, and the Peloponnesus in 1333, the Peloponnesus again in 1335, Athens, Thebes, and Naxos in 1339, the mouth of the Danube in 1341, and Thrace in 1343–4. The emirs of Menteshe were only marginally less enterprising.[26] Altoluogo and Palatia became important centres of the slave trade.[27] In 1333, in Altoluogo, Ibn Battuta 'bought in this city a Greek slavegirl, a virgin, for forty gold dinars'.[28] But although such raiding expeditions were both profitable and directly in the *ghazi* tradition, they did little to affect the dominance of the Christian West over maritime traffic along the sea lanes.

War, piracy, privateering, and peaceful maritime traffic had always existed coterminously in relations between Islam and Christendom. The fourteenth century was no exception to the rule and although the corsairs of the *ghazi* emirates never ceased their depredations against Christian shipping, Western merchants quickly penetrated the markets of Attalya, Palatia, and Altoluogo.[29] Arguably, the development of Western commercial relations with the emirates and the establishment of colonies of Western merchants in their ports was a major influence on mitigating their piratical nature; as perhaps it had been in the case of earlier Muslim societies, as we saw above.[30] Under the terms of agreements with Genoa and Venice the emirs of Menteshe and Aydin undertook to suppress their corsairs' operations against

[25] Imber, 'Ḳurṣān: II', p. 505.
[26] Lemerle, *L'émirat d'Aydin*, pp. 247–53 *et passim*; Wittek, *Fürstentum Mentesche*, pp. 46–7, 56–7, 65, 74–5 *et passim*.
[27] Foss, *Ephesus*, pp. 147, 153; Heyd, *Histoire du commerce*, vol. 1, p. 545; Thiriet, *Romanie Vénitienne*, p. 335; C. Verlinden, 'Venezia e il commercio degli schiavi provenienti dalle coste orientali del Mediterraneo', in Pertusi, *Venezia e il Levante*, 911–29, here pp. 914–15. [28] Ibn Battuta, *Travels*, vol. 2, p. 444.
[29] Tenenti, 'Venezia e la pirateria', pp. 719–23; Thiriet, 'Itinéraires', pp. 597–8.
[30] See above, pp. 108–9, 131.

the shipping of the two cities.[31] Alanya and Attalya became major centres for commerce between Anatolia and Egypt.[32] Much of it was in Western hands and Ibn Battuta reported on the fortified quarter of the Christian merchants in Attalya.[33] Palatia and Altoluogo became emporia for the export of grain, cattle, horses, mastic, alum, cotton, spices, and slaves to the Aegean islands and the West.[34] Altoluogo operated as an exchange point between Genoese Chios and Venetian possessions.[35] Both ports were marked regularly on Italian portolan charts, mentioned in the portolans themselves, and, together with Attalya, figured prominently in Pegolotti's *Pratica della mercatura*.[36] Menteshe, Aydin, and Sarukhan struck gold and silver coins with Latin inscriptions in imitation of Western issues in efforts to stimulate commerce with the West.[37]

The threat to Western dominance of the sea lanes presented by the Turkish acquisition of a North Mediterranean coastline thus never fully materialized in the thirteenth and fourteenth centuries for a variety of social, political, and economic reasons. Once again, the nexus between geography and technology was not a determinant of the course of direction of history but merely one influence on it. In spite of the Turks' superb geographical location, ideally suited to the logistical requirements of a galley operated *guerre de course*, for reasons related both to the internal history and character of the Seljuq sultanate and its successor emirates as well as to the superior qualities

[31] Balard, *Romanie Génoise*, pp. 170, 470–1; Balard, 'Bataille du Bosphore', p. 444; Foss, *Ephesus*, pp. 152–60; Heyd, *Histoire du commerce*, vol. 1, pp. 543–6; Lemerle, *L'émirat d'Aydin*, pp. 230–5; Tenenti, 'Venezia e la pirateria', pp. 721–2; Thiriet, *Romanie Vénitienne*, pp. 175, 207, 335–6, 356.

[32] Heyd, *Histoire du commerce*, vol. 1, pp. 547–9; Inalcik, *Ottoman empire*, pp. 127–8; H. Inalcik 'Bursa and the commerce of the Levant', *Journal of the economic and social history of the Orient*, 3 (1960), 131–47.

[33] Ibn Battuta, *Travels*, vol. 2, pp. 417–18.

[34] Balard, *Romanie Génoise*, pp. 170, 174, 759–60; J. Day, *Les douanes de Gênes 1376–1377* (Paris, 1963), pp. 271–3, 693, 737, 874, 928; Heyd, *Histoire du commerce*, vol. 1, pp. 542, 545; Krekic, *Dubrovnik*, nos. 349, 371, 372, 374, 379, 397, 400, 405, 410, 417, 419; R. Morozzo della Rocca, ed., *Lettere di mercanti a Pignol Zucchello (1336–1350)* (Venice, 1957), pp. 16, 23, 54, 73, 92, 93, 100; Piloti, *Traité*, p. 156; Thiriet, *Romanie Vénitienne*, p. 336; Thiriet, 'Itineraires', p. 597.

[35] Balard, *Romanie Génoise*, p. 779; Thiriet, *Romanie Vénitienne*, p. 336.

[36] F. di Balducci Pegolotti, *La pratica della mercatura*, ed. A. P. Evans (New York, 1970), pp. 43, 55–8, 92, 104, 293, 369–70, 376; *Portolan des Gratiosus Benincasa*, in Kretschmer, *Italienischen Portolane*, pp. 395–6, 413; *Portolan Rizo*, in Kretschmer, *Italienischen Portolane*, p. 521.

[37] Balard, *Romanie Génoise*, p. 667; Heyd, *Histoire du commerce*, vol. 1, p. 546; Thiriet, *Romanie Vénitienne*, p. 307.

of Western battle fleets, the Western maritime powers were able to contain the threat of the *ghazi* corsairs to their freedom of movement along the sea lanes. Not until one of their number, the Ottoman sultanate, managed to unify the *ghazi* emirates were the potentialities of the Turkish position realized.

Bayezid I, 'The Thunderbolt', swept through the emirates in 1390 but the Ottoman sultanate itself was temporarily annihilated by Tamerlane in 1402. The families of the *ghazi* emirs were reinstated in their possessions and a period of chaos ensued to which the Ottomans could not put an end until Murad II did so in 1424.

As *ghazis* themselves, the Ottomans followed policies similar to those of the emirates in their relations with the powers of the Christian West. Like Aydin and Menteshe, they had early had commercial contacts with Genoa. Genoa reached agreement with the Ottomans in 1352, giving her a monopoly over the alum mines of Magnesia, and then in 1387 concluded a general commercial treaty with Murad I.[38] In 1390 Bayezid I confirmed the commercial privileges which both Genoa and Venice had had in Altoluogo and Palatia during the rule of his emir predecessors.[39] In the fifteenth century, the Ottomans continued to allow Europeans to trade with their territories and Bursa, their capital, became an important entrepôt between Asia and the West.[40] Ottoman merchants themselves frequented Western commercial outposts in the Aegean islands, particularly Chios.[41] Throughout the Ottoman domains in Asia Minor and the Balkans, Western merchants sought the spices, dyes, drugs, precious cloths, and porcelain of Asia as well as the grain of Anatolia and Rumelia in exchange for the industrial products of the West, especially the fine woollen cloths of England, Flanders, and Tuscany.[42] As long as the customs duties were paid and the states from which they came

---

[38] Balard, *Romanie Génoise*, pp. 97–8, 174; L. T. Belgrano, *Documenti riguardanti la colonia genovese di Pera* (Genoa, 1888), no. 175 (pp. 146–9); Inalcik, *Ottoman empire*, p. 134; D. Zakythinos, 'L'attitude de Venise face au déclin et à la chute de Constantinople', in H. G. Beck et al., eds., *Venezia: centro di mediazione tra Oriente e Occidente (secoli XV–XVI); aspetti e problemi* (Florence, 1977), vol. 1, 61–75, here p. 64.

[39] Foss, *Ephesus*, p. 162; Thiriet, *Romanie Vénitienne*, p. 356; Wittek, *Fürstentum Mentesche*, p. 82. [40] Heers, *Gênes*, pp. 379–81; Inalcik, 'Bursa', *passim*.

[41] Heers, *Gênes*, pp. 379–81, 399–403.

[42] Balard, *Romanie Génoise*, pp. 752–3, 773–4; Inalcik, 'Bursa', p. 137; Krekic, *Dubrovnik*, pp. 43–8, 54, 85, 94; Luttrell, 'Venice and the Knights Hospitallers', p. 200; Piloti, *Traité*, pp. 155–6; Thiriet, *Romanie Vénitienne*, pp. 373, 426–7; Zakythinos, 'L'attitude de Venise', pp. 64–74.

remained friendly towards the sultans, Western merchants were welcomed. Venice for her part attempted to remain neutral between Byzantium and the Ottomans and to defuse conflict between the two powers of Romania in order to preserve conditions for her own commerce.[43] In the Ottoman mind, however, peaceful commerce coexisted with *jihād*, the *ghazw*, and *guerre de course*. The traditional themes of Mediterranean maritime history became manifest once again.[44] In his *History of the maritime wars of the Turks*, Haji Khalifeh wrote that: before the time of the late illustrious and victorious Sultan Mohammed [Mehmed II, 'The Conqueror'], the Ottomans had not ventured to undertake naval expeditions, or to engage with the European nations. It is indeed related that in the time of Sultan Murad the Second, they occasionally made excursions to the neighbouring shores and islands; but these expeditions are not worth enumerating.[45]

Haji Khalifeh probably knew little about these earlier expeditions, and consequently took his point of departure with Mehmed II's building of a fleet for the conquest of Constantinople in 1453. However, long before that the Ottomans had in fact been continuing the *ghazi* tradition of both *guerre de course* against Christian shipping and *ghazw* operations by their fleet against Christian possessions. The maritime campaigns of Murad II (1421–44) were by no means 'not worth enumerating', as Haji Khalifeh thought. Immediately after his conquest of Aydin, Menteshe, and Karasi, Bayezid I gave a better organization to the corsairs and a new wave of Turkish privateering in the Aegean followed.[46] At the same time he began to build up an Ottoman fleet into which the corsairs and their ships were incorporated. This Ottoman fleet remained active throughout the period to 1453.[47] As early as 1391, 60 ships were sent on a cruise to Chios and

[43] Thiriet, *Romanie Vénitienne*, pp. 354, 373.
[44] Cf. Tenenti, 'Venezia e la pirateria', pp. 719–23.
[45] Haji Khalifeh, *Maritime wars*, p. 12.
[46] Ashtor, *Levant trade*, pp. 119, 215; De Clavijo, *Embassy*, p. 20; Foss, *Ephesus*, p. 166; Imber, 'Ḳurṣān: II', p. 506; H. Inalcik, 'An outline of Ottoman–Venetian relations', in Beck, *Venezia*, vol. 1, 83–90, here p. 85; Tenenti, 'Venezia e la pirateria', pp. 722–3, 745–6, 751–4; Wittek, *Fürstentum Mentesche*, pp. 82–3.
[47] Heyd, *Histoire du commerce*, vol. 2, p. 277; Imber, 'Ḳurṣān: II', p. 506; Inalcik, 'Ottoman–Venetian relations', p. 85; I. H. Uzunçarşılı, 'Baḥriyya, III: the Ottoman navy', in *The encyclopaedia of Islam*, new edn, vol. 1, ed. B. Lewis et al. (Leiden and London, 1960), 947–9, here p. 947; Vaughan, *Europe and the Turk*, pp. 39–40; Wittek, *Rise of the Ottoman empire*, p. 36.

the Aegean to show the Ottoman flag.[48] During his crossing of the Aegean from Rhodes to Athens in 1394, Nicolaus de Marthono was in constant fear of Turkish corsairs, and they actually raided Sykaminon while he was there.[49] In 1399, 27 Ottoman galleys opposed the expedition of marshal Boucicaut to the Bosphorus.[50] Bayezid had 20 ships at Altoluogo and Palatia in 1402, and in the following year de Clavijo numbered the fleet at Gallipoli at 40 ships.[51] In 1413 there were rumours of an impending Ottoman attack on Rhodes,[52] and by 1415 the naval base at Gallipoli had been developed as the major centre of operations for Ottoman corsairs in the Aegean.[53] In that year squadrons attacked Venetian possessions and in revenge Pietro Loredano counterattacked Gallipoli in 1416, triumphing in a pitched battle in the Dardanelles.[54] Yet by 1423 Gilbert de Lannoy reported the port of Gallipoli to be the major Ottoman naval base and that there were four galleys, many small passenger boats ('vaisseaulx passaigiers'), and (corsair?) *fustes* in the port.[55] By 1427 the Gallipoli galleys were again attacking Venetian ships in the straits, with the result that in 1429 Silvestro Mocenigo attacked the port for a second time, this time penetrating the harbour refuge.[56] Moreover, in 1427 50 ships left from Gallipoli for Thessalonica to join the growing Ottoman pressure on that city.[57] In 1442 the Ottomans were again reported to have 60 ships at Gallipoli and in that year a squadron at Lemnos prevented the Despot of the Morea, Constantine Palaeologus, from reaching Constantinople.[58] In 1448 an Ottoman

[48] Wittek, *Fürstentum Mentesche*, p. 83.
[49] Nicolaus de Marthono, *Liber peregrinationis*, pp. 639–53.
[50] H. Inalcik, 'The question of the closing of the Black Sea under the Ottomans', in *ΑΡΧΕΙΟΝ ΠΟΝΤΟΥ. Τομος τριακοστος πεμπτος* (University of Birmingham. Centre for Byzantine studies. Twelfth Spring symposium of Byzantine studies: «The Byzantine Black Sea», 18–20 March 1978) (Athens, 1978), pp. 74–110, here p. 81; H. Inalcik, 'Gelibolu', in *The encyclopaedia of Islam*, new edn, vol. 2, ed. B. Lewis et al. (Leiden and London, 1965), 983–7; A. Luttrell, 'The Crusade in the fourteenth century', in J. R. Hale et al., eds., *Europe in the late Middle Ages* (London, 1965), 122–54, here pp. 149–50; Vaughan, *Europe and the Turk*, p. 40.
[51] De Clavijo, *Embassy*, p. 27; Foss, *Ephesus*, p. 163.
[52] Luttrell, 'Hospitallers at Rhodes', p. 312.   [53] Inalcik, 'Gelibolu', p. 984.
[54] Andrews, *Turkish threat to Venice*, p. 40; Heyd, *Histoire du commerce*, vol. 2, p. 277; Inalcik, 'Ottoman–Venetian relations', p. 85; Inalcik, 'Closing of the Black Sea', p. 81; H. J. Kissling, 'Venedig und der islamische Orient bis 1500', in Pertusi, *Venezia e il Levante*, vol. 1, part 1, 361–87, here pp. 369, 371; Thiriet, *Romanie Vénitienne*, p. 368; Vaughan, *Europe and the Turk*, p. 44; Zakythinos, 'L'attitude de Venise', p. 71.   [55] Gilbert de Lannoy, *Oeuvres*, pp. 160–1.
[56] Inalcik, 'Closing of the Black Sea', p. 81.   [57] Krekic, *Dubrovnik*, p. 47.
[58] Inalcik, 'Gelibolu', p. 984; Inalcik, *Ottoman empire*, p. 21; Thiriet, *Romanie Vénitienne*, pp. 377–9; Vaughan, *Europe and the Turk*, p. 56.

fleet of at least 65 ships demonstrated before Constantinople before going on to Chilia, where it was defeated and burnt in a naval battle.[59] Just as Haji Khalifeh's assertion that Ottoman naval activity was 'not worth enumerating' before 1453 seems self-deprecating in retrospect, so also Thiriet's claim that to *c.* 1450 'la suprématie navale des Vénitiens est encore incontestée' seems exaggerated.[60] But certainly Ottoman naval operations in this early phase of the sultanate's expansion are to be characterized more as a 'hit-and-run', tentative probing of Christian maritime defences than as the full-blooded assault on the sea lanes that they were later to become. Ottoman attention was confined largely to the Bosphorus, the Sea of Marmara, and the Dardanelles.[61] Treaties with Venice virtually recognized defined spheres of authority. Venetian galleys could give chase to Ottoman ships encountered in the Aegean *extra strictum*, but on the other hand Venice had to punch her merchantmen through the Dardanelles by force, providing war galley escorts for the merchant caravans.[62] The Serenissima established a small naval base at Tenedos in an effort to confine the Ottoman galleys to the straits area.[63] Venetian commerce with Constantinople and the Black Sea felt the effects of the Ottoman attempt to control shipping through the straits, but in the same period her commerce in the lower Aegean prospered.[64] The quality and weight of Venetian *galee sottili*, and the experience and expertise of their crews, seem to have maintained that one-to-one superiority over Ottoman *kadirge* noted in the fourteenth century. As late as 1466 a Venetian merchant in Istanbul could say that the Ottomans considered that they needed a superiority of four or five to one before engaging Venetian galleys.[65] If that was true at the time, it was soon to change.

The importance which the naval base at Gallipoli assumed in this initial phase of the struggle between the Ottomans and the West

[59] M. Cazacu & P. S. Nasturel, 'Une démonstration navale des Turcs devant Constantinople et la bataille de Kilia (1448)', *Journal des savants* (1978), 197–210.
[60] Thiriet, *Romanie Vénitienne*, p. 395. Cf. Kissling, 'Venedig', pp. 369–70.
[61] Inalcik, 'Gelibolu', pp. 984–5; Inalcik, 'Ottoman–Venetian relations', p. 85.
[62] Andrews, *Turkish threat to Venice*, pp. 41, 52–3, 63; Heyd, *Histoire du commerce*, vol. 2, p. 268; Inalcik, 'Closing of the Black Sea', p. 81; Inalcik, 'Gelibolu', p. 984; Thiriet, *Romanie Vénitienne*, pp. 364–5, 368; Vaughan, *Europe and the Turk*, pp. 44, 45, 48.   [63] Thiriet, 'Venise et l'occupation de Ténédos', *passim*.
[64] Thiriet, *Romanie Vénitienne*, pp. 424, 433–4; Thiriet, 'Itineraires', p. 588.
[65] A. Tenenti, 'The sense of space and time in the Venetian world of the fifteenth and sixteenth centuries', in J. R. Hale, ed., *Renaissance Venice* (London, 1973), 17–46, here p. 24. Cf. Andrews, *Turkish threat to Venice*, p. 116 n. 79.

underscores at the outset an important fact. In the last days of galley warfare, sea power was just as much a matter of skilful use of coastal geography as it had ever been. Naval forces were in fact amphibious forces. Control of the sea lanes was achieved only through control of the coasts along which they passed. Naval commanders had to be able to manage the logistics and strategy of handling galley fleets by utilization of land-based resources. The base at Gallipoli was established in an attempt to force Western merchantmen to halt for inspection and pay a toll for passage, and to bar their progress if desired.[66] That Venetian squadrons successfully prevented the Ottoman galleys at Gallipoli from achieving these objectives in the case of Venetian ships does not detract from the theme. After 1453, when the struggle moved to a wider arena, that theme remained the same, and the eventual consolidation of Ottoman maritime dominance in the eastern Mediterranean was achieved not by pitched naval battles but by a slow, relentless, and exhausting drive to gain possession of the bases and islands from which war galleys could control shipping along the sea lanes. In the war of 1463–79, galleys of the sultan had not a single success over Venetian squadrons in open battle, yet at the end of the war the Ottoman acquisition of strategic islands and bases, such as Negropont, had strengthened their position at sea immensely.[67] Over the succeeding century, Ottoman fleets won few major fleet battles against Western forces: the two battles of Zonchio in 1499 and 1500, Prevesa in 1538, and Djerba in 1560. From all of these except Djerba the Venetian and allied fleets withdrew with the loss of only a few ships. However, in each case they were out-manoeuvred and severely mauled and the Ottomans achieved their strategic objectives, adding greatly to the consolidation of their maritime regime.[68] Lepanto in 1571 was, of course, an unmitigated disaster for the sultanate. It lost about 200 of its 300 ships. Yet the fleets were quickly reconstituted and the actual battle itself was arguably of little more than symbolic significance in the struggle at sea because it was not followed by any significant Christian strategic gains.[69] The Ottoman conquest of Cyprus in the same year was of infinitely greater significance. There is much truth in the claim that

[66] Vaughan, *Europe and the Turk*, p. 69.
[67] Kissling, 'Venedig', pp. 377–8; W. H. McNeill, *Venice: the hinge of Europe 1081–1797* (Chicago, 1974), pp. 87–8 and n. 101; Thiriet, *Romanie Vénitienne*, p. 435.
[68] F. C. Lane, 'Naval actions and fleet organization, 1499–1502', in Hale, *Renaissance Venice*, 146–73.
[69] Cf. Guilmartin, *Gunpowder and galleys*, pp. 42–56, 123–34, 221–52.

because the only significant Western outpost remaining in the eastern Mediterranean after the loss of Cyprus was Crete, Christian shipping did not sail unmolested in the Levant and the Aegean by the sixteenth century except under the sultan's passport: or, if it did, it did so at its peril.[70]

Prior to the war of 1463–79 with Venice, the Ottomans had barely begun to nibble away at the string of Western possessions in the Ionian and Aegean which gave strength to the Western maritime regime; although they had made some significant gains. Thessalonica had been taken from Venice in 1430 and, following the capture of Constantinople in 1453, the drive against the remnants of Byzantine authority had been brought to a successful conclusion by overrunning the Peloponnesus and Attica in 1458–60. Between 1455 and 1462 Genoa and the Gattilusi family had lost the islands of Lesbos, Imbros, Samothrace, Thasos, and Samos, as well as the mainland port of Enos.[71] Nevertheless, at the outbreak of war the Serenissima and the surviving independent Western lordships still held crucial naval bases on the mainland and also held the islands in the south and west of the Aegean; although some of the independent lordships were by now tributary to the sultan. In fact, during the final 80 or so years of life of the Byzantine empire, Venice had taken advantage of growing insecurity in the face of the Turk to strengthen her *stato da mar*. By purchase, by inheritance, by agreement, and by occupation she had acquired direct suzerainty over most of the remaining Western outposts: Corfu in 1387, Nauplion in 1389, Tinos and Mykonos in 1390, Patras, Navarino/Zonchio, and Lepanto in 1408–10, Thessalonica in 1423 (lost in 1430), Andros in 1440, Aegina in 1451, Skyros, Skyathos, and Skopelos in 1453, and Monemvasia in 1461.[72] With these possessions consolidated into a single regime and added to those which Venice had held since the thirteenth century, the Ottoman expansion can be seen to have had the unlooked-for effect of in fact stiffening the defences of the Christian West.[73]

By 1463 virtually the entire defensive chain of islands and mainland

---

[70] Braudel, *Mediterranean*, p. 906. See also A. C. Hess, *The forgotten frontier: a history of the sixteenth-century Ibero-African frontier* (Chicago, 1978), p. 90; McNeil, *Venice*, p. 136; Vaughan, *Europe and the Turk*, p. 150.

[71] Heyd, *Histoire du commerce*, vol. 2, pp. 320–2; Thiriet, *Romanie Vénitienne*, pp. 371–2, 384–6.

[72] Andrews, *Turkish threat to Venice*, p. 61; Heyd, *Histoire du commerce*, vol. 2, pp. 272, 280, 323–4; Thiriet, *Romanie Vénitienne*, pp. 361–3, 369–71, 378, 389, 393–5.

[73] Heyd, *Histoire du commerce*, vol. 2, p. 323; Inalcik, *Ottoman empire*, p. 134; McNeill, *Venice*, pp. 74–5.

bases was either controlled directly by Venice or else recognized Venetian suzerainty. The Knights Hospitaller of Rhodes added their own small but by no means inconsiderable strength and strategic location to the arc hemming in the sea power of the Turk. Braudel comments that it was 'little short of a miracle then that the barrier held back the swirling tide of Turkish invasion'.[74] But, in fact, the huge Turkish superiority in numbers counted for less than might be expected given the nature and logistical problems of the task. Reduction of every mainland naval base and island required a major assault coordinated by both land forces and fleets against strongly fortified strategic positions. The resolutely tenacious Venetian and Hospitaller resistance to the Ottoman drive is perfectly comprehensible. To be sure, the Venetians and Hospitallers faced great problems in supplying and defending outposts far removed from their sources of logistical support. But their governments were determined, well organized, and resilient. Maritime supply systems could rarely be cut off entirely and were founded upon well armed and skilfully manned battle squadrons which could attack besieging naval forces by sea or break through to relieve exhausted defenders.[75]

The sultans may have had as their objective restoration of the old Byzantine maritime thalassocracy in the eastern Mediterranean under their own rule,[76] but the problems facing them in translating that objective into reality were far from simple. As a first step they needed, of course, to build up their fleets. In all likelihood Mehmed II had about 100 ships of various types and sizes at Constantinople in 1453.[77] From immediately after the fall of the city, Venice daily expected Negropont, its most important Aegean outpost, to be attacked. That expectation remained current through to the actual outbreak of war in 1463.[78] Venetian fears were not at all unrealistic

---

[74] Braudel, *Mediterranean*, p. 846. Braudel refers only to the period after 1540. I mean him no violence in extending the frame of reference of his remark backwards in time for my own purposes.

[75] P. Coles, *The Ottoman impact on Europe* (London, 1968), pp. 133–5.

[76] Inalcik, *Ottoman empire*, pp. 26, 29. Cf. Kritovoulos, *History of Mehmed the conqueror*, trans. C. T. Riggs (Westport, 1970), pp. 141–2, 185–6.

[77] Melissenos, *Chronicle of the siege of Constantinople*, p. 101; Pertusi, *Testi inediti*, pp. 4–5, 35, 39, 67, 96, 98, 105; S. Runciman, *The fall of Constantinople 1453* (Cambridge, 1969), pp. 75–6; R. Schwoebel, *The shadow of the crescent: the Renaissance image of the Turk (1453–1517)* (Nieuwkoop, 1967), p. 4. See esp. the figure of 70 ships given by 'Ašyq Paša-Zâde in his *Tewârîkh-i âl-i 'Osmân (History of the house of Osman)* in Pertusi, *Testi inediti*, p. 241.

[78] Andrews, *Turkish threat to Venice, passim*, esp. pp. 56–62, 180, 191–238; Vaughan, *Europe and the Turk*, p. 69.

for Ottoman squadrons began to operate freely and regularly in the Aegean from 1453 in defiance of the restricting clauses in the Venetian–Ottoman treaties. According to the Hospitallers of Rhodes, Ottoman ships did attack Negropont in 1453, but they were defeated and destroyed by Venetian galleys.[79] An Ottoman squadron showed the flag in the Aegean again in 1454 and in 1455 Naxos was attacked. In 1456 it was the turn of Lesbos and in the following year another large Ottoman squadron came out of the Dardanelles. The Turkish offensive of 1462 finally wrested Lesbos from the Gattilusi.[80]

In the late 1450s Western estimates of the sizes of naval forces needed to contain the Ottoman fleet were still low, in the order of 30 to 40 galleys, although the Venetian Senate was less optimistic.[81] Haji Khalifeh numbered the fleet sent to Negropont in 1470 at 100 ships.[82] In the 1470s the standing fleet grew to about 90 galleys and for the attack on Rhodes in 1480 100 ships were sent out.[83] But between about 1480 and 1496 it doubled in size. In that year Marino Sanudo the younger numbered it at 100 galleys, 50 *fuste* (smaller galleys), 50 *grippi* (*iġribār* – still smaller galleys), three galeasses, two carracks (*naves*), and two *barzoti* (also carracks, but smaller).[84] At the two battles of Zonchio in 1499 and 1500, the Ottoman fleets numbered some 260 and 230 ships respectively, while for the assault on Mamluk Egypt in 1517 about 250 ships put to sea.[85] At Prevesa, Khair-ed-Din Barbarossa had about 90 galleys and 50 galliots, while at Lepanto Ali Pasha had some 230 galleys and 70 galliots.[86] A naval presence of this magnitude could dominate the eastern Mediterranean for the sultans if they could take sufficient bases along the sea lanes for it to operate from.

In fact it was precisely for this purpose that the fleet itself was used. Ottoman fleets never attempted to seek out and destroy Venetian or allied fleets in pitched battle. When fleet engagements did occur, they did so invariably in the context of amphibious assaults by the forces of one of the two faiths against strategic bases or islands held by the

[79] Pertusi, *Testi inediti*, p. 99.
[80] Andrews, *Turkish threat to Venice*, pp. 64 n. 118, 78, 89, 243, 256, 280, 442–5.
[81] Schwoebel, *Shadow of the crescent*, pp. 74–6.
[82] Haji Khalifeh, *Maritime wars*, p. 15.
[83] Schwoebel, *Shadow of the crescent*, pp. 121–2.
[84] V. M. Godinho, 'Venise: les dimensions d'une présence face à un monde tellement changé – XVᵉ–XVIᵉ siècles', in Beck, *Venezia*, vol. 1, 11–50, here p. 32.
[85] Godinho, 'Venise', p. 32; Lane, 'Naval actions', pp. 149, 164.
[86] Guilmartin, *Gunpowder and galleys*, pp. 47, 238–9.

other.[87] The same theme as that noted above in the ninth and tenth centuries recurred. At Negropont in 1470, the failure of Niccolo da Canal to launch an attack on the Ottoman fleet enabled it to achieve successfully its objective of supporting an attack on the Venetian fortress by land forces.[88] In the case of the two battles of Zonchio, both Ottoman commanders, in spite of superiority in numbers of two and three to one, refused to be deflected from their missions of taking their fleets through to join land forces assaulting Lepanto in 1499 and Modon in 1500. Both battles were really running fights, attempts by the Venetians to counter amphibious campaigns by cutting off the naval forces.[89] Similarly at Prevesa Khair-ed-Din Barbarossa's mission was to support a land campaign against Venetian bases and recruiting grounds in Dalmatia. He had no intention of engaging a Christian fleet in open battle. In fact he remained on the defensive throughout, preserving his fleet intact and giving battle only from a position of defensive strength when the Christian fleet was at the end of its logistical capabilities and attempting to withdraw in disorder.[90]

Between 1470 and 1571, by skilful use of their fleet in conjunction with vastly superior land forces, the Ottomans were able to wear down the tenacious resistance of Venice and the Hospitallers of Rhodes and to seize control of most of the important islands and mainland bases on which seapower in the eastern Mediterranean depended. The requirements for an Ottoman maritime regime in the Aegean and the Levant were met by the capture of strategic ports and fortresses rather than by the destruction of Christian war fleets and commercial shipping. Ottoman intentions were signalled in 1467, when in a treaty with Venice the traditional clause prohibiting the Ottoman fleet from leaving the straits area was deleted, in spite of Venetian protests.[91] The loss of Negropont was followed by that of Croia and Skutari on the Albanian coast by the treaty of 1479; by Lepanto, Modon, Coron, Navarino/Zonchio, and the strategic island of Santa Maura/Levkas

---

[87] Cf. Guilmartin, *Gunpowder and galleys*, p. 98. Guilmartin also points out that this fact explains some of the design differences between Ottoman galleys on the one hand and Spanish and Venetian ones on the other.

[88] Haji Khalifeh, *Maritime wars*, pp. 15–16; Hess, 'Ottoman seaborne empire', pp. 1893–4; Heyd, *Histoire du commerce*, vol. 2, pp. 324–6; Lane, 'Naval actions', p. 147; Lane, *Venice*, pp. 358–9; Tenenti, 'Space and time', p. 24.

[89] Haji Khalifeh, *Maritime wars*, pp. 19–22; Lane, 'Naval actions', pp. 149, 162–4.

[90] Haji Khalifeh, *Maritime wars*, pp. 61–4; Guilmartin, *Gunpowder and galleys*, pp. 46–54. Cf. Pryor, 'Roger of Lauria', pp. 185, 205–7.

[91] Tenenti, 'Space and time', p. 24.

in the war of 1499–1502; by Aegina, Patmos, the northern Sporades, Nauplion, and Monemvasia in the war of 1537–40; by Naxos, Andros, and Chios in 1566; and finally by Cyprus itself in 1571. To these acquisitions from the Western powers should be added, of course, the highly important conquest of Syria, Palestine, and Egypt from the Mamluks in 1517.

After a century of exhausting struggle, the map of the strategic command of the eastern Mediterranean looked vastly different from what it had been before 1453. Instead of the endless string of Western possessions covering the sea lanes and providing havens for Christian merchantmen, war fleets, and corsairs, there were now left only the Ionian islands of Corfu, Cephalonia, and Zante, plus Crete and a few unimportant Aegean outposts such as Cerigo, Tinos, and Mykonos. All were exposed to the ravages of Ottoman fleets and corsairs and none could any longer fill the role of providing protection for Christian shipping along the sea lanes in the eastern Mediterranean. A presence by Christian battle fleets east of the Ionian became increasingly rare and Christian corsairs found operations in Aegean and Levantine waters increasingly difficult and dangerous. All the routes to the Levant passed along Turkish coasts, and everywhere they sailed in the eastern Mediterranean Western merchantmen did so under the guns of Ottoman galleys and shore batteries.[92] As well as their main fleets at Galata and Gallipoli, the Ottomans maintained squadrons patrolling the sea lanes from Rhodes, Alexandria, Kavalla, Midilli, and occasionally Menteshe, Sigla, and Alanya.[93]

The late medieval predominance of the shipping of the Christian West and its virtual monopoly of trans-Mediterranean traffic was severely eroded.[94] By the sixteenth century Venice was consciously avoiding confrontation with the Ottomans and was reluctant to become involved in naval leagues against them because continuation of her Levantine commerce was conditional upon peace with the sultans.[95] Indeed, as we saw above, that reluctance had manifested itself from the very emergence of the Ottoman sultanate, long before the sixteenth century. The logistical advantages once possessed by the

[92] Heyd, *Histoire du commerce*, vol. 2, p. 333; Schwoebel, *Shadow of the crescent*, pp. 181–2.   [93] Imber, 'Navy of Süleyman the Magnificent', pp. 222–3, 255–60.

[94] See the comments of Tenenti on the effects of the Ottoman maritime expansion in 'Space and time', pp. 24–9. See also C. M. Kortepeter, 'Ottoman imperial policy and the economy of the Black Sea region in the sixteenth century', *Journal of the American Oriental Society*, 86 (1966), 86–113, here p. 96. See also below, pp. 190–1.

[95] Lane, *Venice*, pp. 246–8; McNeill, *Venice*, pp. 136, 139–40.

Christian West now lay with subjects of the Ottomans in the eastern Mediterranean. Predictably, the period witnessed both a new onslaught by Ottoman corsairs against Western shipping and also a rapid growth of an Ottoman merchant marine. In the second half of the fifteenth century and in the sixteenth, piracy and privateering, the 'little war' of Guilmartin, the *guerre de course*, was the normal form of maritime conflict in the Mediterranean, the interface between Islam and Christendom in Burns's expression[96] (figure 29). In fact it had been throughout the Middle Ages and nothing had changed in this respect. The *guerre de course* was a multi-faceted phenomenon of extreme complexity, with both inter-religious and intra-religious forms, and consequently defies simple analysis. Muslim Barbary and Ottoman corsairs on the one hand and Christian Maltese, Sicilian, Catalan, Tuscan, and Majorcan corsairs on the other, not to mention the Knights Hospitaller of Rhodes and then Malta and the Knights of St Stephen, all wreaked their own special kind of havoc on the sea lanes. Historians have only just begun to examine the parameters of the phenomenon. Significantly, neither Braudel nor Guilmartin attempts to assess any particular directional outcome of piracy and privateering in the period. Earle states quite correctly that no overall estimate of the effects of the various corsairs on Mediterranean maritime traffic has ever been made.[97] Tenenti has, of course, done so, but only for Venice.[98] As far as the synoptic consequences of the corsairs' activities across the sea are concerned, the proceedings of the San Francisco conference on *Course et piraterie* in 1975 were disappointingly inconclusive.[99] Some suggestions are both unavoidable and also most necessary here, but they are made very tentatively.

Fontenay and Tenenti assert that over the period *c.* 1450–1550 the incursions of Christian corsairs into the Ottoman eastern Mediterranean amounted to not a tenth of those made by Ottoman corsairs into the central and western Mediterranean, *la Méditerranée espagnole*.[100] The assessment is intuitive rather than statistically supported, but

[96] Braudel, *Mediterranean*, pp. 865–91; Burns, 'Piracy', *passim*; Fontenay & Tenenti, 'Course et piraterie', p. 95; Guilmartin, *Gunpowder and galleys*, p. 264 *et passim* under *guerre de course*; Hess, *Forgotten frontier*, p. 17; Tenenti, 'I corsari', pp. 261–2, 285–6; Tenenti, *Cristoforo da Canal*, p. 150.   [97] Earle, *Corsairs*, p. 13.

[98] Tenenti, 'I corsari', *passim*; Tenenti, 'Venezia e la pirateria', *passim*; A. Tenenti, *Naufrages, corsairs et assurances maritimes à Venise, 1592–1609* (Paris, 1959); A. Tenenti, *Piracy and the decline of Venice 1580–1615* (Berkeley, 1967).

[99] *Course et piraterie*.

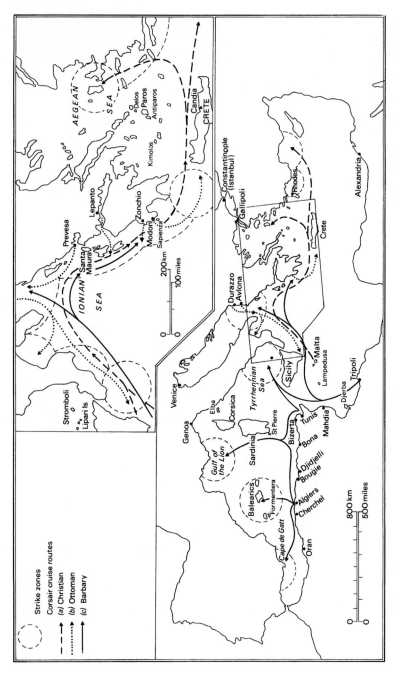

Figure 29 Aspects of the *guerre de course* in the fifteenth and sixteenth centuries

there is no doubt that its sentiment is correct. Operations of Christian corsairs in the East were directed primarily against the growing north–south Ottoman maritime traffic linking Egypt and Syria–Palestine with Asia Minor, Istanbul, and the Black Sea.[101] However, the strike zones along these routes lay some 1000 miles east of Malta and Sicily, beyond the limits of a galley's cruising range without rewatering. Significantly, in the seventeenth century Maltese corsairs abandoned galleys in favour of sailing ships for operations in these waters.[102] But in the fifteenth and sixteenth centuries the galleys of the Western corsairs were hampered severely by a lack of bases in the east and the logistical limitations which that imposed. Before its fall in 1522 Rhodes sometimes provided a base, but at other times the Hospitallers had agreements with the sultans to suppress piracy and privateering and they barred Christian corsairs from their ports.[103] After the fall of Rhodes, the situation became worse.[104] Only Venice could now offer the facilities needed, but Venetian authorities in the islands rarely welcomed corsairs. Venice was both innately suspicious of them because they too often preyed on her own shipping, and also keen to preserve good relations with the Ottomans in the interests of her own commerce. Of course, single galleys and small flotillas could water at deserted coves and victual on islands where Ottoman authority was weak. In the seventeenth century, the small islands of Paros and Antiparos, Delos, and Kimolos, were all used by Western corsairs.[105] Nevertheless, the lack of secure support facilities in immediate proximity to the major strike zones was a fundamental weakness.[106] In the western Mediterranean, Christian corsairs still enjoyed the geographical advantages they had since the thirteenth century, but here the pickings were much slimmer. Muslim shipping was largely limited to Granadan and Maghrebin coastal *cabotage* and to the galleys of the Barbary corsairs themselves. Some maritime traffic plying between Egypt and the Maghreb also fell into their hands, particularly in the eastern approaches to Tunisia.[107]

[100] Fontenay & Tenenti, 'Course et piraterie', p. 102.
[101] Bresc, 'Course et piraterie en Sicile', esp. map 1 (Prises) (p. 754); Braudel, *Mediterranean*, p. 875; Earle, *Corsairs*, pp. 142–4; Inalcik, *Ottoman empire*, p. 128.
[102] Earle, *Corsairs*, pp. 134–6.
[103] Rossi, 'Hospitallers at Rhodes', p. 321; Tenenti, 'I corsari', p. 236–7.
[104] Tenenti, *Cristoforo da Canal*, p. 149.
[105] Earle, *Corsairs*, pp. 144–5, 188–9.
[106] Guilmartin, *Gunpowder and galleys*, pp. 96–7.
[107] Bresc, 'Course et piraterie en Sicile', p. 756 and map 1 (Prises) (p. 754).

No such logistical problems hampered the operations of Ottoman fleets and corsairs in the eastern and central Mediterranean, although they certainly did so whenever the Ottomans attempted to operate in the western Mediterranean.[108] Although the Sultans from time to time made treaties with Venice and the Hospitallers under the terms of which they undertook to suppress piracy and privateering by Ottoman subjects, in practice by turns they turned a blind eye to it, were incapable of controlling it, or actively assisted it.[109] This was an Ottoman rather than a Turkish *guerre de course*, since, as is well known, the contribution of Greek and other populations both to the build-up of the Ottoman navy and to piracy and privateering under the Ottoman flag was very considerable.[110] By the end of the fifteenth century, the corsairs had become a major source of strength for the Ottoman navy.[111] Probably as early as the Turkish capture of Avlona in 1416, there were Ottoman corsairs in the Adriatic.[112] Following the fall of Constantinople in 1453, the threat intensified very rapidly. In that year Jacopo Loredano captured 17 Ottoman corsair *fuste* off the northern approaches to Negropont. At some time prior to 1460 a certain Venetian called Pietro da Mosto and his family were captured by corsairs off Andros, and by the time of the Congress of Mantua in 1459 Venice was advancing to the Papacy her suppression of piracy as one of her major contributions to the defence of Christendom. In 1462 the corsairs were active off Monemvasia against Greek subjects of the despot of the Morea, Thomas Palaeologus.[113] By 1471 Ottoman corsairs were attacking Venetian ships in Syrian ports, and in the second half of the fifteenth century Venetian shipping to the Levant sailed in conditions that became ever more precarious.[114] Both squadrons of the Ottoman navy and also Ottoman corsairs insisted on a right to stop and search ships for merchandise and passengers of hostile powers and, under this pretext, ships were frequently plun-

---

[108] Vaughan, *Europe and the Turk*, pp. 151–2.

[109] Fontenay & Tenenti, 'Course et piraterie', p. 83; Pertusi, *Testi inediti*, p. 98; H. A. von Burski, *Kemāl Re'is: Ein Beitrag zur Geschichte der Türkischen Flotte* (Bonn, 1928); Tenenti, 'I corsari', pp. 236–8, 260; Tenenti, 'Venezia e la pirateria', p. 746.

[110] Hess, 'Ottoman seaborne empire', p. 1891; Fontenay & Tenenti, 'Course et piraterie', pp. 93–4; Kritovoulos, *History of Mehmed the conqueror*, p. 37; Lane, *Venice*, p. 356.

[111] Hess, 'Ottoman seaborne empire', pp. 1905–6; Rossi, 'Hospitallers at Rhodes', pp. 329–31.

[112] Andrews, *Turkish threat to Venice*, p. 46; Vaughan, *Europe and the Turk*, pp. 61, 73.

[113] Andrews, *Turkish threat to Venice*, pp. 57–8, 75, 122, 130, 261.

[114] Ashtor, *Levant trade*, pp. 445, 447, 449, 454. Cf. Casola, *Pilgrimage*, pp. 204, 210, 212–13, 217.

dered or subjected to extortions.[115] Following the Ottoman acquisition of Ionian and Adriatic bases in the war of 1499–1502 with Venice, the corsairs extended the scope of their operations from the Aegean and the Levant to the central and western Mediterranean. Modon, Santa Maura/Levkas, Lepanto, Avlona, Navarino/Zonchio, Durazzo, and Prevesa all prospered as corsair refuges.[116] In 1478 King Ferrante (Ferdinand) I of Naples was allowing Ottoman ships the use of his ports, and in 1480 an Ottoman fleet and army temporarily seized Otranto, thus establishing an Ottoman presence on both sides of the crucial entrance to the Adriatic.[117]

During 1501–2 the Venetians made strenuous efforts to prevent the establishment of Ottoman sea power along the western coasts of the lower Balkans because they saw clearly the consequences that would flow from it.[118] From here the corsairs were never more than a few hundred miles from the major strike zones where Christian shipping agglomerated: around the foot of Italy, from the Straits of Messina to those of Otranto, where the Ionian meets the Mediterranean between Crete and Zante, and in the Sicilian Channel. Tenenti's map of Venetian losses to Turkish and Barbary corsairs in the period 1592–1609 makes the point admirably.[119] No wonder that the pages of the diaries of Marino Sanudo the younger and Girolamo Priuli were so full of the exploits of Ottoman corsairs.[120] Under the impact of their assault, some of them, such as *Camali*, or Kemāl Reis, commanding squadrons sufficiently large to ravage Venetian Crete and to attack Rhodes of the Knights, Venetian control of the sea lanes to the Levant crumbled.

It was not that the causes of this lay in a Venetian loss of superiority in naval technology. Even in the sixteenth century Ottoman galleys were still reputed to be inferior to Venetian ones and were said to be poorly built of inferior materials, to be poorly maintained, and to be less manageable.[121] Although, by this time, the quality of Ottoman artillery seems to have approached that of the Venetians and Spanish,

---

[115] Braudel, *Mediterranean*, pp. 867–8; Schwoebel, *Shadow of the crescent*, pp. 186–7; Tenenti, *Cristoforo da Canal*, p. 151.
[116] Braudel, *Mediterranean*, p. 130; Fontenay & Tenenti, 'Course et piraterie', pp. 81, 85–6, 93–4; Hyde, 'Navigation', p. 530; Kissling, 'Venedig', p. 378; Tenenti, *Cristoforo da Canal*, pp. 9, 124, 160, 163; Tenenti, 'I corsari', pp. 251–9, 281–2.
[117] Vaughan, *Europe and the Turk*, pp. 82–3.
[118] Andrews, *Turkish threat to Venice*, pp. 281–319; Lane, 'Naval actions', p. 165. See also Fasano-Guarini, 'Comment naviguent les galères', pp. 293–4.
[119] Tenenti, *Naufrages*, plate II. [120] Tenenti, 'I corsari', *passim*.
[121] Imber, 'Navy of Süleyman the Magnificent', p. 223.

Venetian galleys were still more than a match for them in one-to-one combat.[122] But the galleys of Venice were too heavy and slow to chase the smaller and faster *kalite* of the corsairs.[123] By the mid sixteenth century, Christoforo da Canal and others were lamenting the poor condition of the maritime defences of the *stato da mar*. From about 1450 any pretence of a maritime *contrôle militaire* in the eastern Mediterranean was abandoned.[124] By the second half of the sixteenth century, even the Adriatic was no longer secure.[125]

The effects were severe. In the case of Genoa, Heers has pointed to a reorientation of her maritime commerce to the West.[126] In the case of Venice, she also reoriented her commerce to some degree; for example, by developing terrestrial trade with the interior of the Balkans through ports such as Spalato (Split).[127] Tenenti has pointed to a loss of sense of maritime security and pride, to a growth of 'restlessness and malaise . . . together with a desire to avoid danger, a feeling of abandon and panic as well as of rage'.[128] The risks of maritime commerce increased perceptibly, and were reflected in increased protection costs and decline of profit margins.[129] Corsair presence led to delays in the departure of galley caravans and to interruption of services, eventually contributing to discontinuation of the merchant galleys.[130] Private voyages to the Levant took their place to some extent, but in the second half of the century even these became less frequent.[131] 'Loss of hegemony in the balance of exchange with the Levant, insecurity on the sea, scanty remuneration from traditional investments, insolvencies, successive bankruptcies: these are the phenomena which historians have clarified in the light of an enormous documentation which leaves little room for divergent interpretations', concludes Tucci for Venice.[132]

No one would for a moment suggest that the sole cause of all this was the creation of an Ottoman maritime regime in the east and the

---

[122] Guilmartin, *Gunpowder and galleys*, pp. 211, 266.
[123] Tenenti, *Cristoforo da Canal*, pp. 43–4. See also Ashtor, 'L'artigleria veneziana'.
[124] Tenenti, *Cristoforo da Canal*, pp. 41, 46, 129–30, 148–9; Tenenti, 'I corsari', pp. 258–9, 276.
[125] Braudel, *Mediterranean*, p. 130; Tenenti, *Cristoforo da Canal*, pp. 9, 124, 160.
[126] Heers, *Gênes*, p. 473.   [127] Tadić, 'Côte occidentale des Balkans', p. 105.
[128] Tenenti, 'Space and time', p. 25; Tenenti, 'I corsari', p. 286.
[129] Coles, *Ottoman impact*, p. 138; Hess, *Forgotten frontier*, pp. 125–6; Thiriet, *Romanie Vénitienne*, p. 442; U. Tucci, 'The psychology of the Venetian merchant in the sixteenth century', in Hale, *Renaissance Venice*, 346–78, here p. 352.
[130] Ashtor, *Levant trade*, pp. 445–7, 475–6; Lane, *Venice*, p. 350; Tenenti, *Cristoforo da Canal*, pp. 163–4; Thiriet, *Romanie Vénitienne*, p. 442.
[131] Thiriet, *Romanie Vénitienne*, p. 442.
[132] Tucci, 'Psychology of the Venetian merchant', p. 352.

operations of Ottoman corsairs. Many other factors influenced not only Venetian maritime traffic but also that of the Mediterranean as a whole at this time: the influx of North European ships, changes in ship design and naval armaments, the oceanic discoveries of Portugal and Spain, the decline of Genoa in the eastern Mediterranean, the rise of France as a power in maritime commerce, and the incorporation of North Africa within the Ottoman sultanate, to mention just a few. But nevertheless, the loss of security on the sea lanes by the maritime powers of the Christian West was certainly a very significant factor in the equation. From the broad perspective in terms of the overall balance of power at sea, the Ottoman realization of the potentialities of the earlier Turkish acquisition of north Mediterranean coastlines, and especially their acquisition of a coastline on the western shores of the Balkans, had meant a reversion to the situation which had prevailed in the ninth and tenth centuries when Islam had also been able to maintain a maritime presence along the trunk routes of the sea.

The situation was complicated somewhat in the case of Venice because the private voyages which succeeded the state galley caravans were made invariably by sailing carracks. Since these could carry much larger cargoes than the galleys, the overall volume of the Egyptian spice trade was not much affected.[133] In spite of the effects of Ottoman sea power on Venetian shipping, the period was by no means a disastrous one for the economy of the city in the lagoons. The sultans were no more opposed now to foreign merchants and ships visiting their domains than they had been in the earlier period. Even Venetians, from whom the Ottoman state had more to fear than from any other Western maritime power, were to be found trading at Bursa and Adrianople, at Thessalonica after 1430, at Istanbul itself after 1453, at Modon and Coron after 1500, and, of course, at Alexandria after 1517.[134] Commercial treaties confirming the Western trading nations in something like their previous status and permitting freedom of trade were concluded after each conquest.[135] But the

---

[133] F. C. Lane, 'Venetian shipping during the Commercial Revolution', and 'The Mediterranean spice trade: further evidence of its revival in the sixteenth century', both rpt. in B. Pullan, ed., *Crisis and change in the Venetian economy in the sixteenth and seventeenth centuries* (London, 1968), 22–46, 47–58.

[134] Heyd, *Histoire du commerce*, vol. 2, pp. 352, 546; Inalcik, 'Ottoman–Venetian relations', p. 89; McNeill, *Venice*, p. 135; Thiriet, *Romanie Vénitienne*, pp. 391, 426–7, 433–4, 437–9.

[135] Ashtor, *Levant trade*, p. 446; Heyd, *Histoire du commerce*, vol. 2, pp. 309–16; Inalcik, 'Ottoman–Venetian relations', pp. 86–8; Inalcik, *Ottoman empire*, pp. 134–5; Runciman, *Fall of Constantinople*, pp. 162–3; Thiriet, *Romanie Vénitienne*, p. 383; Vaughan, *Europe and the Turk*, p. 81.

implications of the Ottoman maritime regime for disruption of the traditional structure of Mediterranean maritime traffic were clearly apparent. On the one hand, Genoa declined as a maritime power in the eastern Mediterranean and turned her commercial interests and maritime activity to the West and to the Iberian world in particular. On the other, in attempts to weaken Venice, the sultans encouraged other Western trading nations to do business with their domains and actually facilitated the growth of their maritime commerce. Particularly, but not only, during periods of war between Venice and the Turks, Florence, Ancona, Dubrovnik, and the French and Catalans partially usurped the place of Venice in the eastern Mediterranean.[136]

The clearest expression of the effects of the Ottoman maritime regime is to be seen not in the confrontation at sea but in the competition for shares of maritime traffic. The predominance of Western shipping which had characterized the late Middle Ages was temporarily negated. Under the influence of conjunctures, that word so beloved by certain historians and so much to be distrusted but which is appropriate here in a perfectly orthodox English sense of the word, created by the Ottoman seizure of a coastline stretching all the way from Dalmatia to the Maghreb, by their deployment of large naval forces, and by the ceaseless harrying of their corsairs, Ottoman subjects recaptured a significant share of trans-Mediterranean traffic.[137] Encouragement of trade with the West by the sultans, progressive exclusion of Westerners from the Black Sea, economic linkage of Egypt and Syria–Palestine with Asia Minor and the Balkans, and programmes of urban development within Ottoman domains all helped to create a new Mediterranean merchant marine in the hands of Ottoman subjects: Jews, Greeks, and Turks at first, later Armenians also.[138] As early as the second half of the fifteenth century, the Venetian government attempted to stop the penetration

[136] Ashtor, *Levant trade*, pp. 495, 505–6; Coles, *Ottoman impact*, pp. 111, 139–45; Heyd, *Histoire du commerce*, vol. 2, pp. 336–7, 340–50; Inalcik, 'Ottoman–Venetian relations', p. 87; Inalcik, *Ottoman empire*, pp. 135–6; Krekic, *Dubrovnik*, p. 258; Vaughan, *Europe and the Turk*, p. 121.

[137] A. Attman, *The bullion flow between Europe and the East 1000–1750* (Göteborg, 1981), p. 20; Braudel, *Mediterranean*, pp. 727–8; Inalcik, *Ottoman empire*, pp. 121–39; Lane, *Venice*, pp. 298–300; McNeill, *Venice*, p. 85; S. Stoianovich, 'The conquering Balkan orthodox merchant', *Journal of economic history*, 20 (1960), 234–313; Vaughan, *Europe and the Turk*, p. 94.

[138] Coles, *Ottoman impact*, p. 111; Kortepeter, 'Ottoman imperial policy', pp. 100–1; Stoianovich, 'Balkan orthodox merchant', p. 235. See also H. Inalcik, 'The Ottoman economic mind and aspects of the Ottoman economy', in Cook, *Studies*, 207–18.

of Venetian Levantine commerce by Jewish and other subjects of the Ottomans.[139] Westerners were not totally excluded from the Black Sea even in the sixteenth century, but long before that the number of their voyages there had dwindled to a trickle.[140] The customs registers of Caffa for 1486–90 and for 1490 show that in 1486–90 of 66 ships calling there, 41 were Muslim and only 4 Italian and that in 1490 of 75 ships calling there in a four-month period, 59 were Muslim and only 7 Italian.[141] Loss of the rich trade in slaves from the Black Sea to Egypt particularly hurt the Italians.[142] Ottoman shipping expanded rapidly in two directions. The old trunk route linking the Black Sea, Istanbul, Asia Minor, and Egypt took on new life, particularly after the conquest of Egypt in 1517. Large convoys of Ottoman merchantmen plied these routes, escorted by war galleys against the dangers of Christian corsairs.[143] By 1559 most of the 50 or so ships which visited Attalya every year were Muslim owned.[144] To the west, Balkan subjects of the Ottomans developed a trans-Adriatic traffic from Dubrovnik to Ancona and later to Venice.[145] Ottoman merchants were already established in Venice before the war of Cyprus and after peace was concluded the *Fondaco dei Turchi* was established by the city in the lagoons.[146] By the late sixteenth century, Braudel estimates the total tonnage of the Ottoman merchant marine at 80 000 tons, double that of Venice and 20 000 tons more than that of Mediterranean Spain.[147] By his own admission the estimate is little more than a guess, but it is nevertheless significant that a historian of his stature believes that the Ottoman merchant marine was easily the largest in the Mediterranean by the end of the sixteenth century.

All this, I would argue, flowed directly, although certainly not

[139] Ashtor, 'Jews in Mediterranean trade', pp. 449–50.
[140] Braudel, *Mediterranean*, p. 392; Inalcik, 'Closing of the Black Sea', pp. 76–7, 107–10; Inalcik, *Ottoman empire*, pp. 128–9; Kortepeter, 'Ottoman imperial policy', pp. 88–93; Lane, *Venice*, pp. 348–9; McNeill, *Venice*, pp. 126–7; Stoianovich, 'Balkan orthodox merchant', p. 240; Thiriet, 'Itineraires', p. 588.
[141] Inalcik, 'Closing of the Black Sea', pp. 91–5; Inalcik, *Ottoman empire*, p. 129.
[142] Lane, *Venice*, p. 349; McNeill, *Venice*, p. 126.
[143] Inalcik, *Ottoman empire*, pp. 127–8; Inalcik, 'Ottoman economic mind', pp. 209–10; Inalcik, 'Bursa', pp. 143–5; H. Inalcik, 'Capital formation in the Ottoman empire', *Journal of economic history*, 29 (1969), 97–140, here pp. 110, 120.
[144] Inalcik, *Ottoman empire*, p. 127.
[145] P. Earle, 'The commercial development of Ancona, 1479–1551', *Economic history review*, 2nd series, 22 (1969), 28–44, here pp. 35–43; Inalcik, 'Capital formation', p. 113 and n. 44; Inalcik, *Ottoman empire*, p. 135; Stoianovich, 'Balkan orthodox merchant', pp. 237–8.
[146] Braudel, *Mediterranean*, pp. 288, 336; Lane, *Venice*, p. 301.
[147] Braudel, *Mediterranean*, p. 446.

exclusively, from the superior quality of the strategic bases acquired for the Ottoman navy and from the logistical advantages held by the Ottoman navy and corsairs in an age when maritime traffic continued to ply the age-old coastal trunk routes of the sea and when the main strike weapon at sea was still the oared galley. No other facet of the *guerre de course* in the fifteenth and sixteenth centuries can be shown to have had such systematic and far-reaching consequences as that of the Ottomans. The case of the Barbary corsairs will illustrate why. Although other corsairs, both Christian and Muslim, undoubtedly contributed much to the creation of a no-man's-land at sea and thus helped all in their own way to establish the conditions and character of maritime traffic in the late Middle Ages and the sixteenth century, only in the case of the Ottoman corsairs can a definite pattern be discerned for the effects of their operations. The consequences of their operations were as clearly apparent as had been those of the corsairs of the Christian West in the twelfth and thirteenth centuries.

8. Epilogue: the Barbary corsairs

In the later Middle Ages the Muslim states of North Africa had by and large been fairly pacific. Although there had always been a certain number of corsairs amongst their populations, they were certainly not renowned for their bellicosity and for their prosecution of *jihād* against the Christian infidel at sea. Indeed, in the fourteenth and fifteenth centuries it had been Christian, and particularly Catalan, corsairs who had been the major threat to maritime traffic in the western Mediterranean. According to Ibn Khaldūn, Maghrebin pirates and corsairs first assumed serious dimensions around 1360 at Bougie.[1] By 1390 corsairs operating from Tunisia had become a severe enough menace to Christian shipping to provoke Genoa to organize a Crusade against Mahdia.[2] Native Maghrebins and Moorish exiles from Spain were always to remain active as corsairs in North Africa throughout the fifteenth and sixteenth centuries,[3] but it was Ottoman corsairs under Kemāl Reis, moving to the Maghreb around 1487, who ushered in the great days of the Barbary corsairs.[4] The move to the Maghreb was a logical extension of the Ottoman push westwards to the shores of the Ionian; however, as we shall see, it was not to offer the Barbary corsairs the same logistical advantages that the push to the west coasts of the Balkans did the Ottomans.

I shall not pursue the political history of the establishment of the

[1] Fontenay & Tenenti, 'Course et piraterie', p. 82. See also Bresc, 'Course et piraterie en Sicile', p. 753; Dufourcq, 'Relations', pp. 46–7; H. W. Hazard, 'Moslem North Africa, 1049–1394', in Hazard, *The fourteenth and fifteenth centuries*, 457–85, here p. 480; Lane-Poole, *Barbary corsairs*, p. 26.

[2] Hazard, 'Moslem North Africa', pp. 481–3; B. Z. Kedar, *Merchants in crisis: Genoese and Venetian men of affairs and the fourteenth-century depression* (New Haven, 1976), p. 30; Lane-Poole, *Barbary corsairs*, pp. 128–9; G. Marçais, 'Les villes de la côte algérienne et la piraterie au moyen-âge', *Annales de l'Institut d'études orientales*, 13 (1955), 118–42, here pp. 135–6. See also Dufourcq, *Vie quotidienne dans les ports*, pp. 131–2; Ferrer i Mallol, 'Corsaris castellans', p. 284.

[3] Coles, *Ottoman impact*, pp. 127–8; Earle, *Corsairs*, p. 35; Hess, *Forgotten frontier*, p. 61; Unali, *Marinai*, pp. 112, 127.   [4] Hess, *Forgotten frontier*, p. 60.

corsairs in North Africa: suffice it to say that by the 1550s they had carved out for themselves three regencies in Tripoli, Tunis, and Algiers, all acknowledging ultimate Ottoman suzerainty.[5] For their raids on Christian shipping the corsairs operated not only from these three ports, of course, but also from smaller ones such as Oran, Cherchel, Bougie, Djidjelli, Bone, Bizerta, and the island of Djerba. However, for our purposes it will be sufficient to refer generally to Tripoli, Tunis, and Algiers.

As always in the *guerre de course*, the Barbary corsairs developed certain favourite strike zones along the sea lanes which they particularly frequented because Christian shipping agglomerated there: the east coast of Sicily and the Ionian Sea;[6] the north coast of Sicily and the southern Tyrrhenian north to the Bay of Naples;[7] the Ligurian Sea between Elba, Corsica, and Genoa;[8] the Gulf of the Lion off the coast of Provence;[9] the south-west coasts of Sardinia;[10] the Balearics;[11] and the Gibraltar approaches.[12] Generally speaking, and for obvious reasons, the corsairs of Tripoli frequented the eastern area from the Ionian to the Tyrrhenian, while those of Tunis frequented the central area from the west coast of Sardinia to the southern Tyrrhenian, and those of Algiers the western areas between Sardinia, the Balearics, and the Gibraltar approaches.[13]

Figure 29 reveals the logistical problems faced by the galleys and galliots of these corsairs. Cruises from Tunis and Tripoli to the Ionian

---

[5] Cf. S. Bono, *I corsari barbareschi* (Turin, 1964); Earle, *Corsairs*; Fisher, *Barbary legend*; Hess, *Forgotten frontier*; J. B. E. Jurien de la Gravière, *Les corsaires barbaresques et la marine de Soliman le Grand* (Paris, 1887); Jurien de la Gravière, *Doria et Barbarousse* (Paris, 1886); Lane-Poole, *Barbary corsairs*; S. Soucek, 'The rise of the Barbarossas in North Africa', *Archivum Ottomanicum*, 3 (1971), 238–50.

[6] Braudel, *Mediterranean*, pp. 117, 851, 973; Earle, *Corsairs*, pp. 56, 58; Fontenay & Tenenti, 'Course et piraterie', p. 86; Lane-Poole, *Barbary corsairs*, pp. 95, 112, 192.

[7] Braudel, *Mediterranean*, pp. 117, 851, 853, 881–2, 992, 994; Earle, *Corsairs*, p. 56; Fisher, *Barbary legend*, pp. 46, 73; Fontenay & Tenenti, 'Course et piraterie', p. 86; Guilmartin, *Gunpowder and galleys*, p. 123; Lane-Poole, *Barbary corsairs*, pp. 86, 126–7, 202.

[8] Braudel, *Mediterranean*, pp. 153–4, 881, 928; Fisher, *Barbary legend*, pp. 45–6; Lane-Poole, *Barbary corsairs*, pp. 35–6, 82, 134, 202.

[9] Braudel, *Mediterranean*, pp. 122, 872, 881–3.

[10] Earle, *Corsairs*, p. 58; Fisher, *Barbary legend*, pp. 52–3; Fontenay & Tenenti, 'Course et piraterie', p. 86.

[11] Colom, 'Navegaciones mediterraneas', pp. 59, 67, 70–73.

[12] Braudel, *Mediterranean*, pp. 789, 839, 880–3, 926–9; Earle, *Corsairs*, pp. 56, 58; Fisher, *Barbary legend*, pp. 53, 57–8, 82, 84; Fontenay & Tenenti, 'Course et piraterie', p. 86; Hess, *Forgotten frontier*, pp. 37, 68; Lane-Poole, *Barbary corsairs*, pp. 186, 202.

[13] Earle, *Corsairs*, p. 56; Lane-Poole, *Barbary corsairs*, pp. 186, 223.

and the Straits of Otranto involved a round trip of about 1100 miles. From Tunis or Algiers to the Gulf of the Lion and back was about 1000 miles. Tripoli to the Tyrrhenian and return was about 1200 miles. All of these cruises were at the extreme limit of galley range. The Ligurian Sea was beyond the range of galleys unless they could water somewhere en route. Only the short trips from Algiers to the Balearics, about 400 miles, from Algiers to the Gibraltar approaches, 700 miles, from Tunis to Sardinia, 400 miles, or the southern Tyrrhenian, 600 miles, and from Tripoli to the east coast of Sicily, 800 miles, were really within the capabilities of galleys operating unsupported. And, even in these cases, except for the very short trips from Algiers to the Balearics and Tunis to Sicily or Sardinia, the amount of time they could spend on station in their strike zones was very limited. In fact it was no greater than that which Fatimid ships operating off the coasts of the Crusader states in the twelfth century had been able to spend.

The Barbary corsairs found hideouts in the western Mediterranean where they could take on supplies of food and water just as did their Christian counterparts in the eastern Mediterranean. Formentera, S. Pietro, Stromboli and the Lipari islands, and Lampedusa were all used, as also were sympathetic communities amongst the Moriscos of Granada and in Calabria. In periods of Franco-Ottoman alliance, Provençal ports could also be used.[14] But such hideouts and refuges were either insecure or available periodically only. In the long term they were incapable of giving to the threat posed by the Barbary corsairs to Christian shipping that permanency and systematic completeness which the Ottoman strategic position in the eastern Mediterranean and Ionian had given to the Ottoman *guerre de course*. The same comment could be made in reverse about the operations of Maltese, Sicilian, and Tuscan corsairs in the eastern Mediterranean in the same period. The failure of the Barbary corsairs and of their Ottoman masters to capture any of the key islands in the western Mediterranean had the most serious long-term consequences for their assault on the Christian maritime regime in the west.[15] The Ottoman attempt to take Malta in 1565 is, of course, famous. However, the attack on the Balearics by Piale Pasha in 1558 was potentially far more

[14] Braudel, *Mediterranean*, p. 994; Earle, *Corsairs*, p. 55; Fontenay & Tenenti, 'Course et piraterie', p. 86; Lane-Poole, *Barbary corsairs*, pp. 10–11, 109–10, 224; Trasselli, 'Naufragi', p. 505.
[15] Coles, *Ottoman impact*, pp. 96, 105.

important and Christendom could be thankful that his French allies persuaded him to withdraw.[16]

It was no wonder that three things happened. Firstly, large numbers of Barbary corsairs went regularly to Avlona, Santa Maura, and Lepanto to enter Ottoman service and to operate from the west coast of the Balkans.[17] Secondly, the greatest permanent threat from the Barbary corsairs developed in the Gibraltar approaches from the corsairs of Algiers.[18] And thirdly, by the end of the sixteenth century, the corsairs began to replace their galleys with sailing ships.[19]

Once more, the old themes were repeated. Because of the coastal nature of the major sea lanes used by maritime traffic, because of the logistical limitations of the oared galley, and because of the distances by which their home ports were removed from their major strike zones, in the sixteenth century the Barbary corsairs proved incapable of upsetting the ultimate predominance of Christian shipping in the western Mediterranean. While we should not underestimate for a moment the seriousness with which their attacks on the sea lanes were regarded at the time, their assault produced none of the lasting consequences which flowed from that of the Ottoman corsairs in the central and eastern Mediterranean.

[16] Braudel, *Mediterranean*, pp. 944–5.
[17] Fontenay & Tenenti, 'Course et piraterie', p. 82; Tenenti, 'Space and time', p. 29.
[18] Braudel, *Mediterranean*, pp. 880–6.
[19] Braudel, *Mediterranean*, p. 885; Earle, *Corsairs*, pp. 30, 49–52; Lane-Poole, *Barbary corsairs*, pp. 226–34.

9. *Conclusion*

In any age or in any society, technology is never more than an imperfect attempt by men to overcome obstacles presented by natural forces to the fulfilment of their needs and desires. No technology is perfect. In one way or another, usually in many, it is inefficient or inadequate and does not allow men to achieve the objectives for which they designed it as easily or as completely as they would wish. In these studies I have focused on one such example: the maritime technology of the Mediterranean world from the seventh to sixteenth centuries. Design characteristics of medieval sailing ships and oared merchant galleys, particularly their inadequate upwind performance capabilities, both limited the extent of the commercial sailing seasons and also greatly restricted the choice of routes. Veritable trunk routes or major sea lanes were established, at least partially because of the inadequate technology of ships. In the fifteenth and sixteenth centuries technological improvements mitigated these limitations and restrictions, but not sufficiently to alter traditional patterns of navigation in any marked way. Inadequate sea-keeping abilities, upwind performance capabilities, and load capacities of war galleys limited their range to a functional minimum. The Mediterranean may appear small on a modern world map but medieval and early modern galleys could barely cope with its distances.[1]

The gap which opened between objectives, needs, and desires on the one hand and actual achievement or degree of their satisfaction on the other offers the historian a fertile field for investigation, for in that gap lie causal explanations for many historical phenomena. One such gap, and one such phenomenon, the success of Christendom in its struggle with Islam at sea until the fourteenth century, and that of the Turks in their struggle at sea with the Christian West in the fifteenth and sixteenth centuries, has been isolated here, but many others spring

[1] Cf. Braudel, *Mediterranean*, p. 355; Udovitch, 'Time, the sea and society', p. 503.

197

easily to mind. In the Middle Ages this gap between objectives and technological achievement was a yawning chasm. Only to a partial degree could the technology available to medieval man surmount the forces of the natural world which surrounded him on all sides, frustrating his ambitions. In the Mediterranean the direction and strengths of the currents, the patterns of the prevailing winds, and the configuration of the coasts all continued to be formidable obstacles to navigation until the very end of the period under discussion here. To a very large degree the secrets of successful navigation never changed. They always remained in avoiding voyages against unfavourable conditions and in utilizing seasonal variations and localized meteorological phenomena to make one's way as much as possible in harmony with the forces of geography and meteorology.

The parameters of the gap between technology and nature, the nexus or structural interrelationships between them, established certain patterns of human behaviour governing the ways in which a particular available technology was normally and most appropriately used and in which men responded most efficiently to the opposition of the forces of nature. Men sought to structure their behaviour in certain optimum patterns in order to achieve their objectives as efficiently as possible given the technology available to them. In the main, men behaved neither in irrational ways which demanded more of their technology than it had to offer nor in illogical ways which failed to extract the maximum that it had to offer. Bunched sailings of merchant fleets at certain times of the year and along certain closely defined routes had technological motivations as well as obvious economic ones. The choice of coastal routes by galley squadrons in preference to shorter high-seas routes offered the best chances of the ships' both reaching their destinations safely and also of their making reasonable time.

These optimum patterns of human behaviour are susceptible to reconstruction by the historian and offer him conceptual frameworks for the interpretation of historical events and phenomena. Particularly when the questions at issue concern conflict or competition of one sort or another between different countries, societies, or civilizations, such conceptual frameworks based on the establishment of optimum patterns of behaviour may help greatly to elucidate and make comprehensible both course and outcome. As in the case studied here, it may be possible to show how one or other of the protagonists was either advantaged by being able to follow optimum patterns of behaviour or disadvantaged by not being able to do so. That is not to say that such patterns are laws of behaviour. Neither levels of technology and natural forces in themselves, nor the nexus between the two, are capable of determining human behaviour. The nexus is a conjuncture in the true and simple sense of that word, and is nothing more. It is comprehensible, not mystical, to be analysed, not fetishized. Conjuncture is not conjecture,[2] but neither is it constricture. Identifying, elucidating, and comprehending patterns of human behaviour given rise to by the nexus between technology and nature does not amount to any form of determinism. Such patterns are but one aspect of the causation which drives human history and must be recognized as such. Circumstances may arise, and indeed probably arise more often than not, in which apparently optimal patterns of behaviour suggested by the nexus between technology and nature will be negated or overridden by other factors and in which other patterns will become optimal instead. In these studies one such example has been identified in the politico-religious concerns which caused Muslim shipping to follow routes along the economically and navigationally less attractive southern shores of the Mediterranean in preference to the natural trunk routes of the sea. But the consequences which were incumbent upon circumstances preventing one or other protagonist from behaving in an optimal way in order to extract the most that technology could offer must be recognized. In the course of the long struggle between Muslim and Christian shipping for shares of Mediterranean maritime traffic, structural inefficiencies flowing from the inability of Muslim shipping to move safely and freely along the trunk routes were highly important. This above all explains how and why Christian shipping was able to penetrate the internal carrying trade between the various Muslim countries and to predominate in trans-Mediterranean traffic between Islam and Christendom from the twelfth to the fifteenth centuries. In the last analysis, geography, technology, and the forms of war had highly influential effects on the general evolution of Mediterranean history.

[2] Cf. G. R. Elton, 'Historians against history', *The Cambridge Review* (18 November 1983), 203–5.

Bibliography

PRIMARY SOURCES

MANUSCRIPT SOURCES

Archivio di Stato di Genova. Antico Commune. Galearum introytus et exitus. No. 690.
Archivio di Stato di Venezia. Senato Misti. Regestro 36.
Biblioteca Nazionale Firenze. Magliabecchiana, MS. Classe 19, palco 7. *Fabbrica di galere.*
Bibliothèque National Paris. MS. Grec 510.
Bibliothèque National Paris. MS. Suppl. lat. 773.
Museo Naval, Madrid. *Coleccion Navarrete.* Vol. XII, dto. 83.

PRINTED SOURCES

Abū Shāma. *Le livre des deux jardins. Historie des deux règnes, celui de Nour ed-Dīn et celui de Salāh ed-Dīn,* in *R.H.C. Or.,* vols. 4–5. Paris, 1898, 1906.
Al-Maqrizi. *Histoire d'Egypte de Makrizi,* trans. E. Blochet, in *Revue de l'Orient latin,* 8 (1900–1), 165–212, 501–53; 9 (1902), 6–163, 465–530; 10 (1903–4), 248–371; 11 (1905–8), 192–239.
Al-Muqqadasi. *Descriptio imperii Moslemici,* ed. M. J. de Goeje, 2nd edn. Leiden, 1906.
Ambroise. *L'Estoire de la guerre sainte,* ed. G. Paris. Paris, 1897.
Ashburner, W., ed. *ΝΟΜΟΣ ΡΟΔΙΩΝ ΝΑΥΤΙΚΟΣ: The Rhodian sea-law.* Oxford, 1909.
Basil of Caesarea, St. *Homélies sur l'hexaéméron,* ed. & trans. S. Giet. Paris, 1949.
Behā ed-Dīn. *Anecdotes et beaux traits de la vie du sultan Youssof (Salāh ed-Dīn),* in *R.H.C. Or.,* vol. 3. Paris, 1884.
The life of Saladin, trans. C. W. Wilson. London, 1897.
Belgrano, L. T. *Documenti riguardanti la colonia genovese di Pera.* Genoa, 1888.
'Seconda serie di documenti riguardanti la colonia di Pera', *Atti della Societá ligure di storia patria,* 13 (1884), 932–1003.
Bellorini, T. & E. Hoade, eds. & trans. *Visit to the holy places of Egypt, Sinai, Palestine and Syria in 1384 by Frescobaldi, Gucci and Sigoli.* Jerusalem, 1948.

Benjamin of Tudela. *The itinerary of Benjamin of Tudela*, trans. M. W. Adler. London, 1907.

Bernard the Wise. 'The voyage of Bernard the Wise: A.D. 867', ed. & trans. T. Wright, in *Early travels in Palestine*. London, 1848. 23–31.

Blancard, L., ed. *Documents inédits sur le commerce de Marseille au moyen-âge*. Marseilles, 1884–5.

Boccaccio. *Decameron*, ed. V. Branca. Florence, 1976.

Bonnardot, F. & A. Longnon, eds. *Le saint voyage de Jherusalem du seigneur d'Anglure*. Paris, 1878.

Brunschwig, R., ed. *Deux récits de voyages en Afrique du Nord au XVᵉ siècle: 'Abdalbasiṭ b. Halil et Adorne*. Paris, 1936.

Caffaro. *Annali genovesi di Caffaro e de' suoi continuatori dal MXCIX al MCCXCIII*, ed. L. T. Belgrano, vol. 1. Genoa, 1890.

De liberatione civitatum Orientis liber, ed. L. T. Belgrano in *Annali genovesi di Caffaro*. Vol. 1, 95–124.

Cantacuzenus, John VI. *Historiarum libri IV*, in J. P. Migne, ed., *Patrologiae cursus completus: series Graeca posterior*, vol. 154. Paris, 1866.

Casola, Pietro. *Canon Pietro Casola's pilgrimage to Jerusalem in the year 1494*, trans. M. Newett. Manchester, 1907.

Choniates, Michael. Μιχ 'Ακομινάτου Σωζόμενα, ed. S. Lampros. Athens, 1879–80.

Choniates, Niketas. *O city of Byzantium, annals of Niketas Choniates*, trans. H. J. Magoulias. Detroit, 1984.

Clavijo, Ruy Gonzalez de. *Narrative of the embassy of Ruy Gonzalez de Clavijo to the court of Timour, at Samarcand, A.D. 1403–6*, trans. C. R. Markham (Hakluyt Soc. Works. First series, 26). London, 1859.

Codex Iustinianus. In *Corpus iuris civilis*, ed. T. Mommsen, P. Krueger, R. Schoell & W. Kroll, vol. II. 15th edn. 1877; rpt. Dublin/Zurich, 1970.

Comnena, Anna. *The Alexiad*, trans. E. R. A. Sewter. Harmondsworth, 1969.

Dain, A. *Naumachica partim ad hunc inedita*. Paris, 1943.

Day, J. *Les douanes de Gênes 1376–1377*. Paris, 1963.

Delaville le Roulx, J., ed. *Cartulaire général de l'ordre des Hospitaliers de St. Jean de Jérusalem (1100–1310)*. Paris, 1894–1906.

Fabri, Felix. *The book of the wanderings of brother Felix Fabri*, trans. A. Stewart, in *P.P.T.S.L.*, vols. 7–10. London, 1896–7.

Filangieri, R., ed. *I registri della cancelleria angioina*, 33 vols. Naples, 1950–81.

Fulcher of Chartres. *Historia Hierosolymitana (1095–1127)*, ed. H. Hagenmeyer. Heidelberg, 1913.

A history of the expedition to Jerusalem, 1095–1127, trans. F. R. Ryan. New York, 1973.

Gilbert de Lannoy. *Oeuvres de Ghillebert de Lannoy: voyageur, diplomate et moraliste*, ed. C. Potvin. Louvain, 1878.

Goitein, S. D., ed. *Letters of medieval Jewish traders*. Princeton, 1973.

Gregoras, Nicephorus. *Byzantina historia*, ed. L. Schopenus & I. Bekker. Bonn, 1829–55.

Hesiod. *Works and days*, in *Hesiod, the Homeric hymns and Homerica*, ed. & trans. H. G. Evelyn-White. London, 1959.

Hoade, E., ed. *Western pilgrims*. Jerusalem, 1952.

Ibn al-Athir. *Extrait de la chronique intitulée Kamel-altevarykh par Ibn-Alatyr*, in *R.H.C. Or.*, vols. 1–2. Paris, 1872–7.

Ibn Battuta. *The travels of Ibn Battuta, A.D. 1325–1354*, trans. H. A. R. Gibb (Hakluyt Soc. Works. Second series, 110, 117, 141). Cambridge, 1958–71.

Ibn Hauqal. *Configuration de la terre (Kitab surat al-ard)*, trans. J. H. Kramer & G. Wiet. Paris, 1964.

Ibn Jubayr. *The travels of Ibn Jubayr*, trans. R. J. C. Broadhurst. London, 1952.

Ibn Khaldūn. *The Muqaddimah: an introduction to history*, trans. F. Rosenthal. Princeton, 1958.

'Imad ad-Dīn. *Al-Faṭḥ al-Qussī fī'l -Fatḥ al-Qudsī*, ed. C. Landberg. Leiden, 1888.

Imber, C. H. 'The costs of naval warfare: the accounts of Hayreddin Barbarossa's Herceg Novi campaign in 1539', *Archivum Ottomanicum*, 4 (1972), 203–16.

Itinerarium peregrinorum et gesta regis Ricardi, ed. W. Stubbs (Rerum Britannicarum medii aevi scriptores, 38). London, 1864.

Jacques de Vitry. *Lettres de Jacques de Vitry (1160/1170–1240) évêque de Saint-Jean d'Acre*, ed. R. B. C. Huygens. Leiden, 1960.

Joinville. *The life of St. Louis by John of Joinville*, trans. R. Hague. London, 1955.

Khalifeh, Haji. *The history of the maritime wars of the Turks*, trans. J. Mitchell. London, 1831.

Kinnamos, John. *Deeds of John and Manuel Comnenus*, trans. C. M. Brand. New York, 1976.

Krekic, B. *Dubrovnik (Raguse) et le Levant au moyen-âge*. Paris, 1961.

Kretschmer, K. *Die italienischen Portolane des Mittelalters*. Berlin, 1909.

Kritovoulos. *History of Mehmed the conqueror*, trans. C. T. Riggs. Westport, 1970.

L'estoire de Eracles Empereur et la conqueste de la terre d'Outremer, in *R.H.C. Occ.*, vol. 2. Paris, 1859.

Louis de Rochechouart. 'Journal de voyage de Louis de Rochechouart évêque de Saintes', ed. C. Couderc, in *Revue de l'Orient latin*, 1 (1893), 168–274.

Ludolph von Suchem. *Description of the Holy Land and of the way thither, written in the year 1350*, trans. A. Stewart, in *P.P.T.S.L.*, vol. 12, part 3. London, 1897.

Mas Latrie, L. de. *Traités de paix et de commerce et documents divers concernant les relations des Chrétiens avec les Arabes de l'Afrique septentrionale au moyen-âge*. Paris, 1866.

Mas Latrie, L. de, ed. *Chronique d'Ernoul et de Bernard le Trésorier*. Paris, 1871.

Melissenos, Makarios. *The chronicle of the siege of Constantinople, April 2 to May 29, 1453*, in George Sphrantzes, *The fall of the Byzantine empire: a chronicle by George Sphrantzes, 1401–1477*, trans. M. Philippides. Amherst, 1980.

Miklosich, F. & J. Müller, eds. *Acta et diplomata graeca medii aevi sacra et profana*, vol. 3. Vienna, 1865.

Morozzo della Rocca, R., ed. *Lettere di mercanti a Pignol Zucchello (1336–1350)*. Venice, 1957.

Motzo, B. R., ed. *Il compasso di Navegare: opera italiana del metà di secolo XIII*. Cagliari, 1947.

Muntaner, Ramon. *The chronicle of Muntaner* (Hakluyt Soc. Works. Second series, 47 and 50). London, 1920–1.

Niccolò da Poggibonsi. *A voyage beyond the seas (1346–1350)*, ed. & trans. T. Bellorini & E. Hoade. Jerusalem, 1945.

Nicolaus de Marthono. 'Nicolai de Marthono, notarii, liber peregrinationis ad Loca Sancta', ed. L. Legrand in *Revue de l'Orient latin*, 3 (1895), 566–669.

Odo of Deuil. *De profectione Ludovici VII in Orientem*, trans. V. G. Berry. New York, 1947.

Pegolotti, F. di Balducci. *La pratica della mercatura*, ed. A. P. Evans. New York, 1970.

Pertusi, A. *Testi inediti e poco noti sulla caduta di Costantinopoli*, ed. A. Carile. Bologna, 1983.

Philip de Novare. *The wars of Frederick II against the Ibelins in Syria and Cyprus*, trans. J. L. La Monte. New York, 1936.

Piloti, Emmanuel. *Traité d'Emmanuel Piloti sur le passage en Terre Sainte (1420)*, ed. P. H. Dopp. Louvain, 1958.

Pisa. *Constitutum usus*, ed. F. Bonaini, in *Statuti inediti della città di Pisa dal XII al XIV secolo*. Florence, 1854–70.

Procopius. *History of the wars: book III. The Vandalic war*, trans. H. B. Dewing, in *Procopius*, vol. 2. London, 1953.

Raymond d'Aguilers. *Historia Francorum qui ceperunt Iherusalem*, trans. J. H. & L. L. Hill. Philadelphia, 1968.

Roger of Hoveden. *Chronica*, ed. W. Stubbs (Rerum Britannicarum medii aevi scriptores, 51). London, 1868–71.

Saewulf. *An account of the pilgrimage of Saewulf to Jerusalem and the Holy Land in the years 1102 and 1103 from our Lord's incarnation*, trans. the bishop of Clifton, in *P.P.T.S.L.*, vol. 4. London, 1896. 1–55.

Sanguineti, A. & G. Bertolotto. 'Nuova serie di documenti sulle relazioni di Genova coll' Impero bizantino', *Atti della Società ligure di storia patria*, 28 (1896–8), 337–573.

Sanudo Torsello, Marino. *Liber secretorum fidelium crucis super Terrae Sanctae recuperatione et conservatione*. Hanover, 1611.

Sarrasin, Jean. 'The letter of John Sarrasin', ed. A. E. Foulet (1924), trans. R. Hague in Joinville, *Life of St. Louis*. 241–6.

Schefer, C., ed. *Le voyage de la sainte cyté de Hierusalem*. Paris, 1882.

Scovazzi, M. 'Il viaggio in Italia del monaco islandese Nikolás', *Nuova rivista storica*, 51 (1967), 358–62.

Theoderich. *Description of the holy places*, trans. A. Stewart, in *P.P.T.S.L.*, vol. 5. London, 1896. 1–86.

The Theodosian Code and Novels and the Sirmondian Constitutions, trans. C. Pharr. New York, 1969.

Usāmah ibn Munqidh. *Memoirs of an Arab–Syrian gentleman or an Arab knight in the Crusades*, trans. P. K. Hitti. Beirut, 1964.

Varaldo, C. 'Inventario ed armamento di una flotta di galee a Savona nel

1476', *Atti e memorie della Società savonese di storia patria*, n.s. 14 (1980), 85–96.

Vegetius. *Epitoma rei militaris*, ed. C. Lang. Stuttgart, 1872.

William of Tyre. *Historia rerum in partibus transmarinis gestarum*, in *R.H.C. Occ.*, vol. 1. Paris, 1844.
A history of deeds done beyond the sea, trans. E. A. Babcock & A. C. Krey. New York, 1941.

SECONDARY SOURCES

UNPUBLISHED THESES

Andrews, A. D. *The Turkish threat to Venice 1453–1463*. Ph. D. thesis, University of Pennsylvania, 1962.

Day, G. W. *Genoese involvement with Byzantium 1155–1204: a diplomatic and prosopographical study*. Ph. D. thesis, University of Illinois, 1978.

Djupedal, K. *The innovation and construction of the wooden sailing ship, 1150–1650*. M.A. thesis, University of Oregon, 1978.

Foster, S. M. *Some aspects of maritime activity and the use of sea power in relation to the Crusading states, 1096–1169*. D. Phil. thesis, Oxford University, 1978.

Van Doorninck jr, F. H. *The seventh-century Byzantine ship at Yassi Ada: some contributions to the history of naval architecture*. Ph.D. thesis, University of Pennsylvania, 1967.

Yarrison, J. L. *Force as an instrument of policy: European military incursions and trade in the Maghrib, 1000–1355*. Ph. D. thesis, Princeton University, 1982.

MONOGRAPHS AND ARTICLES

Abulafia, D. *The two Italies: economic relations between the Norman Kingdom of Sicily and the northern communes*. Cambridge, 1977.

Adam, P. 'A propos des origines de la voile latine', in Mollat, *Méditerranée et Océan Indien*. 203–28.

'Conclusions sur les développements des techniques nautiques médiévales', *Revue d'histoire économique et sociale*, 54 (1976), 560–7.

'Esquisse d'une typologie de la course et de la piraterie', in *Course et piraterie*. Vol. 2, 917–55.

Ahmad, A. *A history of Islamic Sicily*. Edinburgh, 1975.

Ahrweiler, H. *Byzance et la mer: la marine de guerre, la politique et les institutions maritimes de Byzance au VIIe–XVe siècles*. Paris, 1966.

'Course et piraterie dans la Méditerranée orientale aux IVème–XVème siècles (empire byzantin)', in *Course et piraterie*. Vol. 1, 7–29.

'Les liaisons maritimes et continentales dans le monde byzantin', in Ragosta, ed., *Navigazioni mediterranee*. 247–63.

'Les ports byzantins (VIIe–IXe siècles)', in *La navigazione mediterranea nell'alto medioevo*. Vol. 1, 259–83.

Airaldi, G. 'Groping in the dark: the emergence of Genoa in the early Middle Ages', in *Miscellanea di studi storici, II*. Genoa, 1983. 7–17.

Ali, A. 'The Arabs as seafarers', *Islamic culture*, 54 (1980), 211–22.

Anderson, R. C. *Oared fighting ships: from classical times to the coming of steam.* Kings Langley, 1976.

Antoniadis-Bibicou, H. *Etudes d'histoire maritime de Byzance: à propos du 'Thème des Caravisiens'.* Paris, 1966.

'Sources byzantines pour servir à l'histoire maritime', in Mollat, *Sources de l'histoire maritime.* 121–36.

(Antoniadis-) Bibicou. 'Problèmes de la marine byzantine', *Annales: E.S.C.,* 13 (1958), 327–38.

Ashtor, E. 'L'artigleria veneziana e il commercio di Levante', in *Armi e cultura nel Bresciano 1420–1870.* Brescia, 1981. 141–54.

'L'ascendant technologique de l'Occident médiéval', *Revue Suisse d'histoire,* 33 (1983), 385–413.

'Aspetti della espansione italiana nel basso medioevo', *Rivista storica italiana,* 90 (1978), 5–29.

'The economic decline of the Middle East during the later Middle Ages – an outline', *Asian and African studies,* 15 (1981), 253–86.

'The Jews in the Mediterranean trade in the fifteenth century', in J. Schneider, ed., *Wirtschaftskräfte und Wirtschaftswege. I: Mittelmeer und Kontinent. Festschrift für Hermann Kellenbenz.* Nuremberg, 1978. 441–54.

Levant trade in the later Middle Ages. Princeton, 1983.

'Le Proche-Orient au bas moyen-âge: une région sousdévelopé, une économie en déclin', in A. Guarducci, ed., *Sviluppo e sottosviluppo in Europa e fuori d'Europa dal secolo XIII alla rivoluzione industriale.* Prato, 1983, 375–433.

Atiya, A. S. *The Crusade in the later Middle Ages.* New York, 1965.

Attman, A. *The bullion flow between Europe and the East 1000–1750.* Göteborg, 1981.

Ayalon, D. 'Egypt as a dominant factor in Syria and Palestine during the Islamic period', in *Egypt and Palestine: a millennium of association (868–1948).* Jerusalem, 1984. 17–47.

'The Mamluks and naval power: a phase of the struggle between Islam and Christian Europe', *Proceedings of the Israel Academy of Sciences and Humanities,* 1 (1965), 1–12.

Aymard, M. 'Chiourmes et galères dans la Méditerranée du XVIe siècle', in *Mélanges en l'honneur de Fernand Braudel.* Toulouse, 1973. Vol. 1, 49–64.

Baker, W. A. 'Notes' on the papers of Van der Merwe & Friel in 'Session VI: the three-masted ship'. 149–50.

Balard, M. 'A propos de la bataille du Bosphore: l'expédition génoise de Paganino Doria à Constantinople (1351–1352)', *Travaux et mémoires du Centre de recherche d'histoire et de civilization byzantines,* 4 (1970), 431–69.

'Escales génoises sur les routes de l'Orient méditerranéen au XIVe siècle', in *Les grandes escales: Première partie: antiquité et moyen-âge* (Recueils de la Société Jean Bodin, XXXII). Brussels, 1974. 243–64.

'Gênes et la mer noire (XIIIe–XVe siècles)', *Revue historique,* 270 (1983), 31–54.

La Romanie Génoise (XIIe– début du XVe siècle). Genoa, 1978.

Baldwin, M. W., ed. *The first hundred years* (vol. 1 of K. M. Setton, ed., *A history of the Crusades*). Philadelphia, 1955.

'The Latin states under Baldwin III and Amalric I, 1143–1174', in Baldwin, ed., *The first hundred years*. 528–61.

Balletto, L. 'Mercanti, corsari e pirati nei mari della Corsica (sec. XIII)', in *Miscellanea di storia italiana e mediterranea per Nino Lamboglia*. Genoa, 1978. 171–263.

Basch, L. 'A galley in Istanbul: the *kadīrga*', *M.M.*, 60 (1974), 133–5.

Bass, G. F., ed. *A history of seafaring based on underwater archaeology*. London, 1972.

Bass, G. F. & F. H. van Doorninck jr. 'An 11th-century shipwreck at Serçe Liman, Turkey', *I.J.N.A.*, 7 (1978), 119–32.

Bass, G. F. & F. H. van Doorninck jr., eds. *Yassi Ada: Volume I: a seventh-century Byzantine shipwreck*. College Station, 1982.

Bastard de Péré, R. 'Navires méditerranéens du temps de Saint Louis', *Revue d'histoire économique et sociale*, 50 (1972), 327–56.

Bautier, R. H. 'Les sources de l'histoire du commerce international en Méditerranée (XIIᵉ–XVᵉ siècle)', in Mollat, *Sources de l'histoire maritime*. 137–79.

Beck, H. G., et al., eds. *Venezia: centro di mediazione tra Oriente e Occidente (secoli XV–XVI): aspetti e problemi*. Florence, 1977.

Ben-Ami, A. *Social change in a hostile environment: the Crusaders' Kingdom of Jerusalem*. Princeton, 1969.

Blochet, E. *Les enluminures des manuscrits orientaux – turcs, arabes, persans – de la Bibliothèque Nationale*. Paris, 1926.

Bonino, M. *Archeologia e tradizione navale tra la Romagna e il Po*. Ravenna, 1978.

'Lateen-rigged medieval ships: new evidence from wrecks in the Po delta (Italy) and notes on pictorial and other documents', *I.J.N.A.*, 7 (1978), 9–28.

Bono, S. *I corsari barbareschi*. Turin, 1964.

Bradford, E. *Mediterranean – portrait of a sea*. New York, 1971.

Bragadin, M. (A.) *Histoire des républiques maritimes italiennes: Venise – Amalfi – Pise – Gênes*. Paris, 1955.

'Le navi, loro strutture et attrezzature', in *La navigazione mediterranea nell'alto medioevo*. Vol. 1, 389–407.

Brand, C. M. *Byzantium confronts the West, 1180–1204*. Cambridge, Mass., 1968.

Branigan, J. J. & H. R. Jarrett. *The Mediterranean lands*. London, 1969.

Braudel, F. *The Mediterranean and the Mediterranean world in the age of Philip II*, 2nd edn, trans. S. Reynolds. New York, 1973.

Bresc, H. 'Course et piraterie en Sicile (1250–1450)', *A.E.M.*, 10 (1980), 751–7.

Brooks, E. W. 'The Arab conquest of Crete', *English Historical Review*, 28 (1913), 431–43.

Bryer, A. 'Shipping in the empire of Trebizond', *M.M.*, 52 (1966), 3–12.

Burns, R. I. 'Piracy as an Islamic–Christian interface in the thirteenth century', *Viator*, 11 (1980), 165–78.

Burski, H. A. von. *Kemāl Re'is: ein Beitrag zur Geschichte der Türkischen Flotte*. Bonn, 1928.

Cahen, C. 'Commercial relations between the Near East and Western Europe from the VIIth to the XIth century', in K. I. Semaan, ed., *Islam and the medieval West: aspects of intercultural relations*. Albany, 1980. 1–25.

'Douanes et commerce dans les ports méditerranéens de l'Egypte médiévale d'après le *Minhādj* d'Al-Makhzūmī', *Journal of the economic and social history of the Orient*, 7 (1964), 217–314.

Orient et Occident au temps des Croisades. Paris, 1983.

'Orient latin et commerce du Levant', *Bulletin de la Faculté des lettres de Strasbourg*, 29 (1951), 328–46.

Pre-Ottoman Turkey. London, 1968.

'Quelques mots sur le déclin commercial du monde musulman à la fin du moyen-âge', in Cook, *Studies*. 31–6.

'The Turks in Iran and Anatolia before the Mongol invasions', in Wolff & Hazard, *The later Crusades*. 661–92.

Carrère, C. *Barcelone: centre économique à l'époque des difficultés 1360–1462*. Paris, 1967.

'Marseille, Aigues Mortes, Barcelone et la competition en Méditerranée occidentale au XIIIᵉ siècle', *A.E.M.*, 10 (1980), 161–72.

Casson, L. *The ancient mariners: seafarers and sea fighters of the Mediterranean in ancient times*. New York, 1959.

Ships and seamanship in the ancient world. Princeton, 1971.

Cazacu, M. & P. S. Nasturel. 'Une démonstration navale des Turcs devant Constantinople et la bataille de Kilia (1448)', *Journal des savants* (1978), 197–210.

Charanis, P. 'Piracy in the Aegean during the reign of Michael VIII Palaeologus', *Annuaire de l'Institut de philologie et d'histoire orientales et slaves*, 10 (1950), 127–36.

Christides, V. *The conquest of Crete by the Arabs (ca. 824): a turning point in the struggle between Byzantium and Islam*. Athens, 1984.

'Naval warfare in the Eastern Mediterranean (6th–14th centuries): an Arabic translation of Leo VI's Naumachica', *Graeco-Arabica*, 3 (1984), 137–48.

'The raids of the Moslems of Crete in the Aegean Sea: piracy and conquest', *Byzantion*, 51 (1981), 76–111.

'Two parallel naval guides of the tenth century: Qudama's document and Leo VI's Naumachica: a study on Byzantine and Moslem naval preparedness', *Graeco-Arabica*, 1 (1982), 51–103.

Citarella, A. O. 'A puzzling question concerning the relations between the Jewish communities of Christian Europe and those represented in the Geniza documents', *Journal of the American Oriental Society*, 111 (1971), 390–7.

Clarke, J. I., ed. *An advanced geography of Africa*. Amersham, 1975.

Coles, P. *The Ottoman impact on Europe*. London, 1968.

Colom, F. S. 'Navegaciones mediterraneas (s. XI–XVI): valor del puerto de Mallorca', in Ragosta, *Navigazioni mediterranee*. 15–74.

Commissione eletta dalla R. Deputazione Veneta di storia patria. *Sulla scoperta di due barche antiche nel territorio del comune di Contarina in provincia di Rovigo nel gennaio 1898.* Venice, 1900. Rpt. in *Miscellanea di storia veneta edita per cura della R. Dep. Ven. di storia patria*, ser. 2, 7 (1901), 3–64.

Cook, M. A., ed. *Studies in the economic history of the Middle East from the rise of Islam to the present day.* London, 1970.

Course et piraterie (XVᵉ Colloque international d'histoire maritime, San Francisco, 1975). Paris, 1975.

Courtois, C. 'Les rapports entre l'Afrique et la Gaule au début du moyen-âge', *Cahiers de Tunisie*, 2 (1954), 127–45.

'Remarques sur le commerce maritime en Afrique au XIᵉ siècle', in *Mélanges d'histoire et d'archéologie de l'Occident musulman.* Algiers, 1957. Vol. 2, 51–9.

Dachraoui, F. 'La Crète dans le conflit entre Byzance et al-Muʻizz', *Cahiers de Tunisie*, 7 (1959), 307–18.

Davidson, H. R. E. 'The secret weapon of Byzantium', *Byzantinische Zeitschrift*, 66 (1973), 66–74.

Delgado, C. T. 'El Mediterraneo Nazari: diplomacia y pirateria. Siglos XIII–XIV', *A.E.M.*, 10 (1980), 227–36.

Der Nersessian, S. 'The homilies of Gregory of Nazianzus', *D.O.P.*, 16 (1962), 197–228.

De Saint-Denis, E. 'Mare clausum', *Revue des études latines*, 25 (1947), 196–214.

Dimmock, L. 'The lateen rig', *M.M.*, 32 (1946), 35–41.

Dolley, R. H. 'Naval tactics in the heyday of the Byzantine thalassocracy', *Atti del VIII Congresso internazionale di studi bizantini.* Rome, 1953. Vol. 1, 324–9.

'The rig of early medieval warships', *M.M.*, 35 (1949), 51–5.

'The warships of the later Roman empire', *Journal of Roman studies*, 38 (1948), 47–53.

Dotson, J. E. 'Jal's *Nef X* and Genoese naval architecture in the thirteenth century', *M.M.*, 59 (1973), 161–70.

'Merchant and naval influences on galley design at Venice and Genoa in the fourteenth century', in C. L. Symonds, ed., *New aspects of naval history: selected papers presented at the fourth naval history symposium.* Annapolis, 1979. 20–32.

'The voyage of Simone Leccavello: a Genoese naval expedition of 1351', in *Saggi e documenti, VI.* Genoa, 1985. 269–82.

Doursther, H. *Dictionnaire universel des poids et mesures anciens et modernes.* Brussels, 1840.

Dufourcq, Ch.-E. 'Chrétiens et musulmans durant les dernières siècles du moyen-âge', *A.E.M.*, 10 (1980), 207–26.

L'Espagne catalane et le Maghrib aux XIIIᵉ et XIVᵉ siècles. Paris, 1965.

'Les relations de la Péninsule Ibérique et de l'Afrique du Nord au XIVᵉ siècle', *A.E.M.*, 7 (1970–1), 39–66.

La vie quotidienne dans les ports méditerranéens au moyen-âge (Provence – Languedoc – Catalogne). Paris, 1975.

Earle, P. 'The commercial development of Ancona, 1479–1551', *Economic history review*, 2nd series, 22 (1969), 28–44.

Corsairs of Malta and Barbary. London, 1970.

Ehrenkreutz, A. 'The place of Saladin in the naval history of the Mediterranean Sea in the Middle Ages', *Journal of the American Oriental Society*, 75 (1955), 100–16.

Eickhoff, E. *Seekrieg und Seepolitik zwischen Islam und Abendland: das Mittelmeer unter Byzantinischer und Arabischer Hegemonie (650–1040)*. Berlin, 1966.

Elton, G. R. 'Historians against history', *The Cambridge Review* (18 November 1983), 203–5.

Encyclopaedia of Islam, ed. M. Th. Houtsma et al. Leiden, 1913–31.

Fahmy, A. M. *Muslim naval organization in the Eastern Mediterranean*. Cairo, 1966.

Fasano-Guarini, E. 'Au XVIᵉ siècle: comment naviguent les galères', *Annales: E.S.C.*, 16 (1961), 279–96.

Favreau, M.–L. 'Die italienische Levante-Piraterie und die Sicherheit der Seewege nach Syrien im 12. und 13. Jahrhundert', *Vierteljahrschrift fur Wirtschafts- und Sozialgeschichte*, 65 (1978), 463–510.

Ferrer i Mallol, M. T. 'Els corsaris castellans i la campanya di Pero Niño al Mediterrani (1404)', *A.E.M.*, 5 (1968), 265–338.

Fisher, G. *Barbary legend: war, trade and piracy in North Africa 1415–1830*. Oxford, 1957.

Fontenay, M. & A. Tenenti. 'Course et piraterie méditerranéenes de la fin du moyen-âge au début du XIXème siècle', in *Course et piraterie*. Vol. 1, 78–136.

Foss, C. *Ephesus after antiquity: a late antique, Byzantine, and Turkish city*. Cambridge, 1979.

Fotheringham, J. 'Genoa and the Fourth Crusade', *English historical review*, 25 (1910), 26–57.

Friel, I. 'England and the advent of the three-masted ship', in 'Session VI: the three-masted ship', in *Proceedings of the Fourth international congress of maritime museums*. Paris, 1981. 130–8.

Gabrielli, F. 'Greeks and Arabs in the central Mediterranean area', *D.O.P.*, 18 (1964), 57–65.

Garnier, l'abbé. 'Galères et galeasses à la fin du moyen-âge', in Mollat, ed., *Le navire et l'économie maritime*. 37–51.

Gateau, A. 'Quelques observations sur l'interêt du voyage d'Ibn Jubayr pour l'histoire de la navigation en Méditerranée au XIIᵉ siècle', *Hesperis*, 36 (1949), 289–312.

Gibb, H. A. R. 'The Aiyūbids', in Wolff & Hazard, *The later Crusades*. 693–714.

'The career of Nūr-ad-Dīn', in Baldwin, *The first hundred years*. 513–27.

Gille, P. 'Comment' on the paper of P. Adam, 'Voile latine', in Mollat, *Méditerranée et Ocean Indien*. 215–18.

'Jauge et tonnage des navires', in Mollat, *Le navire et l'économie maritime*. 85–103.

Godinho, V. M. 'Venise: les dimensions d'une présence face à un monde tellement changé – XVᵉ–XVIᵉ siècles', in Beck, *Venezia*. Vol. 1, 11–50.

Goitein, S. D. *A Mediterranean society: the Jewish communities of the Arab world as portrayed in the documents of the Cairo Geniza. Volume I: economic foundations.* Berkeley, 1967.

'Mediterranean trade in the eleventh century: some facts and problems', in Cook, *Studies.* 51–62.

'Mediterranean trade preceding the Crusades: some facts and problems', *Diogenes*, 59 (1967) 47–62.

Goldsmith, V. & S. Sofer. 'Wave climatology of the Southeastern Mediterranean', *Israel journal of earth sciences*, 32 (1983), 1–51.

Goudas, M. 'Μεσλιωνικὰ καράγματα πλοίων ᾽επὶ του Θησείου', *Byzantis*, 2 (1910), 329–57.

Graber, A. *Byzantine painting.* New York, 1953.

Grabois, A. 'Navigation méditerranéenne au VIIIème siècle selon quelques sources hagiographiques', in *L'histoire à Nice: Actes du Colloque international de 1980.* Nice, 1983. 7–13.

Great Britain, Admiralty. *Notes on climate and other subjects in Eastern Mediterranean and adjacent countries.* London, n.d.

Great Britain, Admiralty, Hydrographic Department. *Mediterranean pilot*, vol. 1 (8th edn), London, 1951; vol. 3 (9th edn), London, 1970; vol. 5 (4th edn), London, 1950.

Great Britain, Air Ministry, Meteorological Office. *Weather in the Mediterranean*, 2nd edn. London, 1962.

Guillou, A. 'Production and profits in the Byzantine province of Italy (tenth to eleventh centuries): an expanding society', *D.O.P.*, 28 (1974), 89–109.

Guilmartin, J. F. *Gunpowder and galleys: changing technology and Mediterranean warfare at sea in the sixteenth century.* Cambridge, 1975.

Guiral, J. 'Course et piraterie à Valence de 1410 à 1430', *A.E.M.*, 10 (1980), 759–65.

Haldane, D. *Mamluk painting.* Warminster, 1978.

Haldon, J. & M. Byrne. 'A possible solution to the problem of Greek fire', *Byzantinische Zeitschrift*, 70 (1977), 91–9.

Hale, J. R., ed. *Renaissance Venice.* London, 1973.

Halphen, L. 'La conquête de la Méditerranée par les Européens au XIᵉ et au XIIᵉ siècles', in *Mélanges d'histoire offerts à Henri Pirenne.* Brussels, 1926. Vol. 1, 175–80.

Hazard, H. W. 'Moslem North Africa, 1049–1394', in Hazard, *The fourteenth and fifteenth centuries.* 457–85.

Hazard, H. W., ed. *The fourteenth and fifteenth centuries* (vol. 3 of K. M. Setton, ed., *A history of the Crusades*). Madison, 1975.

Heers, J. 'Il commercio nel Mediterraneo alla fine del sec. XIV e nei primi anni del XV', *Archivio storico italiano*, 113 (1955), 157–209.

Gênes au XVᵉ siècle: activité économique et problèmes sociaux. Paris, 1961.

'Le royaume de Grenade et la politique marchande de Gênes en Occident (XVᵉ siècle)', *Le moyen-âge*, 63 (4ᵉ série, 12) (1957), 87–121.

'Types de navires et specialisation des trafics en Méditerranée à la fin du moyen-âge', in Mollat, *Le navire et l'économie maritime*, pp. 107–17.

Hendy, M. F. 'Byzantium, 1081–1204: an economic reappraisal', *Transactions of the Royal Historical Society*, 20 (1970), 31–52.

Herrin, J. 'The collapse of the Byzantine empire in the twelfth century: a study of a medieval economy', *Birmingham historical journal*, 12 (1970), 188–203.

Hess, A. C. 'The evolution of the Ottoman seaborne empire in the age of the oceanic discoveries', *American Historical Review*, 75 (1970), 1892–1919.

The forgotten frontier: a history of the sixteenth-century Ibero-African frontier. Chicago, 1978.

Heyd, W. *Histoire du commerce du Levant au moyen-âge*, trans. F. Raynaud. Leipzig, 1885–6.

Hill, G. *A history of Cyprus. Vols. 2 & 3: The Frankish period 1192–1571*. Cambridge, 1948.

Hocquet, J.-C. *Le sel et la fortune de Venise: Volume 2: Voiliers et commerce en Méditerranée 1200–1650*. Lille, 1979.

Houtsma, M. Th. 'Ueber eine Türkische Chronik zur Geschichte des Seljúqen Klein-Asiens', *Actes du Sixième Congrès international des Orientalistes tenu en 1883 à Leide*, part II. Leiden, 1884. 367–84.

Hyde, J. K. 'Navigation of the Eastern Mediterranean in the fourteenth and fifteenth centuries according to pilgrims' books', in H. McK. Blake et al., eds., *Papers in Italian archaeology I: The Lancaster Seminar. Recent research in prehistoric, classical, and medieval archaeology*, part 2 (British Archaeological Reports Supplementary series, 41 (2)). Oxford, 1978. 521–40.

Imber, C. H. 'The costs of naval warfare: the accounts of Hayreddin Barbarossa's Herceg Novi campaign in 1539', *Archivum Ottomanicum*, 4 (1972), 203–16.

'Ḳurṣān: II. In Turkish waters', in *The encyclopaedia of Islam*, new edn, vol. 5, ed. C. E. Bosworth et al. Leiden, 1980–3. 505–7.

'The navy of Süleyman the Magnificent', *Archivum Ottomanicum*, 6 (1980), 211–82.

Inalcik, H. 'Bursa and the commerce of the Levant', *Journal of the economic and social history of the Orient*, 3 (1960), 131–47.

'Capital formation in the Ottoman empire', *Journal of economic history*, 29 (1969), 97–140.

'Gelibolu', in *The encyclopaedia of Islam*, new edn, vol. 2, ed. B. Lewis et al. Leiden & London, 1965. 983–7.

'The Ottoman economic mind and aspects of the Ottoman economy', in Cook, *Studies*. 207–18.

The Ottoman empire: the classical age 1300–1600. London, 1973.

'An outline of Ottoman–Venetian relations', in Beck, *Venezia*. Vol. 1, 83–90.

'The question of the closing of the Black Sea under the Ottomans', in *ΑΡΧΕΙΟΝ ΠΟΝΤΟΥ. Τομος τριακοστος πεμπτος* (University of Birmingham. Centre for Byzantine studies. Twelfth Spring symposium of Byzantine studies: «The Byzantine Black Sea, 18–20 March 1978». Athens, 1978. 74–110.

Jacoby, D. 'Crusader Acre in the thirteenth century: urban layout and topography', *Studi medievali*, 3rd ser., 20 (1979), 1–45.

'Les gens de mer dans la marine de guerre vénitienne de la Mer Egée aux XIVe et XVe siècles', in Ragosta, *Le genti del mare mediterraneo.* 169–201.

Jenkins, R. J. H. 'Cyprus between Byzantium and Islam, A.D. 688–965', in G. E. Mylonas & D. Raymond, eds. *Studies presented to David Moore Robinson.* Saint Louis, 1953. Vol. II, 1006–1014.

Jurien de la Gravière, J. B. E. *Les corsaires barbaresques et la marine de Soliman le Grand.* Paris, 1887.

Doria et Barbarousse. Paris, 1886.

Kahane, H. & R., & A. Tietze. *The lingua franca in the Levant: Turkish nautical terms of Italian and Greek origin.* Urbana, 1958.

Kazhdan, A. & G. Constable. *People and power in Byzantium: an introduction to modern Byzantine studies.* Washington, 1982.

Kedar, B. Z. 'Discussione' on the paper of Udovitch, 'Time, the sea and society', in *La navigazione mediterranea nell'alto medioevo.* Vol. 2, 558–9.

'Mercanti genovesi in Alessandria d'Egitto negli anni sessanta del secolo XI', in *Miscellanea di studi storici, II.* Genoa, 1983. 19–30.

Merchants in crisis: Genoese and Venetian men of affairs and the fourteenth-century depression. New Haven, 1976.

'Segurano-Sakrān Salvaygo: un mercante genovese al servizio dei sultani mamalucchi, c. 1303–1322', in *Fatti ed idee di storia economica: studi dedicati a Franco Borlandi.* Bologna, 1977. 75–91.

Kissling, H. J. 'Venedig und der islamische Orient bis 1500', in Pertusi, *Venezia e il Levante.* Vol. 1, part I, 361–87.

Kortepeter, C. M. 'Ottoman imperial policy and the economy of the Black Sea region in the sixteenth century', *Journal of the American Oriental Society*, 86 (1966), 86–113.

Kreutz, B. M. 'Ships, shipping and the implications of change in the early medieval Mediterranean', *Viator*, 7 (1976), 79–109.

Krueger, H. C. 'Economic aspects of expanding Europe', in M. Clagett, ed., *Twelfth-century Europe and the foundations of modern society.* Madison, 1961. 59–76.

'The Italian cities and the Arabs before 1095', in Baldwin, *The first hundred years.* 40–53.

Kubiak, W. B. 'The Byzantine attack on Damietta in 853 and the Egyptian navy in the 9th century', *Byzantion*, 40 (1970), 145–66.

Kyrris, C. P. 'John Cantacuzenus and the Genoese 1321–1348', in *Miscellanea storica ligure, III.* Milan, 1963. 9–48.

'The nature of the Arab–Byzantine relations in Cyprus from the middle of the 7th to the middle of the 10th century A.D.', *Graeco-Arabica*, 3 (1984), 148–75.

Labib, S. Y. *Handelsgeschichte Ägyptens im Spätmittelalter (1171–1517).* Weisbaden, 1965.

Labib, S. (Y). 'The era of Suleyman the Magnificent: crisis of orientation', *International journal of Middle East studies*, 10 (1979), 435–51.

Laiou-Thomadakis, A. E. 'The Byzantine economy in the Mediterranean trade system: thirteenth–fifteenth centuries', *D.O.P.*, 34–5 (1980–1), 177–222.

Laiou(-Thomadakis), A. (E.). 'The provisioning of Constantinople during the winter of 1306–1307', *Byzantion*, 37 (1967), 91–113.

Landstrom, B. *The ship: an illustrated history*. New York, 1961.

Lane, F. C. 'The economic meaning of the invention of the compass', *American Historical Review*, 68 (1963), rpt. in his *Venice and history*. Baltimore, 1966, 331–44.

'The Mediterranean spice trade: further evidence of its revival in the sixteenth century', rpt. in Pullan, *Crisis and change in the Venetian economy*. 47–58.

'Naval actions and fleet organization, 1499–1502', in Hale, *Renaissance Venice*, 146–73.

'Progrès technologiques et productivité dans les transports maritimes de la fin du moyen-âge au début des temps modernes', *Revue historique*, 251 (1974), 277–302.

'Venetian shipping during the Commercial Revolution', rpt. in Pullan, *Crisis and change in the Venetian economy*, 22–46.

Venetian ships and shipbuilders of the Renaissance. Baltimore, 1934.

Venice: a maritime republic. Baltimore, 1973.

Lane-Poole, S. *The Barbary corsairs*. London, 1890.

La Roerie, G. & J. Vivielle. *Navires et marins de la rame à l'hélice*. Paris, 1930.

Lemerle, P. *L'émirat d'Aydin, Byzance, et l'Occident: recherches sur «La geste d'Umur Pacha»*. Paris, 1957.

Lev, Y. 'The Fātimid navy, Byzantium and the Mediterranean Sea 909–1036 C. E./297–427 A. H.', *Byzantion*, 54 (1984), 220–52.

Levi della Vida, G., 'A papyrus reference to the Damietta raid of 853 A.D.' *Byzantion*, 17 (1944–45), 212–21.

Lewicki, T. 'Les voies maritimes de la Méditerranée dans le haut moyen-âge d'après les sources arabes', in *La navigazione mediterranea nell'alto medioevo*. Vol. 2, 439–69.

Lewis, A. R. 'Mediterranean maritime commerce: A.D. 300–1100, shipping and trade', in *La navigazione mediterranea nell'alto medioevo*. Vol. 2, 480–501.

Naval power and trade in the Mediterranean A.D. 500–1100. Princeton, 1951.

'Northern European sea power and the Straits of Gibraltar, 1031–1350 A.D.', in W. C. Jordan et al., eds., *Order and innovation in the Middle Ages: essays in honour of Joseph R. Strayer*. Princeton, 1976. 139–64.

Lewis, B. 'Sources for the economic history of the Middle East', in Cook, *Studies*. 78–92.

Lloyd, S. & D. Storm Rice. *Alanya ('Alā'iyya)*. London, 1958.

Lombard, M. 'Arsenaux et bois de marine dans la Méditerranée musulmane: VIIᶜ–XIᶜ siècles', rpt. in his *Espaces et réseaux du haut moyen-âge*. Paris, 1972. 107–51.

'Le bois dans la Méditerranée musulmane: VIIᶜ–XIᶜ siècles: un problème cartographié', rpt. in his *Espaces et réseaux du haut moyen-âge*. Paris, 1972. 153–76.

The golden age of Islam. Amsterdam, 1975.

Lopez, R. S. *The Commercial Revolution of the Middle Ages, 950–1350.* Englewood Cliffs, 1971.

'East and West in the early Middle Ages: economic relations', in *Relazioni del X Congresso internazionale di scienze storiche*, vol. 3. Florence, 1955. 113–63.

'The role of trade in the economic readjustment of Byzantium in the seventh century', *D.O.P.*, 13 (1959), 68–85.

Lopez, R. S. & I. W. Raymond. *Medieval trade in the Mediterranean world.* New York, n.d.

Luke, H. 'The Kingdom of Cyprus, 1369–1489', in Hazard, *The fourteenth and fifteenth centuries.* 361–95.

Luttrell, A. 'The Crusade in the fourteenth century', in J. R. Hale et al., eds., *Europe in the late Middle Ages.* London, 1965. 122–54.

'Gregory XI and the Turks: 1370–1378', *Orientalia Christiana periodica*, 46 (1980), 391–417.

'The Hospitallers at Rhodes, 1306–1421', in Hazard, *The fourteenth and fifteenth centuries.* 278–313.

'Late-medieval galley oarsmen', in Ragosta, *Le genti del mare mediterraneo.* Vol. 1, 87–101.

'Venice and the Knights Hospitallers of Rhodes in the fourteenth century', *Papers of the British School at Rome*, 26 (1958), 195–212.

Lyons, M. C. & D. E. P. Jackson. *Saladin: the politics of the holy war.* Cambridge, 1982.

Malamut, E. 'Les îles de la mer Egée de la fin du XIe siècle à 1204', *Byzantion*, 52 (1982), 310–50.

Mallett, M. E. *The Florentine galleys in the fifteenth century.* Oxford, 1967.

Malowist, M. 'Les fondements de l'expansion Européene en Afrique au XVe siècle: Europe, Maghreb, et Soudan occidental', *Acta Poloniae historica*, 18 (1968), 155–79.

Manfroni, C. *Storia della marina italiana dalle invasioni barbariche al trattato di Ninfeo (anni di C. 400–1261).* Livorno, 1899.

Storia della marina italiana dal trattato di Ninfeo alla caduta di Constantinopoli (1261–1453). Livorno, 1902.

Marçais, G. 'Les villes de la côte algérienne et la piraterie au moyen-âge', *Annales de l'Institut d'études orientales*, 13 (1955), 118–42.

Martin, M. E. 'The Venetian–Seljuk treaty of 1220', *English Historical Review*, 95 (1980), 321–30.

Mas Latrie, L. de. *Histoire de l'île de Chypre sous le règne des princes de la maison de Lusignan*, vol. 2. Paris, 1852.

'*L'Officium Robarie* ou l'Office de la piraterie à Gênes au moyen-âge', *Bibliothèque de l'Ecole des Chartes*, 53 (1892), 262–72.

Meiggs, R. *Trees and timber in the ancient Mediterranean world.* Oxford, 1982.

Mercier, M. *Le feu grégois.* Paris, 1952.

Miles, G. C. 'Byzantium and the Arabs: relations in Crete and the Aegean area', *D.O.P.*, 18 (1964), 1–32.

Mollat, M. 'Essai d'orientation pour l'étude de la guerre de course et la piraterie (XIIIe–XVe siècles)', *A.E.M.*, 10 (1980), 743–9.

'Problèmes navals de l'histoire des croisades', *Cahiers de civilization médiévale*, 10 (1967), 345–59.

Mollat, M., ed. *Méditerranée et Ocean Indien* (VIème Colloque international d'histoire maritime, Venezia, 1962). Paris, 1970.

Le navire et l'économie maritime du moyen-âge au XVIIIe siècle, principalement en Méditerranée (Deuxième Colloque international d'histoire maritime, Paris, 1957), Paris. 1958.

Le navire et l'économie maritime du XVe au XVIIIe siècle (Première Colloque international d'histoire maritime, Paris, 1956). Paris, 1957.

Les sources de l'histoire maritime en Europe du moyen-âge au XVIIIe siècle (IVème Colloque international d'histoire maritime, Paris, 1959). Paris, 1962.

Morgan, G. 'The Venetian claims commission of 1278', *Byzantinische Zeitschrift*, 69 (1976), 411–38.

Muller, R. A. & T. M. Oberlander. *Physical geography today: a portrait of a planet*, 2nd edn. New York, 1974.

Musca, G. *L'emirato di Bari 847–871*. Bari, 1978.

Musso, G. G. 'Armamento e navigazione a Genova tra il Tre e il Quattrocento', in *Guerra e commercio nell'evoluzione della marina genovese tra XV e XVIII secolo*. Genoa, 1973. Vol. 2, 6–77.

McNeill, W. H. *Venice: the hinge of Europe 1081–1797*. Chicago, 1974.

La navigation dans l'Antiquité (Dossiers de l'Archéologie, 29 (July/August 1978)).

La navigazione mediterranea nell'alto medioevo (Settimane di studio del Centro italiano di studi sull'alto medioevo, XXV). Spoleto, 1978.

Nebbia, U. *Arte navale italiana*. Bergamo, 1932.

Occidente e l'Islam nell'alto medioevo, L'(Settimane di studio del Centro italiano di studi sull'alto medioevo, XII). Spoleto, 1965.

Oikonomides, N. *Hommes d'affaires Grecs et Latins à Constantinople (XIIIe– XVe siècles)*. Montreal, 1979.

Painter, S. 'The Third Crusade: Richard the Lionhearted and Philip Augustus', in Wolff & Hazard, *The later Crusades*. 45–85.

Pellat, C. 'Ḳurṣān: I. The Western Mediterranean and the Atlantic', in *The encyclopaedia of Islam*, new edn, vol. 5, ed. C. E. Bosworth et al. Leiden, 1980–3. 503–5.

Pertusi, A., ed. *Venezia e il Levante fino al secolo XV: vol. 1: storia – diritto – economia*. Florence, 1973.

Phillips- Birt, D. *Fore and aft sailing craft and the development of the modern yacht*. London, 1962.

A history of seamanship. New York, 1971.

Pistarino, G. 'Genova e l'Islam nel Mediterraneo occidentale (secoli XII–XIII)', *A.E.M.*, 10 (1980), 189–205.

Pomey, P. 'Comment naviguait-on dans la Méditerranée romaine', *L'histoire*, 36 (July/August 1981), 96–101.

'Discussione' on the paper of Bragadin, 'Le navi', in *La navigazione mediterranea nell'alto medioevo*. Vol. 1, 409–11.

Prawer, J. 'The Italians in the Latin Kingdom', in his *Crusader institutions*. Oxford, 1980. 217–49.

Pryor, J. H. *Business contracts of medieval Provence: selected notulae from the cartulary of Giraud Amalric of Marseilles, 1248*. Toronto, 1981.

'Mediterranean commerce in the Middle Ages: a voyage under contract of commenda', *Viator*, 14 (1983), 133–94.

'The naval architecture of Crusader transport ships: a reconstruction of some archetypes for round-hulled sailing ships', *M.M.*, 70 (1984), 171–219, 275–92, 363–86.

'The naval battles of Roger of Lauria', *Journal of medieval history*, 9 (1983), 179–216.

'Transportation of horses by sea during the era of the Crusades: eighth century to 1285 A.D.', *M.M.*, 68 (1982), 9–27, 103–25.

'Winds, waves, and rocks: the routes and the perils along them'. Forthcoming at the International Congress of historical sciences, Stuttgart, 1985.

Pullan, B., ed. *Crisis and change in the Venetian economy in the sixteenth and seventeenth centuries*. London, 1968.

Purpura, G. 'Un relitto di età normanna a Marsala', *Bolletino d'arte*, ser. 6, 29 (Jan.-Feb. 1985), 129–36.

Raban, A. 'The mercury carrier from the Red Sea', *Sefunim*, 4 (1972), 28–32.

'The "Naamah-South" expedition 1973', *Sefunim*, 4 (1972), 33–41.

'The shipwreck off Sharm-el-Sheikh', *Archaeology*, 24 (1971), 146–55.

Racine, P. 'Note sur le trafic Veneto-Chypriote à la fin du moyen-âge', *Byzantinische Forschungen*, 5 (1977), 307–29.

Ragosta, R., ed. *Le genti del mare mediterraneo*. Naples, 1981.

Navigazioni mediterranee e connessioni continentali (secoli XI–XVI). Naples, 1982.

Richard, J. *Le Comté de Tripoli sous la dynastie toulousaine (1102–1187)*. Paris, 1945.

'La Méditerranée et ses relations avec son arrière-pays oriental (XIᵉ–XVᵉ siècles)', in Ragosta, *Navigazioni mediterranee*. 265–99.

Riefstahl, R. M. *Turkish architecture in Southwestern Anatolia*. Cambridge, Mass., 1931.

Riley-Smith, J. 'Government in Latin Syria and the commercial privileges of foreign merchants', in D. Baker, ed., *Relations between East and West in the Middle Ages*. Edinburgh, 1973. 109–32.

Rizzitano, U. 'Gli Arabi in Italia', in *L'Occidente e l'Islam nell'alto medioevo*. 93–114.

Robson, J. A. 'The Catalan fleet and Moorish sea power (1337–1344)', *English Historical Review*, 74 (1959), 386–408.

Rodgers, W. L. *Naval warfare under oars, fourth to sixteenth centuries*. Annapolis, 1939.

Roger, N. *En Asie Mineure: la Turquie du Ghazi*. Paris, 1930.

Rossi, E. 'The Hospitallers at Rhodes, 1421–1523', in Hazard, *The fourteenth and fifteenth centuries*. 314–39.

Rougé, J. 'Discussione', on the paper of Lewicki, 'Les voies maritimes', in *La navigazione mediterranea nell'alto medioevo*. Vol. 2, 471–2.

'La navigation hivernale sous l'empire romain', *Revue des études anciennes*, 54 (1952), 316–325.

Recherches sur l'organization du commerce en Méditerranée sous l'empire romain. Paris, 1966.

Runciman, S. *The fall of Constantinople 1453*. Cambridge, 1969.

A history of the Crusades. Harmondsworth, 1971.

Santamaría Arández, A. 'La reconquista de las vías marítimas', *A.E.M.*, 10 (1980), 41–134.

Savvides, A. G. C. *Byzantium in the Near East: its relations with the Seljuk Sultanate of Rum in Asia Minor the Armenians of Cilicia and the Mongols A.D. c. 1192–1237*. Thessalonica, 1981.

Scandurra, E. 'The maritime republics: medieval and Renaissance ships in Italy', in Bass, *History of seafaring*. 205–24.

Schreiner, P. 'Zivilschiffart und Handelschiffart in Byzanz: Quellen und Probleme bezüglich der dort tätigen Personen', in Ragosta, *Le genti del mare mediterraneo*. 9–25.

Schwoebel, R. *The shadow of the crescent: the Renaissance image of the Turk (1453–1517)*. Nieuwkoop, 1967.

Semple, E. C. *The geography of the Mediterranean region: its relation to ancient history*. London, 1931.

Senac, P. *Musulmans et Sarrasins dans le sud de la Gaule du VIIIᵉ au XIᵉ siècle*. Paris, 1980.

Sesan, M. 'La flotte byzantine à l'époque des Comnènes et des Anges (1081–1204)', *Byzantinoslavica*, 21 (1960), 48–53.

Setton, K. M. 'On the raids of the Moslems in the Aegean in the ninth and tenth centuries and their alleged occupation of Athens', *American journal of archaeology*, 58 (1954), 311–19.

Sottas, J. 'A model of the Portus ship', *M.M.*, 21 (1935), 145–52.

Soucek, S. 'Certain types of ships in Ottoman–Turkish terminology', *Turcica*, 7 (1975), 233–49.

'The rise of the Barbarossas in North Africa', *Archivum Ottomanicum*, 3 (1971), 238–50.

Steffy, J. R. 'The reconstruction of the 11th-century Serçe Liman vessel: a preliminary report', *I.J.N.A.*, 11 (1982), 13–34.

Stoianovich, S. 'The conquering Balkan orthodox merchant', *Journal of economic history*, 20 (1960), 234–313.

Stratos, A. N. 'The naval engagement at Phoenix', in A. E. Laiou-Thomadakis, ed., *Charanis studies: Essays in honour of Peter Charanis*. New Brunswick, 1980. 229–47.

Strayer, J. R. 'The Crusades of Louis IX', in Wolff & Hazard, *The later Crusades*. 487–518.

Tadić, J. 'La côte occidentale des Balkans et ses liaisons maritimes et continentales (XIᵉ–XVIᵉ siècles)', in Ragosta, *Navigazioni mediterranee*. 99–100.

Talbi, M. *L'émirat Aghlabide 184–296/800–909: histoire politique*. Paris, 1966.

Taylor, E. G. R. *The haven-finding art: a history of navigation from Odysseus to Captain Cook*. London, 1956.

Tenenti, A. 'I corsari in Mediterraneo all'inizio del Cinquecento', *Rivista storica italiana*, 72 (1960), 234–87.

Cristoforo da Canal: la marine vénitienne avant Lépante. Paris, 1962.

Naufrages, corsairs et assurances maritimes à Venise, 1592–1609. Paris, 1959.

Piracy and the decline of Venice 1580–1615. Berkeley, 1967.

'Venezia e la pirateria nel Levante 1300c.–1460c.', in Pertusi, *Venezia e il Levante*. 703–71.

'The sense of space and time in the Venetian world of the fifteenth and sixteenth centuries', in Hale, *Renaissance Venice*. 17–46.

Tenenti, A. & C. Viventi. 'Le film d'un grand système de navigation: les galères marchandes vénitiennes, XIVᵉ–XVIᵉ siècles', *Annales: E.S.C.*, 16 (1961), 83–6.

Thiriet, F. 'Les itinéraires des vaisseaux vénitiens et le rôle des agents consulaires en Romanie Greco-Vénitienne aux XIV–XV siècles', in Ragosta, *Le genti del mare mediterraneo*. 587–608.

La Romanie Vénitienne au moyen-âge: le développement et l'exploitation du domaine colonial vénitien (XIIᵉ–XVᵉ siècles). Paris, 1959.

'Venise et l'occupation de Ténédos au XIVᵉ siècle', *Mélanges d'archéologie et d'histoire publiés par l'Ecole française de Rome*, 65 (1953), 219–45.

Trasselli, C. 'Naufragi, pirateria e doppio giuoco', in Ragosta, *Le genti del mare mediterraneo*. 499–510.

Tucci, U. 'The psychology of the Venetian merchant in the sixteenth century', in Hale, *Renaissance Venice*. 346–78.

'Sur la pratique vénitienne de la navigation au XVIᵉ siècle', *Annales: E.S.C.*, 13 (1958), 72–86.

Udovitch, A. 'Time, the sea and society: duration of commercial voyages on the southern shores of the Mediterranean during the High Middle Ages', in *La navigazione mediterranea nell'alto medioevo*. Vol. 2, 503–46.

Unali, A. *Marinai, pirati e corsari catalani nel basso medioevo*. Bologna, 1983.

Unger, W. 'Commentary' on the papers of Van der Merwe and Friel, in 'Session VI: the three-masted ship'. 147–8.

The ship in the medieval economy 600–1600. London, 1980.

'Warships and cargo ships in medieval Europe', *Technology and culture*, 22 (1981), 233–52 and illustrations.

Uzunçarşılı, I. H. 'Baḥriyya, III: the Ottoman navy', in *The encyclopaedia of Islam*, new edn, vol. 1, ed. B. Lewis et al. Leiden & London, 1960. 947–9.

Vanacker, C. 'Géographie économique de l'Afrique du Nord selon les auteurs arabes, du IXᵉ siècle au milieu du XIIᵉ siècle', *Annales: E.S.C.*, 28 (1973), 659–80.

Van Cleve, T. C. 'The Crusade of Frederick II', in Wolff & Hazard, *The later Crusades*, 429–62.

Van der Merwe, P. 'Towards a three-masted ship', in 'Session VI: the three-masted ship', in *Proceedings of the Fourth international congress of maritime museums*. Paris, 1981. 121–9.

Van Doorninck jr, F. (H.) 'Byzantium, mistress of the sea: 330–641', in Bass, *History of seafaring*. 133–58.

Vaughan, D. M. *Europe and the Turk: a pattern of alliances 1350–1700.* Liverpool, 1954.

Verlinden, C. 'Venezia e il commercio degli schiavi provenienti dalle coste orientali del Mediterraneo', in Pertusi, *Venezia e il Levante.* 911–29.

Vernet, J. 'La navegación en la alta edad media', in *La navigazione mediterranea nell'alto medioevo.* Vol. 1, 323–81.

Villain-Gandossi, C. 'Commentary' on the papers of Van der Merwe and Friel, in 'Session VI: the three-masted ship'. 139–46.

'Notes sur la terminologie turque de la course', in *Course et piraterie.* Vol. 1, 137–45.

Vitale, V., ed. *Le fonti del diritto marittimo ligure.* Genoa, 1951.

Walker, D. S. *The Mediterranean lands,* 3rd edn. London, 1965.

White jr, L. 'The Crusades and the technological thrust of the West', in V. J. Parry & M. E. Yapp, eds., *War, technology and society in the Middle East.* London, 1975. 97–112.

'Introduction: the reticences of the Middle Ages', in R. Berger, ed., *Scientific methods in medieval archaeology.* Berkeley, 1970. 3–14.

Wittek, P. *Das Fürstentum Mentesche: Studie zur Geschichte West-Kleinasiens im 13.–15. Jh.* Istanbul, 1934.

The rise of the Ottoman empire. London, 1938.

Wolff, R. L. & H. W. Hazard, eds., *The later Crusades, 1189–1311* (vol. 2 of K. M. Setton, ed., *A history of the Crusades*). Madison, 1969.

Zachariadou, E. A. 'Prix et marchés des céréales en Romanie (1343–1405)', *Nuova rivista storica,* 61 (1977), 291–306.

'Sept traités inédits entre Venise et les émirats d'Aydin et de Menteşe (1331–1407)', in *Studi Ottomani e pre-Ottomani.* Naples, 1976. 229–40.

Zakythinos, D. 'L'attitude de Venise face au déclin et à la chute de Constantinople', in Beck, *Venezia.* Vol. 1, 61–75.

Zechlin, E. *Maritime Weltgeschichte: Altertum und Mittelalter.* Hamburg, 1947.

Index

230   Index

Past and Present Publications

General Editor: PAUL SLACK, *Exeter College, Oxford*

Family and Inheritance: Rural Society in Western Europe 1200–1800, edited by Jack Goody, Joan Thirsk and E. P. Thompson*
French Society and the Revolution, edited by Douglas Johnson
Peasants, Knights and Heretics: Studies in Medieval English Social History, edited by R. H. Hilton*
Towns in Societies: Essays in Economic History and Historical Sociology, edited by Philip Abrams and E. A. Wrigley*
Desolation of a City: Coventry and the Urban Crisis of the Late Middle Ages, Charles Phythian-Adams
Puritanism and Theatre: Thomas Middleton and Opposition Drama under the Early Stuarts, Margot Heinemann*
Lords and Peasants in a Changing Society: The Estates of the Bishopric of Worcester 680–1540, Christopher Dyer
Life, Marriage and Death in a Medieval Parish: Economy, Society and Demography in Halesowen 1270–1500, Zvi Razi
Biology, Medicine and Society 1840–1940, edited by Charles Webster
The Invention of Tradition, edited by Eric Hobsbawm and Terence Ranger*
Industrialization before Industrialization: Rural Industry and the Genesis of Capitalism, Peter Kriedte, Hans Medick and Jürgen Schlumbohm†*
The Republic in the Village: The People of the Var from the French Revolution to the Second Republic, Maurice Agulhon†
Social Relations and Ideas: Essays in Honour of R. H. Hilton, edited by T. H. Aston, P. R. Coss, Christopher Dyer and Joan Thirsk
A Medieval Society: The West Midlands at the End of the Thirteenth Century, R. H. Hilton
Winstanley: 'The Law of Freedom' and Other Writings, edited by Christopher Hill
Crime in Seventeenth-Century England: A County Study, J. A. Sharpe†
The Crisis of Feudalism: Economy and Society in Eastern Normandy c.1300–1500, Guy Bois†
The Development of the Family and Marriage in Europe, Jack Goody*
Disputes and Settlements: Law and Human Relations in the West, edited by John Bossy
Rebellion, Popular Protest and the Social Order in Early Modern England, edited by Paul Slack
Studies on Byzantine Literature of the Eleventh and Twelfth Centuries, Alexander Kazhdan in collaboration with Simon Franklin†

The English Rising of 1381, edited by R. H. Hilton and T. H. Aston*

Praise and Paradox: Merchants and Craftsmen in Elizabethan Popular Literature, Laura Caroline Stevenson

The Brenner Debate: Agrarian Class Structure and Economic Development in Pre-Industrial Europe, edited by T. H. Aston and C. H. E. Philpin*

Eternal Victory: Triumphal Rulership in Late Antiquity, Byzantium, and the Early Medieval West, Michael McCormick*†

East-Central Europe in Transition: From the Fourteenth to the Seventeenth Century, edited by Antoni Mączak, Henryk Samsonowicz and Peter Burke†

Small Books and Pleasant Histories: Popular Fiction and its Readership in Seventeenth-Century England, Margaret Spufford*

Society, Politics and Culture: Studies in Early Modern England, Mervyn James*

Horses, Oxen and Technological Innovation: The Use of Draught Animals in English Farming 1066–1500, John Langdon

Nationalism and Popular Protest in Ireland, edited by C. H. E. Philpin

Rituals of Royalty: Power and Ceremonial in Traditional Societies, edited by David Cannadine and Simon Price*

The Margins of Society in Late Medieval Paris, Bronisław Geremek†

Landlords, Peasants and Politics in Medieval England, edited by T. H. Aston

Geography, Technology and War: Studies in the Maritime History of the Mediterranean 649–1571, John H. Pryor*

Church Courts, Sex and Marriage in England, 1570–1640, Martin Ingram*

Searches for an Imaginary Kingdom: The Legend of the Kingdom of Prester John, L. N. Gumilev

Crowds and History: Mass Phenomena in English Towns, 1780–1835, Mark Harrison

Concepts of Cleanliness: Changing Attitudes in France since the Middle Ages, Georges Vigarello†

The First Modern Society: Essays in English History in Honour of Lawrence Stone, edited by A. L. Beier, David Cannadine and James M. Rosenheim

The Europe of the Devout: The Catholic Reformation and the Formation of a New Society, Louis Châtellier†

English Rural Society, 1500–1800: Essays in Honour of Joan Thirsk, edited by John Chartres and David Hey

From Slavery to Feudalism in South-Western Europe, Pierre Bonnassie†

Lordship, Knighthood and Locality: A Study in English Society, c. 1180–c. 1280, P. R. Coss

English and French Towns in Feudal Society: A Comparative Study, R. H. Hilton

An Island for Itself: Economic Development and Social Change in Late Medieval Sicily, Stephan R. Epstein

Epidemics and Ideas: Essays on the Historical Perception of Pestilence, edited by Terence Ranger and Paul Slack

* Published also as a paperback
† Co-published with the Maison des Sciences de l'Homme, Paris

Lightning Source UK Ltd.
Milton Keynes UK
16 November 2010

162934UK00001B/36/A